CATHOLIC LIVES,

CONTEMPORARY AMERICA

CATHOLIC LIVES,

CONTEMPORARY AMERICA

THOMAS J. FERRARO, EDITOR

Duke University Press   Durham and London 1997

© 1997 Duke University Press
"My Parents, My Religion, and My Writing" © 1994 David Plante
"Virtually Normal" © 1994 Andrew Sullivan
Frank Lentricchia, "Making It to Mepkin Abbey," was originally published in
slightly different form as "En Route to Retreat: Making It to Mepkin Abbey,"
Harper's Magazine (January 1992): 68–78; used by permission; it also appeared
in *The Edge of Night* © 1994 Frank Lentricchia. Reprinted by permission of
Random House, Inc. Paul Crowley, "An Ancient Catholic: An Interview with
Richard Rodriguez," was originally published in slightly different form in
America 173 (23 September 1995): 8–11; used by permission.
Printed in the United States of America on acid-free paper ∞
Typeset in Adobe Caslon by Tseng Information Systems, Inc.
Library of Congress Cataloging-in-Publication Data
appear on the last printed page of this book.
The text of this book originally was published without the present
introduction, index, and essays by Lentricchia, Giles, and Crowley as
volume 93, no. 3 of the *South Atlantic Quarterly*.

For Louis Camardella and Anthony Emmi—
great uncles, diverse spirits

CONTENTS

Acknowledgments

This collection had its origins in an invitation by Fredric Jameson, incoming editor in chief of *SAQ*, to guest edit a special issue. My proposal for the issue met with encouragement from the "whole damn crew" at the journal, including outgoing editor in chief Frank Lentricchia, whose recent essay on Mepkin Abbey had fueled my thinking. I received early counsel from Stanley Hauerwas (for a decade, guardian spirit of Catholic inquiry at Duke University) and from his then graduate student in arms Mike Baxter, C.S.C.

From start to finish, corresponding with the contributors was a privilege and a delight — so savvy their letters, so expert the essays and interviews (generously conceived, freely given) that followed. An especial thank you, one and all.

Melissa Malouf guided me through the editorial process at *SAQ* and at times threw her hand in, with characteristic élan. Copy editor Candice Ward gave of her heart and memory as well as her pencil. Mike Young lent designer Anne Keyl his painting, *Bob's Congo*, to work with, producing an evocative cover that runs against type.

In shepherding the journal issue into book form, editor Rachel Toor reminded me, fortunately, that what is worth doing is worth doing well; Steve Cohn and Peter Guzzardi, *menschen*, sustained the faith from "above"; and editor Ken Wissoker not only took on the project at the eleventh hour, but formulated questions I still needed to hear—in the ways I needed to hear them.

Thank you, finally, to Paul Elie, James W. Arnold, Susan Bello, Mary Lee Freeman, Jon Butler, Lisa Mulman, Thomas Pfau, Sarah Beckwith, and Beth Eastlick (in-house editorial), for nays and yeas at crucial moments, in forums public and private.

THOMAS J. FERRARO

Not-Just-Cultural Catholics

In the film *Big Night* (1996), set largely in a restaurant in the
early 1950s, there is not a crucifix or a medallion, not a plaster cast
of the Blessed Virgin or a picture of Pius XII anywhere in sight—at
least not in plain sight. Yet its evocation of "gustatory sacramentalism"
speaks with unprecedented power and clarity to a complex of Catholic practices that I was raised with (among other forms) and continue
to pursue (with difficulty but not alone). By gustatory sacramentalism I
mean food prepared with fierce dedication and fiercer hope: a banquet
table made open to those who have always been there *and* to those this
day passing by, and a resplendent insistent conviviality that renews love
while forcing the hand of integrity. "To eat well—good food, really
good food—is to come closer to God," the traditionalist chef, Primo,
sputters in halted and exasperated English: the one obvious reference
to what the nineteenth century denominated *religion*—inserted, alas, to
make sure the philistines (as Primo terms them) get it.

Stanley Tucci and Campbell Scott, the directors, mean not just to
preach at the audience, but, ultimately, to seduce it, by performing,

not just intoning, Primo's creed.[1] *Big Night* aspires to what is almost a missionary practice: tempting, indeed graced hospitality *in cinematic form*. Such a practice is rooted in a single ethnic tradition—not just excellence, but gastronomic excellence, and not just any gastronomic excellence, but the traditions of Naples, Rome, and especially Bologna—yet it constitutes a *religious vision* that even in today's world has the hubris to claim universal wisdom and the chutzpah to imagine for itself a form—the movie—that calls to others beyond its institutional boundaries into identity, into communion, however liminally. Not just Italians and not just Christians, evidently enough, come to eat at Primo and his brother's place, and we in the audience are supposed to, too.

This collection of essays is meant as a banquet like Primo's, in which the food being served is splendiferous conversation and debate, autoethnography to revisionist purpose especially; the myriad cooks are spirited virtuoso writers, within and along the borders of the academy, who have thought much about contemporary Catholicism, yet through diverse professional lenses and with regard to different phenomenological foci; the topic is how Catholics have gotten and should go from here to there (from fifties self-assurance to nineties self-challenge, from intellectual insularity to congress, and from second-class cultural citizenship to center stage); and the guests of honor are our readers, of whatever experience or persuasion, who seek stronger, more original "stuff"—probing or subtle or just plain forthright—than what either the mass media can afford or the academic establishment has heretofore seen fit to circulate. It is a party of the intellect and the word, I wish to suggest, a long time in the making.

It ought to be a commonplace that there has long been, and to a certain extent continues to be, a marked discrepancy between the hypersalience of Catholic matters in public discourse (especially contemporary matters) and their relative absence in academic discourse other than that sponsored by the Church and its orders (medieval and colonial history notwithstanding). In October of 1996, for instance, when a Durham, North Carolina, parish with an African American mission announced it was discontinuing its Sunday afternoon Spanish mass, the resultant walkout, modeled of course on black civil rights praxis, made front page and prime time.[2] What resulted was sustained (if not always accurate) coverage, coverage explicable in part by the perceived threat, both within and without the parish, of ethnic disenfranchisement—a new pastor lacking Spanish but seeking unity, an African American community's rich traditions and meager resources put at risk by the migrant influx from Mexico and Central America—but also, on a larger scale, by a general fear of Catholic inroads into what is statistically the most Protestant fundamentalist state in the nation: if the U.S. Catholic hierarchy is once again fumbling the ball of Latino renewal, can massive conversions to Evangelical and Pentecostal Christianity be far behind?

It would come as a surprise, then, given such intensity of local interest and activity (we support two synagogues, one mosque, and more churches than you could count), that during my first five years in this very town, 1988–1993, Duke University carried on its books only one religious studies course in "The Roman Catholic Tradition," at the introductory level, and without regular faculty qualified to teach its developments after the Reformation; and not even one course in history and the social sciences focused on the Catholic presence *in the United States* after the French and Spanish conquests. A fact sobering in itself; disturbing, perhaps, given university demographics. In 1990, upwards of 40 percent of the undergraduate population at the university had at least one Catholic parent, or so one well-placed sociologist at the time discreetly estimated; whatever their backgrounds, 23 percent of the entire student body did in fact identify themselves, officially, as Catholic; and a startling 11 percent of the total student body attended the Sunday night (9:30 PM) mass on campus each week.[3] Hereabouts folks refer ruefully to the undergraduate program as the State College of New Jersey at Durham, North Carolina, not without reason. It is into the breach between the anxious talk of the public at large ("What is to be done?") and the anxious silence of the non-Catholic academy ("Hopefully nothing has to") that this collection is launched.

As an American studies major in college—at Amherst, in the late 1970s—the only version of twentieth-century U.S. Catholicism that made a lasting impression on me was that of Garry Wills: a hermetic, near-singular Catholicism put into crisis in the mid-1960s by the symbiosis of its own design and the national moment. In *Bare Ruined Choirs,* Wills paints a lucid picture of midcentury homogeneity, of intellectual enclosure, of a world taken for granted, with enough detail and texture that to reread it today is to be taken in once again: yes, it was — wasn't it? — that way. "The church was enclosed, perfected in circular inner logic, strength distributed through all its interlocking aspects; turned in on itself, giving a good account of itself to itself — but so vulnerable, so fragile, if one looked outward, away from it." For Wills, the Church offered the near-true and hence unpenetrated illusion of *changelessness* as its primary value. The sixties were a wake-up call to another sense, another idea, entirely: "*it let out the dirty little secret. It forced upon Catholics, in the most startling symbolic way, the fact that the church changes.*"[4]

The inspiration for this volume was the sense that coming on the scene was a coterie of writers raised largely if not entirely after Vatican II, whose work treated Catholic lives — and the life of Catholicism — in the recent and contemporary United States in wondrous new ways: work that on the one hand was tutored outside the Catholic academy by the paradigms of self-division, dissensus, and contestation entailing gender and sexuality, ethnicity if not race, and blue-collar alienation; and that on the other hand (re)turned to disparate Catholic materials to recover for critical interrogation less-official, often unsuspected, and at critical points unsanctioned forms of Catholic practice. In their writing to date and here, these scholars and essayists identify disjunctive forms of experience and even dissensus predating Vatican II — tensions and fissures held in check by uniform liturgy and a web of familiarity, "changes" already under way or roads not taken; and they trace the trajectories of such modalities across the putative sixties watershed and its related passages (secularization, ethnic assimilation) — countervailing *continuities* that continue to surprise, or revolutionary pushes not yet in effect.

The practices these writers bring forward include street festivals and Mardi Gras, devotions to Mary and the communion of saints, the sanctification of the cripple, and the martyring ethos of the hospital auxiliary; New Left and Brown Power civil disobedience, the conservative think tanks and organs of policy debate, and quietist communions centered on working-class bars and professional playing fields; the visual and performing arts, not only Flannery O'Connor and *Going My Way,* but the films of Frank Capra and Alfred Hitchcock, beat writing and postmodern art, the stadium rock of Madonna and Springsteen, and cops-and-robbers TV; as well as the revisionary responses, active and contemplative, to the "gender crisis" (make that *crises*) in the Church, the topical but no less insistent matters of reproductive responsibility, the ordination of women, gay personhood, and AIDS devastation. What has emerged is a remarkable constellation of writing, known but not quite well enough known—a constellation warranting the refocus and provocation that dissemination across disciplinary boundaries begets.[5]

During the postwar era of "consensus," U.S. academics, as a group, found ethnicity (including the ethnicities of Catholic immigrants) easy to talk about, and religion (Puritanism excepted) difficult, except (this may be a tautology) in sociological terms. We can begin to account for this. In the mid-1950s what John Murray Cuddihy has called the "no offense" pact was struck, on a brilliantly Protestant foundation of compromise, entailing a separate peace between private matters of the spirit and the American civil religion of liberal individualism. Tensions between cultures of faith and national vision were to be kept quiet, voiced only at home if at all, in houses of worship set apart.[6] By 1955, sociologist Will Herberg had given denominational pluralism its classic articulation as a tripartite melting pot: *Protestant–Catholic–Jew.* The Catholics, especially, demurred. "The orthodox have no need of consolation," Mary Gordon recalls, "and a closed world has no need of descriptions of itself."[7]

A problem, then: if the U.S. legacy of Protestant exceptionalism incorporated Catholicism as a minority sect, one denomination among others, what was supposed to happen to its antisectarian ideals; its dissent from Enlightenment individualism, from ethnic factionalism, from European-style nationalism; its belief in common humanity, common condition, common cause? Had the Roman Catholic conscience on such matters disappeared, or somehow gone underground, become

a family secret?[8] U.S. Catholic historiography, which flourished during the postwar period (under the rapprochement of John Tracy Ellis),
suggested that what was actually going on behind immigrant doors was
assimilation: the rededication of paganish folk Christianity to "Truth,
Justice, and the American Way." Notre Dame's Touchdown Jesus
existed; his flock was becoming legion; was it not he who stood for
Catholic modernity in America? In the early 1970s, with the popular
renewal of ethnic self-consciousness and the concomitant rise of the
new social history, most chroniclers of immigration weren't so sure. But
however much they emphasized cultural continuity—immigrants and
their descendants now figured as the transplanted, not the uprooted—
the social historians still weren't themselves talking *faith*, at least not
very much, and not very loudly.

It was in the early 1990s, during the final stages of finishing a book
on immigrant literature, that I first noticed testings of the accommoda-
tionist waters from the Catholic side—testings nearly as tough-minded
and provocative as the rise of Black Atlantic studies, which took the
lead. One monograph in particular, from 1985, recognized the vexed
nature of the ethnicity/Catholicism dialectic, and went after it. In *The
Madonna of 115th Street: Faith and Community in Italian Harlem, 1880–
1950*, Robert A. Orsi investigated the reciprocal shaping, through the
female-centered "domus" of East Harlem, between Italian migration
and uncertain mobility on the one hand and immigrant women's piety
and popular devotions to Mary on the other. Awarded the John Gilmary
Shea Prize of the American Catholic Historical Association (ACHA),
The Madonna of 115th Street was hailed by Philip Gleason (a former
ACHA president) as the first "comprehensive analysis of the place of
religion in the life of an American ethnic group" since 1932 (the publication year of a volume on Lutheran Swedes).[9] To the Orthodox, the
coming of the Italians must have felt like a mixed blessing, as usual: in
crediting Italian-American spirituality, Orsi not only foregrounded the
home over the institutional church, and the Sunday family meal over
the eucharist, but went on to demystify the Marian Catholicism that
reigned there. For my part, however, I sensed that the maternal focus
and sublime empathy of *The Madonna of 115th Street* harbored more

6   Thomas J. Ferraro

of a residual Marianism than Orsi (an offspring of its world) let on; and I believed, more importantly, that it was his combination of testament and suspicion (love *and* irony) that made the work, whatever its wellspring, so persuasive to almost all who read it: a natural crossover study if ever there was one.

Yet I remained unsure whether Orsi's *Madonna*, as well as several superb case studies that soon followed (by Paula Kane on the Irish of Boston, Ana María Díaz-Stevens on Puerto Ricans in New York, and Ramón A. Gutiérrez on mestizos in New Mexico), would find a significant audience outside the subdiscipline, and if so whether they would be read as complicating the rule of multiculturalism in American studies, or simply confirming it.[10] What I feared was the long-standing strategy of intellectual containment, in which the sociology rubric enabled attention to Catholicism while circumscribing its impact; what I wondered about was the potential of Catholic history for reconceiving U.S. culture writ large, and the potential of a Catholic sensibility for reimagining the subject of history.

Thus my surprise—and pleasure—when in the early nineties I also began hearing religious inflections in cultural history more broadly, in art and literary criticism, and in intellectual journalism. In *The Catholic Counterculture in America, 1933–1962* (1989), for instance, James T. Fisher relied upon the usual coterie of twentieth-century converts—Dorothy Day, Thomas Merton—to identify a counterhegemonic American mysticism, only to give us, in stunning illumination, beat icon Jack Kerouac and jungle doc Tom Dooley. In *Sexual Personae: Art and Decadence from Nefertiti to Emily Dickinson* (1990), Camille Paglia, at the time of publication an unknown professor at the Philadelphia College of the Arts, deployed a vivid catechistic style to pay homage to the visual mystery of a canonical line, with an irreverence toward humankind (especially mankind) foreign to the optative mood of U.S. criticism. Richard Rodriguez, whose analysis of the impact of Vatican II in *Hunger of Memory: The Education of Richard Rodriguez* (1981) went virtually unnoticed in the controversy surrounding its politics of race and language, was now writing on sanctity and mourning in gay San Francisco, and on the Murrietta cult that possesses Mexican California, including its Jesuit priesthood—a trajectory that soon culminated in *Days of Obligation: An Argument with My Mexican Father* (1992).[11] Increasingly I was intrigued: who were these folks, and what did these apparent convergences mean? How aware were they of one another? Had anyone else taken notice?[12]

Rodriguez likes to kvetch that as a writer he still gets classified as ethnic, Chicano, or, as he sardonically puts it, *pocho*, so that the full force of what he is doing—in *Days of Obligation*, especially—doesn't register. Like other things worth objecting to, the problem is not just Rodriguez's, but reflects several decades of decorous attribution, in which acknowledging ethnic identity screens out fundamentally religious energies. The label *Latino* might be said to be doing Rodriguez a favor—it is meant to incorporate him under current dispensations, however reluctantly—yet the scope and quality of his inquiry requires that that which dare not speaketh its name "on the American campus" be addressed head-on.[13]

In an interview with Rodriguez, published in the Jesuit organ *America* in September 1995, Paul Crowley, S.J., a theologian, puts one and one together, ventures to name what he sees, and lays down an implicit challenge: "In recent years there has been a wild, sometimes heretical cultural Catholicism abroad in 'post-Protestant' America. I'm thinking of Camille Paglia, Andy Warhol, Madonna, Martin Scorsese. Do you consider yourself part of this renegade Catholic movement?" As a catchphrase, *cultural Catholicism* suggests the development and deployment of Catholic ways of knowing and habits of being outside the official precincts and sanction, if not purview, of the Church. Although *movement* is perhaps too concerted, too teleological a term, Crowley has indexed a remarkable demographic cohort: a coterie of artists and intellectuals, once raised in but now somewhat distant from immigrant devotionalism, whose work is deliberately, often tantalizingly, at times insistently, "religious"—without being or wanting to be catechistic.

Madonna, Richard Rodriguez, Andy Warhol, Camille Paglia, Martin Scorsese: when cultural Catholicism first gets noticed, those intellectuals meant to exemplify it (a high-end essayist, a lit-crit agent provocateur) are observed side by side with, and are not distinguished from, those operating in the visual and performing arts (pop art's late icon, rock music's dancing queen, the cinematic auteur of the mean streets).[14] In a history that is just beginning to be recovered, Catholics in the United States have gravitated into the arts more easily than into the academy, not just because the parochial environment has been anti-intellectual and the secular academy anti-Catholic, but because populist forms of Catholic knowing reside more in gesture than in explication, more in the mass of common spectacle than in the monastery of individual contemplation, and more in public theaters of aesthetic transformation than in the sequestered libraries of its preservation.[15] It should come as no surprise, then, that as folks with Catholic backgrounds move forthrightly into "secular" intellectual ranks and the academy, the Catholic culture that they bear (and reproduce and transform) reemerges as a cluster of performative predispositions — not only or primarily a choice of subject or pronounced belief.[16] The national *habitus* affords critical distance on the Church and its members, yet even the criticism that ensues may exhibit Catholic modalities, tutored in the catechism and confessional, of course, but also in the pews, playgrounds, kitchens, bedrooms, and hospitals, where the lay practicum — including much of its mysticism — really happens.

I am especially interested in how fundamental Catholic discourses — iconicity and ritual, original sin and sacramentality, intercessory mediation and corpus christi — function in social and cultural contexts beyond the narrowly religious, including where least expected. To me, *cultural* as a qualifier to *Catholicism* does not necessarily mean dilution or dissolution — a draining of the religious imagination into banal secularity — but can in fact signify the opposite, a form of transfigurative reenvisioning that refuses to quarantine the sacred.[17]

The Catholicizing of culture is to be found in how, not just what, culturally Catholic intellectuals do: in the style and rhythms and unstated operations of their writing and scholarship, yet also in how they approach the classroom and public lecture hall, departmental meetings and the conclaves of their universities and professional organizations — for which, indeed, many will feel tempted to give either more or less emphasis than is the profession's wont. The dynamics of the Catholic/non-Catholic interface are thus overdetermined. Intellectuals of Catholic bent are going to attract or, as frequently, discomfort non-Catholics—not just because of their ideas, but because of how they hold and conduct themselves, because of how they understand ideas to be generated in the first place, and what in the final analysis they feel ideas are for. In short, the business of the intellectual community at large, not just the keeping or discarding of an individual tradition, is fundamentally *at stake*. Which is to say, from the hegemonic perspective of those who do not share those emphases, *at risk*.

Richard Rodriguez and Camille Paglia, Crowley's nominees among the intellectuals, are disaffected academics of some notoriety, both of whom have stepped off and/or have been excused from the fast track they were once groomed for, at Berkeley and Yale, respectively. Paglia in particular makes no bones about why, guaranteeing by her bluntness that the feeling is mutual. Such alienation is *not* characteristic of cultural Catholics—gathered here, as well, are everyday citizens of the university, distinguished chaired faculty, and respectful fellow travelers—but it may be suggestive nonetheless. Why are both of them so readily, often preemptively dismissed? Why do they touch the nerves that they do? I think answers lie in how these "academic renegades," in other ways distinctive, challenge professional protocol and writerly norms—that is, in where their intellectual personae meet.

The principal paradox is that Rodriguez and Paglia are both ethnically and class-consciously trenchant, transnationalist in impulse, and gender bending, thus in tune with "the times," yet somehow beyond academic sanction, neither politically correct nor happily neoconservative, at once too down-to-earth and too venturesome. Philosophically, each is acutely aware of the idealist (Protestant) liberatory impulse underlying mainstream Americanist work (the jeremiad, the manifesto), but does not capitulate to it, ideologically or formally; each is fatalistic with regard to matters social and psychological, yet holds the line crucially, one might even say "religiously," as an aficionado unwilling to dissolve the aesthetic into the mist of postcanonical relativism.[18] Learned *and* highly stylized, serious of purpose yet wickedly witty, locally sensuous but with mythic reach, their writings produce aftershocks that cannot be reduced, I believe, to temperament ("mavericks") or posture ("iconoclasm for iconoclasm's sake") alone. One dresses up and the other down, one tends to intone liturgically and the other to sermonize improvisationally, one is diplomatic and the other is not, yet both are hell on wheels in front of the classroom, an audience, and the camera, where they practice, quite emphatically, what they preach.

Crowley asks Rodriguez, "Do you consider yourself part of this renegade Catholic movement?" The point Rodriguez makes in response is that his experience of ethnic, including racial, marginality has reinforced his sense of spiritual difference, and thus has prompted him to sustain or renew (it's not clear which) actual sacramental practice (that by implication could be understood to constitute a form of ethnic resistance). At least that would appear to be Rodriguez's argument when rendered, according to academic custom, in propositional logic. What Rodriguez actually says, or rather how he says it, offers a provocative illustration, in miniature, of how intellectual performance enacts (I really should say *embodies*) Catholic sensibility.

In Rodriguez's response, ideation emerges with necessary sound-bite compactness, but only so far as it is induced from narrative, which takes precedence and generates the oomph. That is, Rodriguez deals in the actions of the body (personal, social, personal because social) before the mind, assuming that worship is the precondition of belief, not the other (Protestant) way around. I quote in full: "In blond, crewcut America, my soul is hairy and dark. And has a mouth! So I need to be a communicant; I am more than a 'cultural Catholic.' But yes." He's a glamorous man of reddish-brown hue and spirit (dark of skin, dark of philosophy) at risk in straitlaced white-bread (because white-bred) America, despite his upper-middle-class status; and that fact— of a difference read semiotically but experienced *materially*—sends him to Mass, where he goes to partake of what is there made available. The idiom here ("my soul is hairy and dark") begins as familiar ethnic shorthand, then metamorphoses almost instantaneously ("And it has a mouth!") into the signal metaphoric regime of gustatory sacramentalism: the medium, to cite an earlier Canadian Catholic visionary (whose message we've let lie fallow), is Rodriguez's massage.[19]

He is not alone.

The group of writers who have contributed to this volume is by no means exhaustive, no more so than Crowley's short list of the wild and wooly. But this group is, I hope, illustrative: conflicted, polysemous, and syncretic, within themselves as well as among one another—but a cohort nonetheless, with intersecting religious trajectories, social concerns, and constructions of knowledge. Like Rodriguez and Paglia, these renegade Catholics have proven hard to classify. In their works, the idioms and topoi of devotional Catholicism have a way of popping up in fascinating, heretofore unexplored, even unsuspected places—in places where the competing claim of ethnicity is expected and would do. But the Catholic thematics are not the half of it. For what characterizes the writing they do is its capacity for crossing boundaries, be they disciplinary, generic, or institutional; its tendency to resist being mapped onto the left-right spectrums of social vision and intellectual change, definitive of American intellectual hegemony and confirmed in part (in the moral sphere primarily) by John Paul II's Vatican; and its talent for making itself felt viscerally, so that it seduces even those readers (myself included) whose established understandings and commitments it contravenes. Such writing achieves, I believe, a mysterious "catholicity"—in which the force of its relevance is felt beyond the borders of a faith community, semi-universalized as it were, without its author necessarily having abandoned the more narrowly Catholic within.

If there is a turn of professional fashion that much of the work in this volume could be said to participate in, it is what has been called *autobiographical criticism*. These writers distinguish what in their memories deserves a public airing and what does not; they know when what they have experienced speaks not individually, in one fallen version of Emerson, but corporately, so that the articulation they achieve is on behalf of others (what Emerson actually envisioned for his "representative men," though in a strangely disembodied, socially unmediated way); and they demonstrate how religious habits of inquiry, even when (perhaps especially when) held provisionally, may enhance the still honorable pursuits of critical self-reflection, ethnographic understanding, and objective knowledge.

The *Chronicle of Higher Education*'s "Hot Type" column generously issued an advance notice about the special issue of *SAQ* that constituted the earlier, shorter form of this book.[20] The *Chronicle* proclaimed, "God is Back"—the implication being that God had disappeared as a legitimate academic subject but was about to be resurrected, perhaps too conveniently, as a site for poststructuralist theorization: that is, divinity as the final frontier of theory's imperial reach. My own sense is that religious energies—a certain form of mysticism—have fueled theory, particularly in its more eloquent reaches, since the very beginning, at times unbeknownst to itself. If poststructuralism has anything to teach its own adherents, however, it is that the discursive formation of religion means that God may not be abstracted from the interpretive community and practices that recognize him, and that any effort to do so will invariably enact, despite itself, for good as well as for ill, one form of religious discourse at the expense of others.[21] It is my conviction that such a revelation comes as no surprise to those working on or out of Catholic sensibility, since if there is anything that runs bone-deep, in the laity especially, and in the Mediterranean diaspora especially, it is the fact that transcendence and immanence work hand in hand, often ferociously so.

The essays and interviews gathered here, do, I hope, represent an emergent intellectual force, but it is not one that was or can be understood as an effort to get God "back," as if once gone. The *donné* of these essays, in most cases individually but more importantly as a group, is not God in his Radical Otherness, but rather embodied spirit: the impress of the Church on its people, including forms of worship it generates yet knows not how to sanction. So I have titled the collection *Catholic Lives, Contemporary America,* to foreground the lived experience of those who once were or are expected to be in the pews of the Roman Catholic Church in the United States—where, for instance (among the rich instances investigated here), the "cripple" is sanctified so as to be silenced, the ethnic barfly cityscape is understood in terms of Christ's mystical body, male celibacy takes on an invulnerable (inhuman, de-incarnated) erotic force, or communal hospitality to children makes a different kind of reproductive choice possible. In locating religion at the nexus of ethnicity, gender, and class (at the nexus, that is, of what cultural anthropologists call *symbolic contestation*), the writers assembled here are able to take us intimately into the God-tangles of actually lived lives; and, in doing so, in writing as it were *incarnationally*, they are able to illuminate the spiritual trajectories of American persons and, in the essays of larger scope, of American personhood, with critical (by which I mean discomfiting) revelatory power.

As my father says at our table, in deep seriousness, especially when guests abound, *buon appetito.*

NOTES

1 The film is in a technical sense nostalgic—the fifties once again!—but not necessarily rose-colored, since the historical lesson it seems to insist on is fatalistic, anti-immigration, anticapitalist, and ferociously suspicious of America: the restaurant has failed economically, the United States is given over to glitzy joints whose offerings of spaghetti and meatballs Primo likens to *raping* the customer (Pizza Hut not long in coming). The vision that the film overtly, indeed melodramatically, mourns is, paradoxically, at the same time already being resurrected (this is transfigurative Catholicism, after all) by the film, not only in what it recovers but by whom *and* for whom. It was a cohort of contemporary Americans—Stanley Tucci, his Italian American cowriter, codirector Campbell Scott, plus the magnificent performance of Tony Shalhoub(!) as Primo—who made *Big Night* in the mid-1990s; and they found a very enthusiastic audience for it, not a mass audience, but one of intellectuals and aesthetes, well outside of any inner ethnic or religious circle.

2 The Holy Cross walkout and its aftermath received front-page coverage in the Durham *Herald Sun* from Monday, 14 October 1996, through Wednesday, 23 October 1996 (with follow-ups thereafter). The 14 October headline read, "Catholic church to drop bilingual service" and featured a full-color photograph of the procession out of the front door of Holy Cross, framed frontally (like a post-courtroom scene), with a woman of determination in the lead cradling the church's statue of the Virgin of Guadalupe, with the caption, "Hispanic parishioners walk out in protest."

3 Tom Curley, "ASDU Debates Clubs' Budgets," *Chronicle*, 27 October 1990,

1 ff.; Timothy Stephen Hohman, "Aspirations and Transformations: A Study of the Roman Catholic Church at Duke University" (unpublished undergraduate essay on file at University Archives, Perkins Library, Duke University, 1 April 1991).

4 Garry Wills, *Bare Ruined Choirs: Doubt, Prophesy, and Radical Religion* (New York, 1972), 33, 21. I have treasured this book, yet on rereading it recently I have also come to suspect how it won its honored place as the at-large report on fifties Catholicism. "It may look contradictory for the liberal to escape Catholic parochialism and chauvinism—what would come to be called 'triumphalism' in the Sixties—by creating a cult of Catholic authors, heralding a Catholic renascence, chanting Gregorian, and trying to start Catholic farms, restaurants, film studies, newspapers, and social organizations. But the liberals' most acutely experienced urge was to prove that something recognizably Catholic need not be as cramped, ugly, and anti-intellectual as they found at the corner church" (44–45). Not only does Wills's irony cut in both directions—as it ought to—but so does his condescension. It is my suspicion that those "Catholic restaurants"—and bars!— were always already there, around the corner from the rectory-school complex, and even in certain places frequented by Catholic liberals, if not quite near Columbia uptown, then crosstown, hard by Fordham or St. John's.

5 What do I mean by "not quite well enough known"? For instance, Jenny Franchot has offered a rundown of recent major works in "religion, anthropology, and art history" that have or should become of interest to Americanists in literary and cultural studies. The works she enumerates—entailing the recovery of the Black Atlantic especially, but also of latter-day European-descended "paganism," including goddess worship—are in fact revitalizing and reshaping critical inquiry along lines at once religious and social, spiritual and material. Tellingly, however, no work in Catholicism or Catholic syncretism is cited. This apparent oversight reflects honorable modesty—Franchot is the author of the formidable *Roads to Rome: The Antebellum Protestant Encounter with Catholicism* (1994)—but it is also indicative of cross-disciplinary inattention (disinterest, incomprehension, resistance, or a lack of awareness) more generally. See Jenny Franchot, "Invisible Domain: Religion and American Literary Studies," *American Literature* 67 (December 1995): 838.

6 John Murray Cuddihy, *No Offense: Civil Religion and Protestant Taste* (New York, 1978).

7 Mary Gordon, *Good Boys and Dead Girls and Other Essays* (New York, 1991), 171.

8 Eugene Kennedy suggests that the laity practice a form of universalism

("largeness of heart" in "social context"), but do so quietly, without adopting "the pinched cheeks of austere and uncomforted piety" (Kennedy, *Tomorrow's Catholics, Yesterday's Church* [San Francisco, 1990], 25).

9 Philip Gleason, *Speaking of Diversity: Language and Ethnicity in Twentieth-Century America* (Baltimore, 1992), 251.

10 Ana María Díaz-Stevens, *Oxcart Catholicism on Fifth Avenue: The Impact of the Puerto Rican Migration upon the Archdiocese of New York* (Notre Dame, 1993); Ramón A. Gutiérrez, *When Jesus Came, the Corn Mothers Went Away: Marriage, Sexuality, and Power in New Mexico, 1500–1846* (Stanford, 1991); Paula M. Kane, *Separatism and Subculture: Boston Catholicism, 1900–1920* (Chapel Hill, 1994).

11 James T. Fisher, *The Catholic Counterculture in America, 1933–1962* (Chapel Hill, 1989); Camille Paglia, *Sexual Personae: Art and Decadence from Nefertiti to Emily Dickinson* (New Haven, 1990); Richard Rodriguez, "Credo," in *Hunger of Memory: The Education of Richard Rodriguez* (Boston, 1981), 75–110; Rodriguez, *Days of Obligation: An Argument with My Mexican Father* (New York, 1992).

For other significant work from outside the academy see Paul Elie, "The Everlasting Dilemma: 'Young' Catholics and the Church," *Commonweal* 118 (27 September 1991): 537–42; Elie, "Hangin' with the Romeboys," *New Republic* 206 (11 May 1992): 18–26; occasional pieces by David Gonzales, Bronx bureau chief of the *New York Times,* such as "A Haven for Hopeless Causes," *New York Times,* 10 November 1993, B1, 10; and Rubén Martínez, *The Other Side: Notes from the New L.A., Mexico City, and Beyond* (London, 1992). For an overview of the seminal work of Andrew Greeley—sociologist, novelist, and agent provocateur in his own right—see Ronald D. Pasquariello, *Conversations with Andrew Greeley* (Boston, 1988).

12 As regards artists, writers, and public intellectuals, the fact is others had noticed, and noticed well. I learned belatedly of a book of interviews, whose author I would like to meet: Peter Occhiogrosso, *Once a Catholic: Prominent Catholics and Ex-Catholics Reveal the Influence of the Church on Their Lives and Work* (Boston, 1987); the book includes interviews with Mary Gordon, Bob Guccione, Jimmy Breslin, George Carlin, Robert Stone, Frank Zappa, José Torres (the boxer), Martin Scorsese, Eugene McCarthy, and a dozen others. Occhiogrosso writes, "Both those Catholics who emphatically defend Church orthodoxy and those most evidently at odds with the Church, including ex-Catholics, . . . form a communion, I would even presume to say a mystical body, of Catholics aware of one another and of their divergent and consonant viewpoints" (ix).

13 Stanley Hauerwas ends his homage to Notre Dame, "I suspect that the

last legitimate prejudice on the American campus is against the Catholics." Hauerwas is by no means the first non-Catholic who has put the problem in such powerfully denominational terms. At Amherst College in the late 1970s, a great Americanist scholar and teacher, of German Jewish birth told me, in private but in no uncertain terms, that "the real bias in the secular academy is anti-Catholicism." His advice was akin to the parting words of the Amish farmer in *Witness* to the Harrison Ford character, "watch it out there amongst them English, John Book."

14 It's hard to resist noting the short announcement in the 15 October 1996 Durham *Herald Sun,* placed above the treatment of the Holy Cross walkout, "Madonna and Child Doing Well after Birth": a tongue-in-cheek reference to Madonna Louise Veronica Ciccone and Carlos Leon's firstborn, whom they christened Lourdes Maria Ciccone Leon. *Oy, vay.*

15 See, for instance, Leo Braudy, "The Sacraments of Genre: Coppola, DePalma, Scorsese," in *Native Informant: Essays on Film, Fiction, and Popular Culture,* ed. Leo Braudy (New York, 1991), 240–52; Thomas J. Ferraro, "Catholic Ethnicity and Modern American Arts," *New Ethnic American Literature and the Arts: Vol. 1, The Italian American Heritage,* ed. Pellegrino D'Acierno (forthcoming); Peter Gardella, *Innocent Ecstasy: How Christianity Gave America an Ethic of Sexual Pleasure* (New York, 1995), chap. 6; and Paul Giles, *American Catholic Arts and Fictions: Culture, Ideology, Aesthetics* (Cambridge, 1992), esp. the introduction and chaps. 12–14. To uncover a related and older genealogy of Protestant aesthetic investments in Catholicism see Jenny Franchot, *Roads to Rome: The Antebellum Protestant Encounter with Catholicism* (Berkeley, 1994), esp. chaps. 7–13; Jackson Lears, *No Place of Grace: Antimodernism and the Transformation of American Culture, 1880–1920* (New York, 1981), esp. chaps. 4–5; and the critical bibliographies of such writers as Nathaniel Hawthorne, Henry James, Ernest Hemingway, F. Scott Fitzgerald, Eugene O'Neill, Willa Cather, and James T. Farrell.

16 "There is a saving earthiness to sacramental Catholicism. . . . Faith . . . is realized in a social context as much as in church, and is marked by a largeness of heart rather than by the pinched cheeks of austere and uncomforted piety" (Kennedy, *Tomorrow's Catholics,* 25).

17 For debate over the term *cultural Catholic* see parts one and two of "The Intellectual Life: Essays in Memory of John Tracy Ellis," *U.S. Catholic Historian* 13 (winter 1995), esp. essays by Philip Gleason and James T. Fisher in part one and the short pieces constituting the review symposium on Patrick Allitt's recent book in part two; and the "Catholicism and Popular Culture" issue of *Commonweal* 122 (22 September 1995).

18 For analysis of how Protestant typologies, jeremiadic rhetorical con-
ventions, and romantic Emersonian individualism continue to undergird
American studies in the United States, even under the multicultural rubric,
see Werner Sollors, introduction to *The Invention of Ethnicity*, ed. Werner
Sollors (New York, 1989), ix–xx; Sacvan Bercovith, *The Rites of Assent:
Transformations in the Symbolic Construction of America* (New York, 1993),
1–28; and Paul Giles, "Reconstructing American Studies: Transnational
Paradoxes, Comparative Perspectives," *Journal of American Studies* 28
(1994): 335–58.

19 Marshall McLuhan and Quentin Fiore, *The Medium Is the Massage* (New
York, 1967).

20 "Hot Type," *Chronicle of Higher Education* 40 (2 February 1994): A10.

21 Giles, "Reconstructing American Studies," 344.

ROBERT A. ORSI

"Mildred, is it fun to be a cripple?":
The Culture of Suffering
in Mid-Twentieth-Century
American Catholicism

On the first Saturday of every month in the 1960s my Uncle Sally, who has cerebral palsy, used to go to a different parish in New York City or its suburbs for Mass and devotions in honor of Our Lady of Fatima and then afterwards to a Communion breakfast sponsored by that month's host church. These special outings for "shut-ins" and "cripples"[1] were organized by the Blue Army of Mary, an association of men and women dedicated to spreading the messages of apocalyptic anti-Communism and personal repentance delivered by Mary at Fatima in 1917.[2] My uncle would be waiting for me and my father in the hallway of his mother's apartment, dressed in a jacket and tie and smoking cigarettes in a long, imitation tortoiseshell holder that my grandmother fitted between the knotted fingers of his left hand. He smoked by holding his hand stiff on the green leatherette armrest of his wheelchair, then bending his torso forward and bringing his legs up until his lips reached the burning cigarette. He was always afraid that my father wouldn't show up, and as his anxiety mounted my uncle clenched again and again over his cigarettes so that by the time we got there—always early—the foyer was dense with smoke.

We laid Sally down on his back on the front seat of the car. My grandmother, in an uncharacteristic moment of hope and trust, had taken my uncle as a boy to a mysterious doctor on the Lower East Side who said he could make him walk; instead, he had locked Sally's legs at the knees, sticking straight out in front of him, fusing him into a ninety-degree angle, and then had vanished. Sally reached back, hooked his right wrist into the steering wheel, and pulled himself in while we pushed. When he was in the car up to his legs, my father leaned in over him and drew him up. He angled my uncle's stiff limbs under the dashboard and wedged them in.

My father went around the car and dropped into the other side. He looked over at his brother-in-law, the two of them sweating and panting. "Okay?" he asked. My uncle nodded back.

We drove to a designated meeting place, usually another church's parking lot, where members of the Blue Army, wearing sky-blue armbands printed with an image of the Virgin of Fatima and the legend "Legion of Mary," helped us pull my uncle out of the car. Other cripples were arriving. The members of the Blue Army knew who wanted to sit next to each other, and they wheeled my uncle's friends over to him, locking them in place beside him. He greeted them solemnly, not saying very much. From here a big yellow school bus would take the cripples out to the church; we'd follow in the car. My uncle was anxious to get going.

The wheelers teased him in loud voices whenever they brought a woman over. "Here's your girlfriend!" they shouted. "I saw her talking to So-and-So yesterday! Aren't you jealous?! You're gonna lose this beautiful girl! Come on, Sal, wake up." They pounded my uncle on the back. "Don't you know a good thing when you got it?" Their voices and gestures were exaggerated, as if they were speaking to someone who couldn't understand their language.

The women rolled their heads back and laughed with bright, moaning sounds, while their mothers fussed at their open mouths with little embroidered handkerchiefs, dabbing at saliva. "Calm down, calm down," they admonished their daughters, "don't get so excited."

My uncle laughed too, but he always looked over at me and shook his head.

There was a statue of San Rocco on a side altar of the Franciscan church of my childhood. The saint's body was covered with open, purple sores; tending to the bodies of plague victims, he had been infected himself. A small dog licked the sores on his hands. The Franciscans told us that St. Francis kissed a leper's sores; once he drank the water he had just used to bathe a leper.

One woman, a regular of the First Saturday outings, came on a stretcher covered with clean sheets in pale pastel colors; her body was immobile. She twisted her eyes up and looked out at us through a mirror fixed to the side of the stretcher, while her mother tugged at her dress to make sure it stayed down around her thin ankles.

These were special people, God's children, chosen by him for a special destiny. Innocent victims, cheerful sufferers, God's most beloved— this was the litany of the handicapped on these First Saturdays. Finding themselves in front of an unusual congregation, priests were moved to say from the pulpit at Mass that the prayers of cripples were more powerful than anyone else's because God listened most attentively to these, his special children. Nuns circulated among the cripples, touching their limbs kindly and reverently, telling them how blessed they were, and how wonderful. To be standing these mornings in a parking lot or church basement was to be on ground made holy by the presence of beds and wheelchairs and twisted bodies.

At breakfast, the mothers of the cripples hovered over them. They held plastic straws, bent in the middle like my uncle, while their children drank coffee or juice; they cut danishes into bite-sized pieces; they cleaned up spills. Volunteers from the parish and members of the Blue Army brought out plates of eggs and sausage.

"You have such a big appetite this morning!"

"Can you eat all that? God bless you!"

"If I ate like you I'd be even fatter than I am!"

But why had God done this to his most beloved children? What kind of love was this? What kind of God?

When he was done with his coffee, my uncle cupped himself around his cigarette.

Physical distress of all sorts, from congenital conditions like cerebral palsy to the unexpected agonies of accidents and illness, was understood by American Catholics in the middle years of this century as an individual's main opportunity for spiritual growth.[3] Pain purged and disciplined the ego, stripping it of pride and self-love; it disclosed the emptiness of the world. Without it, human beings remained pagans; in physical distress, they might find their way back to the Church, and to sanctity. "Suffering makes saints," one hospital chaplain told his congregation of sick people, "of many who in health were indifferent to the practices of their holy religion."[4] Pain was a ladder to Heaven; the saints were unhappy unless they were in physical distress of some sort. Catholic nurses were encouraged to watch for opportunities on their rounds to help lapsed Catholics renew their faith and even to convert non-Catholics in the promising circumstances of physical distress.[5]

Pain was always the thoughtful prescription of the Divine Physician. Thomas Dooley's cancer was celebrated in Catholic popular culture as a grace, a mark of divine favor. Dooley himself wrote, "God has been good to me. He has given me the most hideous, painful cancer at an extremely young age."[6] So central was pain to the American Catholic ethos that devotional writers sometimes went so far as to equate it with life itself—"The good days are a respite," declared a laywoman writing in a devotional magazine in 1950, "granted to us so that we can endure the bad days."[7]

Catholics thrilled to describe the body in pain. Devotional prose was generally overwrought, but on this subject it exceeded itself. There was always an excess in Catholic accounts of pain and suffering of a certain kind of sensuous detail, a delicious lingering over and savoring of other people's pain. A dying man is presented in a story in a 1937 issue of the devotional magazine *Ave Maria* as having "lain [for twenty-one years] on the broad of his back, suffering from arthritis . . . his hands and fingers so distorted that he could not raise them more than an inch . . . his teeth set . . . so physically handicapped that in summer he could not brush away a fly or mosquito from his face because of his condition." It was never enough in this aesthetic to say simply "cancer," stark as that word is; instead, it had to be the "cancer that is all pain."[8] Wounds always "throbbed," suffering was always "untold," pain invariably took its victims to the very limits of endurance.

The body-in-pain was itself thrilling: flushed, feverish, and beautiful—"The sick room is rather a unique beauty shop," one priest mused, where "pain has worked more wonders than cosmetics"[9]—it awaited its lover. A woman visiting a Catholic hospital in 1929 came upon a little Protestant girl who was dying and reported:

> He has set His mark upon her. Somehow you guess; those frail little shoulders are shaped for a cross, those eyes are amber chalices deep enough for pain, that grave little courteous heart is big enough to hold Him! He will yet be her tremendous lover, drawing her gently into His white embrace, bestowing on her the sparkling, priceless pledge of His love—suffering.[10]

Pain had the character of a sacrament, offering the sufferer a uniquely immediate and intimate experience of Jesus' presence.[11] Walking amid the "couches of pain" laid out for the sunset service at Lourdes, an American visitor suddenly sensed that "he is here now. . . . Almost I can hear him speak, —almost I can reach out and touch his garment." Another writer reported that she knew "a very holy nun who is herself one of God's chosen ones" (that is, afflicted with the most severe pain), "and one day she said something to me that I have never forgotten. She said, 'Sometimes God's hand seems to rest so heavily upon our shoulder, and we try to squirm away, and we cry, Oh, let me be! And then we begin to realize how tender as well as how heavy is His hand, and we want it there.'"[12]

This was a darkly erotic aesthetic of pain, one expression of the wider romanticism of American Catholicism in this period;[13] but for all this culture's fascination with physical distress, the sensual pleasure it took in feverish descriptions of suffering, it was also deeply resentful and suspicious of sick persons—a nasty edge of retribution and revenge is evident in these accounts. In one priest's typical cautionary tale of pain, "a young woman of Dallas, Texas, a scandal to her friends for having given up her faith because it interfered with her sinful life, was severely burned in an explosion. Before her death, through the grace of God, she returned to the Church."[14] According to a nursing sister, writing in the leading American Catholic journal for hospital professionals, *Hospital Progress,* in 1952: "Physical disability wears off the veneer of sophistication and forces the acceptance of reality. It is difficult for a patient imprisoned for weeks in a traction apparatus to live in a state of illusion."[15] Pain gives people their comeuppance; it serves as chastisement and judgment.

The Catholic tradition was ambivalent about the moral status of the sick. Despite constant injunctions to the contrary, a persistent identification was made between sickness and sin—not only sin in general or Original Sin, but the specific sinfulness of the person in pain—and the suspicion of all physical suffering as merited was never completely absent from devotional culture.[16] "You may complain and moan about a single toothache," Father Boniface Buckley chided the readers of *Sign* in 1945, but be "woefully forgetful of the fact that this particular pain may be due in justice for some sin of that very day."[17] God always has a reason for sending pain. Theology's restraint is evident here in Father Buckley's use of the conditional; more commonly, devotional writers threw such theological caution to the winds in order to score moral points with pain. Learn to take your pain the way a man takes his hangover, another priest scolded, and admit that you "asked for it."[18]

The association between physical sickness and moral corruption was reinforced throughout American Catholic popular literature by the persistent use of metaphors of illness to describe threats to the social fabric and sources of political and moral decay. As the editor of *Ave Maria* put it, aphoristically, in 1932, "Error is due to thought germs," against which only mental and moral hygiene is an effective prophylactic.[19] Another writer even suggested that to visit the sick was to "stand by the bedside of our soul-sick world."[20] The persistent metaphorical use of leprosy to excoriate various moral dangers was so egregious in the Catholic press that missionaries among sufferers of Hansen's disease regularly complained of the effect this usage was having on the people in their care.[21] This was not an unusual rhetorical device, of course, but it achieved its own peculiar, disorienting resonance in Catholic devotionalism, where images of the body-in-pain were used to suggest both the depths of corruption and the highest reaches of spiritual glory. In the case of the leper, the two discrepant usages converged: the leper was at once physically—and morally—scrofulous and (potentially) sacred.[22]

As American Catholics interpreted an ancient tradition in their contemporary circumstances, the idea that sickness was punishment for something the sufferer had done took deeper hold. The more sentimental view of sickness as the training ground for saintliness was commonly reserved for people with congenital conditions, such as Sal and his friends; their suffering, at least, could not be attributed to any moral failure since they were born this way. The innocence of handicapped people made them central to the elaboration of the gothic romance of suffering; because they were "innocent," unalloyed spiritual pleasure could be taken in the brokenness of their bodies. There was a cult of the "shut-in" among American Catholics in the middle years of this century, a fascination with "cripples" and a desire to be in some relation to them, which was thought to carry spiritual advantages. In the summer of 1939, *Catholic Women's World,* one of the most modern and upbeat of the Catholic magazines, set up a pen-pal system so that readers going away on vacation could write to shut-ins about their trips; the project was so popular that "many readers have written to us requesting that we put them in touch not only with one, but as many as three or four shut-ins."[23] There were a number of organizations dedicated to harnessing the spiritual power of shut-ins and putting it to work for the rest of the Church, such as the Catholic Union of the Sick in America (CUSA), which formed small cells of isolated handicapped persons who communicated through a round-robin letter and whose assignment was to direct their petitions, more powerful by virtue of their pain, toward some specific social good.[24] The spiritual pleasure taken by the volunteers on the First Saturdays in their proximity to the handicapped was a reflection of this cult as well.

But the mistrust of the sick, the suspicion that their physical distress was the manifestation of a moral failing, lurked just below the surface of even the fantasy of the holy cripple. The eleventh-century "cripple" Hermann, who composed the Marian hymn "Salve Regina," is described in one article as having been "pleasant, friendly, always laughing, never criticizing, so that everybody *loved* him." Concluding, "What a record for a cripple!" the author implies that just the opposite could have been expected from a man like this.[25] The subtext here is that if Hermann had not been so delightful, he would not have deserved love—there was nothing unconditional about this culture's affection for cripples.

Apart from these "fortunate unfortunates," a favorite Catholic term for the handicapped, however ambivalently construed, sick people were guilty people, and, not surprisingly, they behaved as such. Sick people were generally depicted as malingering, whining, selfish, overly preoccupied with their own problems, indolent, maladjusted, and self-destructive. They exaggerated the extent of their distress; they were quick to yield to despair and loneliness. Wake up to the fact that life is a vale of tears, one priest scolded the ill, and get rid of your "Pollyanna attitude," by which he meant stop hoping for relief. Above all, the sick could not be trusted. Without the astringent of religion, for example, lepers—even beloved lepers—would be "spiteful, cynical, and debauched," according to one visitor to Molokai, and this was maintained as generally true of all sick people.[26] As late as 1965, a Dominican priest writing in *Ave Maria* derided a sick person as a "spoiled child" and warned against "the tendency to remain in our suffering, to exaggerate the injustice, to pout."[27]

But what exactly constituted complaint? Were devotional teachers warning in these passages against the sometimes dark and self-defeating human impulse to protest the will of God, or to rebel against the facts of life?

One Saturday the bus didn't come. Something had happened somewhere along its route. The hot summer's morning dragged on; the sidewalk around Sal's chair was littered with cigarette butts; and the garbled messages—there'd been a crash, no, it was just a flat tire, he'll be here any minute, he's upstate—from the people in charge of the outing, meant to be reassuring, just made the confusion and anxiety worse.

A man I didn't recognize, not one of the Blue Army regulars, strolled over to the back of Sal's chair and gripped its rubber handles as if he were going to push my uncle off someplace. He winked at me and my father. Maybe Sal knew him from someplace. "So, Sal," he boomed at the back of my uncle's head, sounding pleased with his own cheerfulness, "looks like you're gonna have to spend the night in this parking lot, hunh?"

My uncle gave an angry wave of dismissal, but the man behind him, comfortably resting his weight on the chair, went on, "Hey, Sal, you hear what I said? You're gonna have to spend the night out here in the parking lot! I hope you got your blankets! Maybe we can get the girls over there to sing you a lullaby."

My uncle rocked himself from side to side in his seat, as if he wanted to dislodge the man's grip on his chair and move him out from behind his back. Bored with the game, the man let go. "Jesus, I hope we get the hell out of here soon," he said to my father, and walked away.

Sal smacked the brakes off his chair with his hard, calloused hands and began to spin himself around in circles. My father tried to calm him down. "Sally," he said, "the bus'll be here any minute, I know it. It's probably just a flat tire. Come on, don't get like this, you're gonna make yourself sick." But my uncle went on spinning. "Ahhhhhh," he roared, "ahhhhhh."

Everyone teased the cripples, joked with them and needled them almost all the time; this may have been what the man behind Sal's chair was doing, but I don't think so. He was sweaty and angry. Maybe he was only there that morning because of his wife's devotion to Our Lady of Fatima; maybe he hated cripples and the stories they told about the human body, of all that could and did go wrong with it. He had bent forward over the back of Sally's head and stared down at his bald crown and coarse gray hair. Maybe he hated the way the cripples drooled when they sucked up their coffee and juice on these Saturday mornings, or the mess they made of Communion breakfast.

My uncle began to push himself along the parking lot's chainlink fence, hitting the wheels of his chair with hard shoves; when he got to the end of the fence, where it connected with the church, he spun himself around and began pounding his way back.

Maybe the man found it hard to sustain the idea that Sal and his friends were holier than he was, closer to Heaven, when they sprayed him with saliva and bits of egg.

My uncle wheeled around again and started back along the fence.

"This is the only guy I know," my father said to me, "who can pace in a wheelchair."

Someone came over and demanded that Sal stop. "Control yourself! These things happen, Sal," she yelled at him, bending to lock his chair in place, but my uncle pushed her hand away and kept moving.

The morning wore on, and the fortunate unfortunates, disappointed and upset, got on everybody's nerves.

"Complaint" meant any sound that the sick might make, any use of their voices, whether it was to ask for a glass of water in the middle of the night, to question a doctor's decisions, to express a spiritual doubt, or to request that their bodies be shifted in bed. Hospitalized sick people who complained of physical discomfort were referred to in the *Voice of Saint Jude,* a periodical published at the Chicago shrine of the patron saint of hopeless causes, as "c.t.m.p.'s" ("cantankerous, tempestuous, maladjusted patients").[28] There was only one officially sanctioned way to suffer even the most excruciating distress: with bright, upbeat, uncomplaining, submissive endurance.[29] A woman dying horribly of an unspecified cancer was commended by *Ave Maria* for having written "cheerful newsy notes" home from the hospital, with "only casual references to her illness."[30] In the spirit of a fashion editor, one devotional writer counseled the chronically ill to "learn to wear [your] sickness becomingly. It can be done. It has been done. Put a blue ribbon bow on your bedjacket and smile."[31] Visitors were instructed to urge their sick friends and kin to make the best use of their time; the sick should be happily busy and productive even in the most extreme pain.[32] "Only two percent of the various types of pain are permanent and continual," wrote Mary O'Connor in an *Ave Maria* article for the sick in 1951. She was onto their games; she knew they were likely to "wallow in the muck of self-pity or sympathy": "[I]f the sieges of pain let up a little now and then, take up an interesting hobby and throw yourself into it with all you've got. You'll be delighted to find that your pain is lessening as a result." Her own experience was exemplary in this regard: since the onset of her pain a decade earlier, she had written over two thousand poems, articles, and stories.[33]

If such pitiless badgering failed to arouse the sick, against their sinful inclinations, to saintliness, there was always the scourge of the suffering of Jesus and Mary: no matter how severe your suffering, the sick were told, Jesus' and Mary's were worse, and *they* never complained. What is a migraine compared to the crown of thorns?[34] Who could ever suffer a loss like Mary's? Jesus' suffering served the same purpose as Mary's virtue in devotional culture: to diminish the integrity and meaning of ordinary persons' difficulties and experiences. Indeed, there was a hierarchy of scorn for sick people: just as Jesus' suffering outweighed all human pain, so truly awful pain was used to dismiss anything less, and all physical distress was greater than any psychological trouble, in a pyramid of suffering with Jesus, all bloody, and Mary, modestly sorrowing, at its top. Leprosy, in particular, functioned in this ethos as a means of denying other forms of physical distress, which partially accounts for its ubiquity. The message to sick people was: someone else is always suffering more than you are—look at the lepers!—and besides, Jesus suffered most of all, so be quiet!

In this way, the priests, nuns, and lay people writing for the many devotional magazines and diocesan newspapers that made up the popular literary culture of American Catholicism waged a campaign against men and women in physical or emotional distress. The saint offered as patron to the sick in this century was Gemma Galgani, who used violence against herself when she was ill, adding self-inflicted pain to the distress of disease so that she might "subdue even the faintest sugges-tion of rebellion on the part of the flesh against the spirit";[35] and if sick people would not subdue their own flesh as St. Gemma did hers, if they could not bedeck their own pain in ribbons, it would be done for them. The language used against people in pain was harsh and cruel, devoid of compassion or understanding, and dismissive of their experience. As one priest demanded, if a child spends "seven or nine years" in an iron lung, "what of it?"[36] There was only scorn, never sympathy, for the sick who failed to become saintly through pain.[37] Bending the images and idioms of popular religion against them so that even the suffering Christ emerged as a reproach, devotional writers crafted a rhetoric of mortifi-cation and denial for the sick. This was particularly cruel since they were doing so in the language and venues of popular devotionalism, to which sick people customarily turned for spiritual and emotional comfort.

The consequence of this rhetoric was that pain itself—the awful, frightening reality of something going wrong in the body—disappeared. It was hidden behind the insistence that the sick be cheerful, produc-tive, orderly; it was masked by the condescending assurances offered to the shut-in handicapped by those who were not that it was better to be a cripple; it was occluded by the shimmering, overheated prose, the ex-cited fascination with physical torment, and the scorn and contempt for the sick.[38] There is not nearly as much suffering in the world as people complain of, chided a writer in the pages of *Ave Maria*—two years after the end of the First World War.[39] "I enjoyed my week with the lepers of Molokai," a traveler exclaimed as if he had not been sojourning among people he had just described as looking "more like corpses than human beings."[40] Chronic illness brought families together in special joy and intimacy, according to these writers.[41] Even Jesus' pain could be denied: lest they find in his Passion an expression of the reality of their own ex-perience, the sick were occasionally reminded that, since he had been conceived without Original Sin, Jesus himself was never sick—the risk of Docetism apparently less troubling than that of compassion.[42] It was in this spirit that William P. McCahill, executive secretary of the Presi-dent's Committee on National Employ the Physically Handicapped Week, could report with approval a child's question to a handicapped person: "Mildred, is it fun to be a cripple?" Yes, it is! McCahill assured his readers.[43]

Physical distress that had been thus purged of its everyday messiness, of the limitations it imposed on the body, and of the dreariness of its persistence could be transmuted into its opposite: "pain" became a "harvest" ripe for the gathering, a spiritual "powerhouse" that could light the Church, a vein of gold to be mined, minted, and spent. "It isn't suffering that's the tragedy," one of CUSA's mottoes proclaims, "only wasted suffering."[44] In a 1953 meditation that mixed several of these transformative metaphors, Florence Waters urged the readers of *Ave Maria* to "travel the length and breadth of the country and add them up—the cardiacs, and arthritics, the cerebral palsied, the paraplegics, the amputees, the blind, the congenitally malformed, and the victims of countless other ills that tie human bodies to beds, wheelchairs, crutches, to one room or one house." What does all this add up to? —"A vast storehouse of spiritual power." In "stark, unadorned pain, mental and physical," Waters concluded, there is "a subtle but true coin that may be exchanged for spiritual goods for ourselves."[45]

So pain was alienable: coined from the bodies of the (untrustworthy) sick, it could be taken away and applied to the welfare of the healthy in a redistributive economy of distress.[46] God apparently sent pain to some people so that others might be edified, making the bodies of the sick conduits of communications and benefits from heaven to earth. But, again, the actual sick people, the real persons suffering from specific illnesses in precise ways, got lost in this process.

Since all pain was God-sent and good, and since it was never in any case as bitter as weak, whining sick people made it out to be, there was no need to account for its place in the universe, to respond to the spiritual and intellectual distress it might have occasioned. Protestants required this, perhaps, but not Catholics, who knew that God sent pain always for a purpose;[47] and priests, who might have been expected to sympathize most compassionately with the spiritual and physical dilemmas of the sick, were said to be always cheerful in the presence of suffering because, unlike their counterparts in other faiths, they knew that the problem of pain had been "solved."[48] In any case, as American devotional writers reminded the sick, comprehensible suffering was not real suffering. Catholics were said to prefer to suffer humbly and submissively, in recognition of their own guilt, rather than attempting to lessen the sting of it through understanding. Only spoiled children required such reassurance.[49]

The crew of Italian, Irish, Puerto Rican, and West Indian janitors, kitchen workers, handymen, and gardeners who hid out from their supervisors in the boiler room of the House of the Holy Comforter (a residence on the Grand Concourse to which my uncle moved in the mid-1960s) had a lot to say about the sexuality of the cripples in the rooms above them. A soft-voiced Italian-American man named Aldo usually started these conversations. "Hey, I was up there the other night, they had them in the showers—Jesus Christ, have you ever seen Jimmy's dick? It's like this. . . ." He opened his hands about a foot wide. "They all got big dicks," someone else affirmed knowledgeably, and then the men would speculate about whether or not having such huge organs was another consequence of their being cripples, as if nature compensated there for the ravages elsewhere. Aldo was always kind and extremely attentive to the men with cerebral palsy who lived at the "home," stopping on his rounds through the floors to talk with them, bringing them things to eat and drink from the kitchen between meals, but in the boiler room he returned again and again to the subject of cripples and sex. I was shocked, when I went to work at the House of the Holy Comforter in the summer after my first year of college, to encounter this other Aldo, so different from the one I knew upstairs, and he didn't spare me his fantasies of my uncle's sex life.

Often Aldo, less frequently one of the other men, sat next to Sally on the long back porch of the home and commented on the women walking past them along the garden walkways below. Leaning into Sally, he'd murmur, "Look at that one, Sal. What would you like to do with her?" He made a cupping motion with his hands. "Just one night, hah Sally, what we couldn't do. Jesus, Mary, and St. Anthony." My uncle seemed comfortable and happy during these conversations, apparently delighted with Aldo's company and enjoying their salacious bond, although I'm not sure of this.

The men in the boiler room claimed that in the early hours of the morning the cripples crawled out of bed and wheeled themselves into the shadows for blow jobs from the few women with cerebral palsy living at the home. This was absolutely impossible, of course, if only for practical reasons: none of the residents could get out of their crib-like beds by themselves, and there were no deep shadows in the well-lit building and no times when there were not nurses and orderlies everywhere. But none of the men in the boiler room, who were cynical and skeptical about everything else, ever questioned Aldo's tales of the cripples' nocturnal sexual carnival.

Devotional writers did not shrink from the hard God implied by their celebrations of pain; indeed, they delighted in him. In the winter of 1949, Jerry Filan, a man with cerebral palsy who was slightly younger than Sally, was badly burned in a fire at his home in Brooklyn. Filan had made two arduous trips to Lourdes in the hope of a miracle sometime before this, capturing the imaginations of devotional writers so that, by the time of the fire, Jerry Filan was a well-known "shut-in," admired and loved (in the way that "shut-ins" were, in the culture). The young man died after two months of excruciating pain. In their stories of his last days, Jerry Filan's admirers calmly affirmed, with the pride that American Catholics took in making such hard statements, that the fire was God's will; that God would burn a young man in a wheelchair to death never seems to have occasioned any doubt or grief.[50]

This God reflected all the anger, resentment, scorn, and denial of the Catholic ethos of suffering and pain. A paralyzed woman, bedridden since she was seventeen, admonished herself to remember that "it is God who sends such things as cold toast."[51] Writing about a nun dying slowly of cancer, a priest concluded that God "had planned to fill her last days on earth with pain so that she might have greater glory in heaven."[52] The family of a little girl stricken with polio was told to marvel that God loved them (not necessarily her) so much as to send them this gift.[53] If anyone dared to register dismay at the handiwork of a deity who was mean-spirited and petty enough to chill a sick woman's toast, he or she would have met with derision from devotional writers, and with even harsher injunctions to silence. American Catholic religious teachers practiced an antitheodicy in which a cheerful, compliant silence was deemed the only appropriate response to human sorrow.

But what was it like to believe that this mean God wanted you to suffer like this? Or to hear from the mouths of the ambulatory and the healthy calm affirmations of your distress, to receive from them the word that you were better off bedridden, poor, and alone?

"They hid us away," my uncle shouted at me one afternoon on the back porch of the home, long after my days there as a summertime janitor. He lifted himself off his chair by his elbows and rasped at me, "You don't know what it was like!"

We were in the middle of a conversation—an "interview," I was calling it—about Sal's favorite saints for a new project of mine when he began telling me how the families of his friends, ashamed of them, hid them away in back rooms so that their neighbors wouldn't see them. "We talk to each other about these things," Sal said over and over to me, and, "You don't know what I know."

My grandmother never hid Sal away. Before the operation on his knees, he used to crawl out of the apartment and slide down the building's steps on his rear end, then sit on the stoop watching over First Avenue. Later on, his brothers carried him downstairs or he would lean sideways out his bedroom window on a pillow. But not all the neighbors were comfortable with the sight of him. One crazy woman taunted my grandmother constantly about Sal. She called him "a diseased piece of meat." "May the doors of Calvary"—a cemetery in Queens—"close behind you," she screamed at my grandmother on the street, announcing to the stoops and sidewalks that Sally was a judgment on his family.

"They left them alone all day in dark rooms. I know these things—they told me about them—you don't know."

Sal has always had many friends, male and female, all over the city, and he's had a number of extended, monogamous, romantic engagements over time, as have most of his acquaintances. Sal's closest friends belong to the United Cerebral Palsy Federation, which has a large, modern building on 23d Street between Lexington and Park Avenues where Sal and the others go for classes and social events. This is where Sal said he'd heard stories of people being abandoned in back rooms, left all day without even water to drink.

The UCP has been Sal's special domain for many years, his place away, like his younger brothers' offices and social haunts. A couple of times a week he dresses up in his good clothes and wheels himself out to the curb to wait for the van that takes him to his downtown world. Whenever I visited him at the House of the Holy Comforter, I heard stories about the UCP, about the pretty girls volunteering there, whose pictures Sal sometimes put up on his dresser, about a discussion of abortion he had with his friends in psychology class or some hilarious tale of woe involving one or the other of his more maladroit or flamboyant friends.

"You know Irving, right?" Sally'd start, wheezing with laughter, his eyes tearing. "The other night, down at the UCP...."

He's asked me to come and visit him there, but I've never gone; for some reason, I feel uncomfortable about dropping in on him at that place. Recently, I passed by there on a wet summer night, very late in the evening. A solitary figure was sitting under the blue fluorescent lights of the building's entryway, waiting to go home. I thought I recognized the silhouette, and I stopped, standing just off to the side. The man didn't move; he stared ahead, gently nodding his head in response to some inner thought. His face was smooth, his forehead uncreased. He seemed to be supremely at peace.

I did know him, actually, or I think I did—he looked like Jimmy, from the old House of the Holy Comforter. When the home closed some years ago, the men and women with cerebral palsy had moved to other residences across the city. My uncle still saw them all at the UCP, but I didn't anymore. Jimmy was a man of astounding self-confidence. For all of the many years that I knew him, he was working on an autobiography, a book that combined—he told me once—his understanding of things, his life's philosophy, with stories about what it was like growing up with cerebral palsy. Whenever he was not at the UCP or visiting in the garden of the home with his girlfriend, whose parents brought her every week from another residence across the city, Jimmy was in his room, working on his autobiography.

A West Indian orderly would come in after breakfast and fix a tight elastic band around Jimmy's head; his forehead was permanently grooved at this spot, like a trumpeter's lips. Affixed to this band so that it stuck out from the middle of Jimmy's forehead was a long, thin rod with a round, cushioned button at the tip. Jimmy was now ready to work: bending forward again and again over his electric typewriter, he touched the tip of the rod to the keys. The last time I checked with Jimmy, his manuscript was more than eight hundred pages long.

At a time when several American industries were dedicated to the desperate work of helping people avoid or deny pain, which was increasingly understood as an obstacle to performance, achievement, and consumption in a culture that has treated physical distress and difference as sources of embarrassment and shame as well as signs of personal failure, the Catholic ethos posed (as Catholics themselves recognized) a powerful alternative. Catholics offered a storehouse for what everyone else was disposing of; the notion of sickness as a source of spiritual energy for the whole Church recast the uselessness and isolation of sickness into participation and belonging. Organizations like the Catholic Union of the Sick in America assigned the physically distressed a privileged place in the spiritual economy and offered them a way to reconnect themselves to the world around them literally *through,* not despite, their illnesses.

American Catholics in these years were enraptured and enthralled by physical distress. They presented themselves to the rest of the nation as a people experienced in pain. This was what set Catholics apart, and above others: in such an elitism of pain, rebelling against illness, whining, and complaining were seen as characteristically Protestant responses, while Catholics were stronger, better able to endure, better prepared to suffer. "It's how I react to cancer" that is important, Dooley wrote, not the suffering itself, because "people will see how I react" and draw spiritual lessons from it.[54] This was one of the things that

Catholics could teach American Protestants and, beyond them, the world.[55] There was a specular quality about the way in which Catholics understood their suffering. The devotional press severely and coldly admonished Catholics to suffer well in the sight of others, particularly Protestants, as if everyone were taking note of how they handled their distress. Pain served in this way as both a test of Catholic presence in the United States and a guarantee of it.

But there is an irony here: these romantic evocations of pain without analgesia and of the spiritual glories of leprosy were appearing just when the children and grandchildren of Catholic immigrants were beginning to leave the old ethnic neighborhoods of the Northeast and Midwest for the middle-class suburbs and American way of life beyond, just when the fantasy that scientific medicine could cure almost everything was becoming pervasive and Catholics themselves were developing a sophisticated network of up-to-date hospitals. The ethos of pain was being elaborated in Catholic magazines alongside tips for arranging new furniture, recipes, beauty hints, and ways to throw successful birthday parties for children, all written in the upbeat prose of women's magazines.

Elaborated in a particular way, physical distress was regularly counterposed in devotional culture to middle-class achievement. What good is success, money, power, or fame in this vale of tears? Catholic writers asked, over and over again—in the same periodicals that regularly celebrated the success, money, power, and fame of Catholic film stars, business tycoons, and athletes. Historian James Terence Fisher suggests that the pervasive preoccupation with pain in American Catholic culture of this time was a way for the children of immigrants to articulate and respond to their uneasiness with their success in the United States.[56] Young American Catholics with Southern- or Eastern-European or Irish parents and grandparents were caught in a terrible double bind after the First World War. American culture, as they encountered it in advertising, films, school, and the workplace, proclaimed that ambition was good, that material achievement and consumption were worthy goals, but they had grown up in cultures, religious and ethnic, that advocated self-control and self-denial, sacrifice and delayed gratification. These were the values of the Catholic family economy; they were taught by parish priests and nuns, expressed in the stories of saints and the old countries that they were told as children, and evident in the iconography surrounding them in church. They may have begun to "disdain" the culture of the enclaves, as Fisher writes, but the immigrants' children could not free themselves of it. This clash of moral sensibilities was exacerbated, furthermore, by the fact that the immigrants' children were trying to make it—and were by then succeeding—in a society that had not welcomed their parents and in which they were uncertain of their own places. These were the roots of the anger, resentment, and self-recrimination that found expression in the discourse of pain and the broken body, and of its ambivalence.

In other words, the modern American Catholic cult of pain and suffering cannot simply be attributed to the European heritage. This was not peasant fatalism reborn in the industrial working class: the parents and grandparents of the people writing about how wonderful it was to suffer cancer without recourse to painkillers had come to America to escape pain, after all, not to make a fetish of it. American Catholics of the second and third generations improvised an ethic of suffering and pain out of elements available in their tradition, in conscious and unconscious response to their contemporary circumstances. What they made lent an aura of spiritual heroism to the frustrations and setbacks they experienced in moving, with guilt and uncertainty, out of the ethnic enclaves, and it assured them of their moral superiority over the culture they were ambivalently striving toward. The constant refrain that pain mocked the pretensions of the world transformed their resentment of the people who appeared to be more successful than they were (among whom they were not sure of finding the place they desired) into a satisfying reaffirmation of traditional Catholic values.

The discourse of pain was similar in this regard to that of ethnicity in American Catholic communities of the 1930s (and later).[57] Both were made here, not inherited; both were produced through the constitution of necessary Others—racial or cultural in one case, the depraved, malingering sick person in the other—against which one's own identity and that of the community could be secured and affirmed. Finally, both ethnic nostalgia and the ethos of suffering and pain articulated the complex and ambivalent feelings that erupted out of the changing social circumstances of American Catholics in these years, when the immigrants' children found themselves pulled in different directions by memory and desire, parents and spouses, Catholic and American values. Denial and displacement gave to each discourse its rigidity and harshness.

"You can get up and go get yourself a glass of water," Sally was saying to me in a tense, hoarse voice, "whenever you want. You can get up and walk out of here today, but I can't!" He waved his arm in the direction of the front door.

First the stories of friends hidden in back rooms, and now this; Sally had never been so angry with me before. In between his accusations and challenges my uncle took deep breaths and held himself rigidly against the back of his chair with his long arms, looking away from me, shaking his head.

A new holy figure had recently entered Sal's customary pantheon of saints: Blessed Margaret of Castello.[58] Sal kept an image of her propped up on his messy, cluttered desk alongside holy cards of St. Francis and St. Anthony and pictures of his girlfriend, his nieces and nephews, and himself with various camp counselors and UCP staff. I'd never heard of her before or seen her image anywhere else. The holy card showed a small, bent figure leaning on a rough wooden staff; her eyes are closed, and her feet are turned in (Figure 1a and b). A pamphlet from Margaret's shrine in Philadelphia describes her as "A PATRON OF THE UNWANTED . . . A SAINT FOR OUR TIMES . . . BLIND . . . CRIPPLED . . . HUNCHBACKED . . . DWARF."

Sal had heard about Margaret at one of the First Saturday gatherings he still attended occasionally; a Dominican priest talked to the group about her. "If she'd been born today," Sally said to me, "she'd 'a been an abortion." Margaret's father was Captain of the People of the Umbrian city-state of Metola; his thirteenth-century victory over the neighboring Republic of Gubbio had brought him great fame and wealth. The Captain hoped that his first child would be a son to carry on the family's name and increase its glory, but his wife had given birth instead to a tiny girl, blind and horribly misshapen, in 1287. The bitterly disappointed couple hid the infant away in the castle, refusing even to give her a name. A gentle servingwoman called the baby "Margarita." The child was not only blind, but had a twisted foot and a hunchback; she was also a dwarf.

Sally interrupted himself. "She wouldn't have been born today," he said again, "she would have been an abortion." I didn't quite understand what Sally meant by this, but later I learned that Margaret's devout say that modern technology would have allowed her wealthy parents to discover her congenital conditions in the womb and that legalized abortion would have permitted them to kill her. For this reason "little Margaret," as her devout call her, has been proposed as the patron saint of the unborn and unwanted and of the anti-abortion movement.[59] Sally was starting to get agitated, and the mood of the conversation was growing darker.

When Margaret was six years old, her father, terrified that the lively child would wander out of the castle's shadows and be seen by someone, to the disgrace of his name, had her walled up in a room. The child was fed through a small window. She remained in this cell for seven years, and it was here that Margaret, cheerful and forgiving even in these circumstances, according to her biographers, began experiencing Jesus' presence in an unusually vivid way. She fasted continually from the age of seven on and mortified her flesh by wearing a hairshirt to increase her discomfort in the cell, which was hot in the summer and freezing in the winter. (It was also here that Margaret, as an adolescent, began struggling with temptations against her purity, as most popular biographies of her say. Sally must have known about this, although he didn't mention it to me.)

Sal paused again, this time to tell me about his friends who'd been hidden in the back rooms of their families' apartments; "May the gates of Calvary close behind you!" the crazy old woman had screamed at my grandmother.

When she was thirteen years old, Margaret was taken by her mother to the nearby town of Città di Castello and abandoned there in a

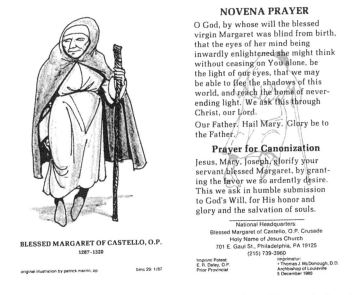

NOVENA PRAYER

O God, by whose will the blessed virgin Margaret was blind from birth, that the eyes of her mind being inwardly enlightened she might think without ceasing on You alone, be the light of our eyes, that we may be able to flee the shadows of this world, and reach the home of never-ending light. We ask this through Christ, our Lord.

Our Father. Hail Mary. Glory be to the Father.

Prayer for Canonization

Jesus, Mary, Joseph, glorify your servant blessed Margaret, by granting the favor we so ardently desire. This we ask in humble submission to God's Will, for His honor and glory and the salvation of souls.

National Headquarters:
Blessed Margaret of Castello, O.P. Crusade
Holy Name of Jesus Church
701 E. Gaul St., Philadelphia, PA 19125
(215) 739-3960

Imprimi Potest:
E. R. Daley, O.P.
Prior Provincial

Imprimatur:
+ Thomas J. McDonough, D.D.
Archbishop of Louisville
5 December 1980

BLESSED MARGARET OF CASTELLO, O.P.
1287-1320

original illustration by patrick marrin, op   bmc 29: 1/87

Figure 1a and b. Front and back of prayer card. Distributed by the Order of Preachers, Holy Name Priory, Philadelphia. Reproduced with permission.

church. Her devout vividly imagine the little girl groping her way along the cold walls of the sanctuary, calling out for her mother, with the church bell marking the hours of the day's passing as she gradually realizes what has happened to her. Margaret lived on the streets for a while, begging for her food, until the townspeople became aware of her sanctity and took her into their homes. She eventually entered a Dominican order of lay women and died in 1320, when she was thirty-three years old.

"You know what I like about her?" my uncle asked me at the end of the story. "I like it that there's somebody up there"—he glanced Heavenward—"like us." He was smiling, and the way he rolled his eyes up reminded me of the looks he'd given me when Aldo was teasing him about girls.

"Don't you think," I asked him, trusting the calm that seemed to have returned between us, "that St. Francis and St. Anthony can know what you feel, since they're saints?"

This was when Salvatore began shouting about water and the front door. I'd never know—nor would St. Francis or St. Anthony—what it was like to be crippled.

One of the pictures on his desk showed Sally with a beautiful young woman from the South Bronx named Silvia, a counselor at the UCP summer camp whom my uncle was crazy about. Sometimes Silvia came by the home to visit him in the winter. He said that once, when Silvia's little sister had been hit by a car, he and Silvia had prayed together to Blessed Margaret to heal the girl. She did.

"But I never asked her to make me walk," he snapped.

Finally, I had to leave. I got up, kissed my uncle on the top of his head like I always did, and then—just as he had said I would—I walked out. The last thing my uncle said about Blessed Margaret was, "She has a little bit of all the things we have."

Margaret's case for canonization is unaccountably stalled right now.[60] She has performed all the necessary miracles, there is evidence of a continuous cult, and she has a skilled advocate from the Dominican order who appears to be sincerely interested in seeing her made patroness of "the handicapped." But six hundred years after her death, Margaret has still not been elevated to the ranks of the saints. Perhaps not everyone is happy with the idea of "someone like us" in Heaven.[61]

The devotional ethos of suffering and pain failed actual sick people. It deepened the silence already threatening persons in pain with its constant injunctions to be quiet, denying them even the dignity of crying out in distress or unhappiness. It intensified the isolation and claustrophobia of the sick. Devotional writers castigated sick people for asking to be positioned more comfortably on beds that such writers liked to see as miniature calvaries rather than as the lumpy, lonely places of human suffering they actually were. The ethos confronted the sick with an image of the suffering Christ and then, in a perverse inverted Christology, told them that this image mocked any suffering of theirs: Did Jesus ask for a pillow on the Cross? Furthermore, by making pain a challenge, or test, of spiritual capacity, devotional culture added a layer of guilt and recrimination to the experience of bodily disease, as it proclaimed that most humans would fail this test. The ethos denied the social, communal, and psychological consequences of illness.[62]

Not surprisingly, given all this, few priests undertook ministry among the sick as their main work, and even visiting hospitals was not always a high priority among parish clergy, as the periodic admonitions in clerical journals suggest.[63] The parish clergy of the time held hospital chaplains in contempt (many still do), as the chaplains were well aware. In a typical lament, a former chaplain complained in 1937 that most parish priests "seem to have the foolish idea that a chaplain is a kind of second-rater, and that the very fact that he is stationed in the hospital is enough to guarantee that he has some failing which labels him 'unfit for real work.'"[64] Often enough, these suspicions were well-founded. The Catholic hospital chaplaincy has been a scandal until relatively recently, having been the place to assign—and to hide—priests with emotional or physical troubles of their own, particularly alcoholism, and the dumping ground for men who could not make it in the high-pressure, big-business, hearty male world of the American parish.[65] As late as 1965, when the National Association of Catholic Chaplains was founded, men (and women, although their spiritual work in the hospitals was generally accorded more respect from the first) who had chosen the hospital ministry as their vocation were complaining that they were forced by local church authorities to accept "a semi-invalid or problem personality" on their increasingly professional staffs.[66]

The rapid shift and reorganization of health care from the home to the hospital in the first three decades of this century posed a daunting challenge to an already overburdened Church, and the inadequacy of spiritual care for the sick can be at least partly attributed to this broader development. But American Catholics succeeded in building a network of modern, technologically sophisticated hospitals of their own; Catholic doctors and nurses were trained well in denominational schools; Catholic hospital professionals in the United States were up-to-date and well-informed on matters ranging from the latest surgical equipment to the best cafeteria designs, as the publications of the

American Catholic Hospital Association show. The Church was also capable of providing—and of treating as heroes—military chaplains in several wars. All of this contrasts sharply with the dismal level of pastoral care for the sick and suggests that the latter reflected the impact of the ambivalent ethos of suffering and pain rather than the economic or social state of the community.

The ethos also shaped the culture's stance toward religious healing. Healings had taken place at American shrines before this century, and charismatic healers, usually members of religious orders who scrupulously muted their own place in the thaumaturgic event in deference to ecclesiastical authority, were not unknown in the community before the widely publicized revival of faith healing among Catholics in the 1970s.[67] But Catholic culture was cautious and suspicious of popular healing of all sorts. The traditional curative arts of Irish and of Southern- and Eastern-European women were mostly lost within a generation of their immigration to this country, under the combined pressures of their children's assimilation to the world of modern medicine and the clergy's denunciations of "superstition" and "magic."[68] After the revival of faith healing among American Protestants in the early part of the century, and its subsequent association with flamboyant and disreputable characters, many American Catholics sought to distance themselves from what they saw as an example of Protestantism's tendency toward excess and anarchy. Insecure enough in their own middle-class status, Catholics had no desire to get out on anyone else's margin, and faith healing was definitely on the American margins.

But it was the romance of pain itself that made it so complicated for Catholics to hope for healings of any sort. Their yearnings were supposed to be pointed in the opposite direction, toward a deeper, sustained engagement with the promise and loveliness of "pain" (as opposed to the distress and loneliness of pain). Devotional culture taught that to alleviate pain was to deny the Cross; to seek relief was understandable, perhaps, but still an instance of human selfishness, a denial of the soul's superiority to the body and a rejection of the opportunity for saintliness. In a meditation published in *Catholic World* in 1929, a very sick woman warned others in similar distress that to be healed meant that "you might lose the shining thread of Him" in a misplaced quest for happiness, "only to discover that you had it once when you were bedridden, poor, and alone."[69] Some Catholics opposed painkillers and anesthetics even for the most extreme distress on the grounds that they interfered with an experience intended by God for the good of the afflicted person and intruded upon the intimacy with him available only to those in pain. Father Jerome Dukette celebrated a man, "quite crippled with arthritis," who, after traveling all the way to the Shrine of St. Anne de Beaupré in hopes of a cure, decided—on the steps of the shrine—that his suffering was a grace after all and turned away. Thirteen years later, according to Father Dukette, this man (still deformed) came back to the shrine to tell St. Anne that he was "grateful [to her] for not curing me" because "healthy, I stood a chance of damning myself, [whereas] I prefer to crawl up to Heaven on hands and knees than to run off to Hell on two good legs."[70] The Dominican theologian Bede Jarrett told a story with a similar theme:

> I remember a woman once in a parish where I worked, down in terribly poor streets. I remember her dying of cancer—a terrible cancer, that type of cancer that is all pain. One day she said to me, "Need I take morphia? The doctor wants me to. Need I?" "No," said I, "there's no need to; but why not?" "I think it would be better for me not to. You remember my boy?" Yes, I knew and remembered all about her boy. "It would be better for me not to because then I could offer all my sufferings for him. I'd love to make an offering of them. I can, can't I? That is the teaching of our faith?" What could I answer except that this was indeed our faith. She died in very great agony but wonderfully happy. The worse her pains grew, the happier she became.[71]

What other answer, indeed? Healing would shut off the spiritual dynamo of pain, squandering its exploitable energy. It would be like turning off Niagara Falls.[72]

Everyone agreed that Joey was a saint. Joey was one of Sal's roommates at the home, a short, stocky Italian-American man from the Bronx, with a tonsure of wooly brown hair ringing his huge head. His plump thighs strained the cloth of his pants and his wide hips filled the wheelchair, and he always rested his thick arms snugly at his sides. The nurses teased him about his weight, pinching his cheeks and kissing his head; the orderlies giggled and poked him while they shaved him in the early mornings. No one could resist touching Joey, stroking his hair, patting his round belly. Joey was a devout Yankees fan. On hot summer afternoons and evenings, he sat in front of the enormous window in his room, watching the cars stream by on the Concourse below, nestling his ear against the small transistor radio he held tightly in his hand. There'd almost always be one or two orderlies sitting on the bed beside him, bending close to hear the play-by-play or just staring out the window at the pigeons on the adjacent rooftops while Joey sat rapt in the game. When he wasn't listening to the Yankees or visiting with his mother, who came to the home almost every day, bringing food in foil-covered Pyrex dishes, Joey stared at the clock on his bureau. He was mesmerized by the sweeping second hand. Everyone who came into the room teased him about this.

During one of the summers I worked at the home, I was sunk in a terrible depression because I was having trouble taking my leave of the old neighborhood to go away to college. Unfamiliar with these awful feelings, I was terrified that I was going crazy; as I went about my chores on the floors or in the garden of the home, my skin prickled with anxiety. Occasionally, the terror was so intense that I raced in panic down the hallways—or so it seemed to me—or hid away in the darkest corners of the boiler room. My green janitor's uniform was always wet with sweat or rain. It never stopped raining that summer. The northern blocks of the Concourse dissolved in the steady drizzle and in the grey steam rising from the hot, wet concrete. My supervisor ran out of jobs for me to do, so we avoided each other on those long, wet days. I hid out in Sal's room, listened to the pecking of Jimmy's typing, or watched the clock with Joey.

Sometimes Joey rested his head on my shoulder, and I held his strong hand. He seemed content to have me sitting next to him, and I needed the comfort he provided me. I never told Joey my problems (although I imagined that he knew them anyway). I'd ask how the Yanks were doing or tease him about the clock, but Joey never said much to me. When I came into the room (terror-stricken and forlorn, as I imagine now), he'd smile and pat the arm of his chair, inviting me to sit next to him. I was always on the edge of tears there beside Joey in the cool, humid room, with the smells of the wet streets coming in the windows. Joey patted my hand. My uncle, working at the edge of his bed on a heap of papers or coming in from sitting on the porch with his girlfriend, shook his head sarcastically at me and, pointing to Joey, twirled a bony finger at his temple, letting me know what he thought of Joey, his clock, and me.

Sally will be eighty years old soon. About ten years ago something obscure and terrible happened to his digestive system, and now his diet is limited almost completely to liquids. He weighs about seventy pounds. He smokes a pack of cigarettes a day, down from his usual three. He keeps a leather bag tucked into his chair at his hip, filled with matches, coins, cigarettes, and the chewed and broken stumps of countless cigarette holders. Joey has been dead for a long time.

My uncle was born in the early years of this century at the beginning of a period of intense devotional creativity and improvisation in American Catholic culture, when the community was working to transform European spiritual idioms into forms that addressed and reflected the experiences, needs, and fears of the second and third generations in their American lives. The ethos of suffering and pain was central to this work, for reasons I have already discussed, and Sal—along with people afflicted by cancer, migraines, pneumonia, and other physical troubles—had no choice but to live within it and contend with it, making what they could of the ethos and of themselves within it.

The discourse of pain generally, and of the holy cripple specifically, offers historians a lens on some inner dimensions of American Catholic culture at midcentury, if the crafting of that discourse is understood as a practice situated in the social circumstances of the various communities at the time and not simply as a reflection of perennial Catholic theology. The children of immigrants, in transition from one way of life to another, constructed for themselves an ethos that proclaimed pain (not hard work, ambition, or a desire for success) as the road to the greatest achievement (which was sanctity, not a bigger apartment, a new car, or a good job). They clung to an image of themselves as sufferers while their circumstances steadily improved, which in turn allowed them to transform their envy and uneasiness into judgment on the social world they aspired to when those circumstances did not improve quickly enough. The elaboration of the ethos in this century has given suburban Catholic culture a distinct tone.

Living within this story, however, had many consequences for the everyday experience of the sick and handicapped, who were pivotal to its construction. These consequences were not all bad, as Sal's history shows: because others said his body made him special, closer to Heaven than they were, those who could walk out the door paid more attention to him than they might have otherwise and did nice things for him. They organized outings for him, visited him, made sure that some of his needs were met. The handicapped had a distinct place in American Catholic imaginations and public life. Because of this story, the world of Catholic devotionalism was seen as Sal's natural domain. He has always been a devout man (what else could he be in this culture?). He says the rosary daily, surrounds himself with images of the saints, and plans to be buried in the robes of the Third Order of St. Francis. Sal made a home (and a future grave) for himself in these idioms; through them, he could find comfort, consolation, and meaning for himself. In the prayer books tightly wrapped with rubber bands and jammed into a duffel bag fixed to the back of his chair, Sal had access to an intimate language for discovering, making, and naming his desires, fears, and hopes, and a language in which to address them to powerful figures who, he was told, would be listening closely to him. Devotionalism also gave Sal a set of practices—making the sign of the cross, fingering his beads, touching holy water, and so on—through which he could embody the prayers he was saying. It was in this world that he found Margaret of Castello.

But Sal also had to contend with the covert and unacknowledged implications and consequences of the discourse of the holy cripple. This spiritual fantasy was elaborated out of a disjuncture. Ambulatory

Catholics expected the handicapped to respond to the circumstances of their lives in ways that they knew they would not be capable of themselves were they trapped in a chair, strapped to a bed, unable to eat by themselves or get themselves a drink of water. Cripples were "better," which really meant that cripples were not like us—so the discourse of the holy cripple turned people like Sal, Jimmy, and Joey into inhuman Others whose inner lives were radically unlike everyone else's, and ultimately unrecognizable. First it made them into Others—and then devotional culture celebrated them for this otherness and difference, which was called holiness.

But in its insistence on the innocence, nearness to Heaven, purity of heart, and resilient cheerfulness of handicapped people, the fantasy drained away the lived reality of their days. It was the spiritual equivalent of the back rooms into which Sal's friends were tucked. It obscured the anger and resentment of handicapped persons, their struggles to overcome the physical limitations that mattered to them and their frustrations when they could not; it denied them the full range of human desires and hopes, including those for love, mastery, and independence; and it hid their dismay at the condescension and good intentions of the volunteers who spoke to them in loud voices and simple words. Holiness ensured the absence of the Other.

The discourse of the holy cripple accomplished this, furthermore, because it obscured the unequal relationships between those who could walk out the door and those who could not. The pretense of the discourse was that the latter were better than the rest of us—holier, more noble, more cheerful, better spirited. As Margaret Lehr concluded in *Ave Maria*, "Many of us [who can walk] are moral failures, while you almost invariably hear it said of the handicapped, 'My, isn't he wonderful! Always cheerful—always overcoming obstacles and surprising people with his achievements.'"[73] But the power of those of us who could walk out the door over those who could not was evident in the fact that *we* were the ones defining—and limiting—*their* inner lives for them. Their holiness was the practice of our power, and woe to the cripples who would not conform to our prescription. Then "many of us" would taunt them like the man who came up behind Sally on the morning the bus was late, or tell them to shut up, or write them off as complainers and stop taking their distress seriously.

Thus emptied of all but their holiness and innocence, cripples became blank slates for the articulation and vicarious experience of desire. Holiness became the space into which all kinds of unacknowledged needs and impulses could be driven, an exercise of fantasy that was unimpeded by the resistant facts of the Other's actual experience, since these did not exist. Holiness became a compelling and productive psychic zone for everyone but the "cripples" it was defining. Aldo's fantasies emerged ineluctably from within the narrative of holiness: once the emptiness of the holy cripple had been opened up, the cripple-with-the-big-penis was sure to fill it. Aldo's were not the only fantasies, though, nor were all the desires articulated through the handicapped sexual. "The physically sound," according to Lehr, "often turn to the afflicted for strength—for moral courage," and so they—we—did.

The cruelty of the discourse of the holy cripple is fully evident in a 1950 "Letter to Shut-Ins" by Thomas A. Lahey, C.S.C., in *Ave Maria*.[74] "This letter is written to you as one of God's favorite children," Lahey begins. He assures his "dear suffering shut-in" and his "dear fortunate shut-in" that he understands what their lives are like.[75] "The music of the theater, the laughter of the banquet table, the natural and normal consolations which come from human relationships—all these are denied you. No matter how helpful those around you try to be, the inevitable fact confronts you that during most of your life you will have to put up with the four walls of your room and the somewhat impersonal companionship which your books and radio can furnish." This will not be easy, Father Lahey concedes. "I do not have to tell you how slowly the clock will tick under such circumstances, and how agonizing will be some of the hours that follow."[76] He attributes such distress, though, to "your own natural weaknesses," not to the awful loneliness of life within those four walls; if his shut-ins are miserable, Lahey wants them to know that it is a sign of their corruption.

But "suffering would not be suffering" if it were not so miserable and painful; so Lahey urges his shut-ins not to try to relieve their distress, since "it is the very fact of your suffering which has marked you out as one of the favorite children of God." Are there any consolations? Of course: "Sealed up as he is from the direct sense-appeals of various earthly attractions," the shut-in is freer of temptation, more likely to look to Heaven for satisfaction. Lahey closes by warning the fortunate unfortunates not to squander their time on earth. Join the Franciscans' Apostolate of the Way of the Cross, he encourages them, through which they will receive "free and without any obligation" a crucifix "so indulgenced" that, by holding it and saying certain prayers, the shut-in can release an untold number of souls from Purgatory. Stuck within their own rooms, cripples get to be the liberators of the dead. "Since those indulgences can be received over and over almost without end, you can spend your wakeful hours in helping to deliver not only hundreds but thousands of those poor souls who are pining for release . . . a wonderful missionary project you will admit."[77]

Father Lahey's "Letter to Shut-Ins" was not idiosyncratic; indeed, letters like this were a popular feature of American Catholic devotional discourse. Under the guise of compassion and understanding, their authors defined what they imagined and wanted the cripples' lives to be. Their accounts were prescriptive, pretending to be descriptive. While Sally and his girlfriends were in fact dancing and eating together, holding hands and kissing, the devotional press was telling us and them that they did not laugh or enjoy uproarious company and did not feel any human bond, let alone engage in sex, romance, dancing. But Father Lahey and the others did not want their beloved shut-ins to live like the rest of us, to enjoy what we enjoy (and the sound of his satisfaction can be heard in the prose): "the music of the theater, the laughter of the banquet table." Rather, they wanted them to be holy. When you get to Heaven, Lahey assured his readers in conclusion, you will find millions of souls freed from Purgatory by your prayers waiting to thank you.

I hope that when Sally gets to the Heaven he imagines, he finds Blessed Margaret waiting to wheel him quickly away from these grateful souls—who think that their Heaven was secured by his (and her) isolation and denial on earth—to a place where there are others like them.

Sal discovered Margaret in the devotional world, and he prayed to her and other saints in the idioms of devotionalism, which is just what Father Lahey told him to do with himself. But Father Lahey did not understand that there were enough ruptures, fissures, and contradictions in this world for my uncle and the others to find ways within it of living against it. Catholic devotionalism offered a complex field of expression and experience, polysemous, internally contradictory. These were flexible idioms, subject to improvisation; this world afforded many guises and voices, some of them (at least) at odds with the narrative of the holy cripple promulgated elsewhere in the same devotional culture.

I cannot say much about Sal's relationship with Margaret of Castello since we had only the one, difficult (for me) conversation about her, but I do know that in this conversation, Margaret served as the "articulatory pivot" through which Sal was able to express his experience and emotions.[78] She permitted Sally to uncover the fact of hiddenness: the details of her story created a context in which he could rage against his own sense of isolation and abandonment. The refrain "she would have been an abortion" may have echoed his own anger and anxiety. I do not fully understand how satisfying and empowering it can be to discover oneself reflected in Heaven—to see someone up there like me; to see not simply my actual experience embodied in the narrative of a person understood to be close to God now, but my hidden fears and anger as well; or to see my sense of myself as a special, noteworthy person reflected in the adulation given to someone like me. We will have to take Sal's word for this. But as Sally told me, while he was talking about Margaret, there was a lot I did not understand about his experience.

Through the crippled saint, Sally momentarily breached the otherness constituted for him by the same devotional culture that gave him Margaret. He asked, demanded, through her that I imagine myself in his place—did I know what it was like to be unable to walk out the door?—and that I think about his experience as he lived it, not as I fantasized it. By his work of appropriation within a tradition complex enough to allow for such discrepancies, Sal inverted the meaning of holiness: Margaret's holiness became a sign of his own presence. If there were someone up in Heaven like him, Sal taught me, then people like him could be recognized on earth. In Heaven as on earth, Margaret subverts the narrative of the holy cripple, and this may be why she will not be admitted into the ranks of the saints.

Holiness itself turns out to be a peculiarly unstable cultural construction. Because it emerged out of desire and denial, it seemed to mutate almost organically into its opposite, as Aldo's relentless fantasizing shows. Even though they were themselves a reflex of the emptying discourse of holiness, Aldo's fantasies exposed, through the endlessly, compulsively reiterated image of the large phallus, precisely what holiness was meant to deny: that Sal, like the rest of us, was motivated and inspired by powerful, fully human needs, desires, and hopes. They certainly affirmed that he was a person, present, not absent, and that he would in fact seek the "natural and normal consolations which come from human relationships" that Father Lahey wanted to deny him. Thankfully, Sal, Jimmy, and the others had their own ways of doing so and ultimately did not need Aldo's obsessions to live against Father Lahey's denials.

My uncle is desire and will incarnated now. His flesh has shrunk back to the bone; he looks like a dark, knotted piece of leather. He sits in his chair breathing smoke, the cigarette holder clamped in his teeth. Many times in the last ten years my mother and father have been summoned to the residence late at night with the word that Sal was close to death, and each time Sal has fought his way back. St. Francis's shroud may be waiting for him, but Sal is not slipping easily into it; holding onto his rosary, he is still fighting the story that was written for him out of the needs of ambulatory Catholics. He is not cheerful, compliant, or uncomplaining. He resists what others want from him, perversely (as everyone else sees it) putting up obstacles to what others want to do for (or, as he sees it, to) him. He is not offering up his suffering for anyone. Jerry Filan's God is not going to get him.

Joey died at just the age when men of his generation with cerebral palsy were expected to die.

A terrible storm hit New York on a recent summer's night when Sal was scheduled to go down to the UCP. The trees outside on Mosholu Parkway were bent to the ground by the wind, and rain poured from a black sky. My father happened to be at the residence that night on some errand and, thinking that my uncle would be frightened by the storm, went looking for him. Sal wasn't in his room or the corridors of his floor, not in the chapel or the lounge. My father finally found him waiting at the front door, all dressed up to go out, a wide, colorful tie completely covering his thin chest. An old black raincoat was crushed between his stiff legs.

"It's the middle of a hurricane," my father yelled at Sally. "What are you doing? You don't really think you're going out in this tonight, do you?!"

An iron table was blown off one of the upper porches and came crashing into the street outside.

"Ahhhh," my uncle said, "it's not that bad."

"The highway's closed," my father said, laughing in his fury at Sal's stubbornness. "Are you kidding? No one's gonna drive in this!"

"Go see when the bus is coming," Sally commanded. Then he turned back to face the front door, ready to go out.

NOTES

When I was five years old someone asked me what I wanted to be when I grew up, and I said, "Uncle Sally." Sal was a good friend of my childhood, and this essay is affectionately dedicated to him.

What I say here about American Catholic popular theology is based on my readings of the many devotional periodicals that made up the everyday literary culture of the community for most of this century. Some of these, such as the *Voice of St. Jude,* were published by the shrines that proliferated on the American Catholic landscape in these "heyday" years of devotionalism (as Jay Dolan has called them); others (*Catholic World, Ave Maria,* and *America*) were the work of specific religious orders; still others were more or less trade journals for clergy (*Homiletic and Pastoral Review* and *American Ecclesiastical Review*). *Hospital Progress* was published for Catholic hospital professionals.

While it is impossible to give a history of American Catholic journalism here, I need to note, first, that this kind of popular journalism has existed among American Catholics since the early nineteenth century. These periodicals have always appealed mainly to a middle-class, not a working-class, readership, for obvious reasons, and they have always promoted the devotional piety that has been seen since the early modern period as the foundation of Catholic life and a bulwark against modernity. In the decades considered here, Catholic magazines slowly became attractive, accessible, upbeat family periodicals in a self-consciously American voice, offering articles and fiction on subjects of interest to the middle-class children of immigrants. (A popular feature was nostalgic presentations of "authentic" Old World customs.) By the middle of this century, Catholic popular magazines and newspapers together sustained Catholics' sense of their distinction in American culture as they described the aesthetics of assimilation, articulated the moral ideals of an emerging middle class, served as the training ground for Catholic intellectuals like John Cogley and Donald Thorman, supported a host of Catholic entrepreneurs, gave a Catholic gloss to every dimension of American culture from highways and kitchen designs to foreign policy, and thus became visible expressions of the coherence, integration, and unity of American Catholic culture— which did not really exist outside of these magazines and newspapers.

Catholics had other sources for their theology: the pastors and prelates of the airwaves, Catholic fiction, catechisms, sermons, religion classes, book clubs, moral handbooks, and so on. All of these other idioms converged in the devotional magazines, however, which regularly printed excerpts from popular theological books, condensations of Catholic novels, articles by or about Catholic television and film personalities, and the sermons of famous Catholic preachers, along with the usual fare of American family magazines.

Devotional periodicals could be found everywhere. Salesmen sold subscriptions door to door in cities, suburbs, and rural areas, often traveling in big cars with the name of the magazine painted on the doors. Magazines were offered as promotions in local parish fundraising drives, stocked in the libraries of Catholic hospitals, schools, convents, and rectories, and given as gifts, prizes, and incentives. By 1959, at the end of the most intense period of devotional improvisation in American Catholic history, the Catholic Press Association reported that there were 24,273,972 subscribers to 580 Catholic publications. See Jay P. Dolan, *The American Catholic Experience: A History from the Colonial Times to the Present* (Garden City, NY, 1985), 394. I have also been helped in preparing these brief comments on the history of American Catholic journalism by Arnold J. Sparr, "The Catholic Literary Revival in America, 1920–1960." Ph.D. diss., University of Wisconsin-Madison, 1985; and Apollinaris W. Baumgartner, *Catholic Journalism: A Study of Its Development in the United States, 1789–1930* (New York, 1967).

Popular theologizing was practiced with considerable fervor and verve in devotional journals—which until recently have been overlooked as sources for the study of American Catholic culture—literally in response to current events as they unfolded. This was where Catholics commented on what they were becoming as they were becoming it. Clergy read the magazines and talked about them in their sermons, and issues of particular magazines were discussed in Catholic schools. Ample space was allotted for readers' comments, and their letters were generally lively, provocative, and sometimes at odds with editorial positions. This was a thriving and important idiom, in which modern American Catholics not only discovered who they were, but constituted themselves as well.

1 "Cripple" is an ugly word and strikes contemporary ears (rightly) as harsh and demeaning. But it is the word that everyone used in the years under consideration to talk about my uncle and his friends. This is what my family called Sal; priests used it to refer to the handicapped in the sermons delivered on devotional outings; and this was the term applied to men and women like my uncle in the devotional press. It should become clear that my uncle was anything but "crippled," in spirit or mind. His body was strong too; he hugged his nephews and nieces with powerful arms. But "cripple" was the standard nomenclature of the times, and I use it as such throughout.

The word is, not surprisingly, undergoing a revolutionary repositioning right now. Handicapped persons are adopting it in self-conscious political anger and personal defiance, just as gay men and women have done with "queer." As Joseph P. Shapiro notes in his recent, excellent study of the struggles of persons with disabilities for civil rights, "In reclaiming 'cripple,' disabled people are taking the thing in their identity that scares the outside world the most and making it a cause to revel in with militant self-pride." See his *No Pity: People with Disabilities Forging a New Civil Rights Movement* (New York, 1993), 34.

2 On the devotion to Our Lady of Fatima in contemporary Catholicism, see Sandra Zimdars-Swartz, *Encountering Mary: From La Salette to Medjugorje* (Princeton, 1991), 67–91, 190–219. The Blue Army still exists. The National Shrine of the Blue Army of Mary is located in Washington, New Jersey, where a periodical, *Soul Magazine,* is published.

3 For this theology of sanctification through suffering, as it was elaborated in American Catholic devotional journals in this century, see, for example, Marcella Murray, O.S.B., "Magazines in the Catholic Hospital Library," *Hospital Progress* 21 (February 1940): 50–51; M. Teresita, C.M.H., "Opportunities for the Promotion of Catholic Action in the Teaching of Professional Adjustments in the Catholic Schools of Nursing," *Hospital Progress* 21 (June 1940): 206–12; Thomas A. Fox, "Drama with a Happy Ending," *Homiletic and Pastoral Review* 49 (April 1949): 565–67; Joachim DePrada, C.M.F., "To Whom Shall We Turn?" *Voice of St. Jude* 24 (December 1958):

34; E. J. Garesché, S.J., "Catholic Hospital Apostolate," *Ave Maria* 73 (5 May 1951): 551-55; and Jerome F. Wilkerson, "Patient-Care Spiritual Needs," *Hospital Progress* 46 (December 1965): 76-80. The ethos was pervasive, and virtually any issue of any devotional periodical contained some expression of it. The ambivalent ethos of suffering and pain in modern American Catholicism is evident in the following examples, among many others: "Our Foolish Discontent," *Ave Maria* 11 (10 April 1920): 469; "Sympathy for the Sick," *Ave Maria* 11 (12 June 1920): 757-58; "A Virtue More Admired Than Cultivated," *Ave Maria* 15 (21 January 1922): 84-85; "The Best of All Devotions," *Ave Maria* 26 (16 July 1927): 84-85; "Relief of the Holy Souls," *Ave Maria* 36 (5 November 1932): 595-96; see also Jane Sprenger, "Do It for Mom, Patty," *Sign* 32 (July 1953): 51-52; Ed Willock, "Suffering and Spiritual Growth," *Ave Maria* 88 (12 July 1958): 23-26; and Jerome Dukette, O.F.M., Conv., "Salvation in Suffering," *Homiletic and Pastoral Review* 58 (October 1957): 77-79.

4 Joseph L. Healy, S.J., "Opportunities for Religious Education in the Hospital," *Hospital Progress* 18 (August 1937): 259-61.

5 For examples of such advice to nurses, see Bakewell Morrison, S.J., "Religion in the Curriculum of the Catholic School of Nursing," *Hospital Progress* 20 (December 1939): 419-27; and "The Nurses' Apostolate," *Catholic Women's World* 2 (February 1940): 30.

6 On Dooley's cancer in American Catholic popular culture, see James T. Fisher, *The Catholic Counterculture in America, 1933-1962* (Chapel Hill, 1989), 187.

7 Katherine Neuhaus Haffner, "One Day at a Time," *Ave Maria* 72 (9 September 1950): 343.

8 Healy, "Opportunities for Religious Education," 261.

9 Rev. Lincoln F. Whelan, "The Sick and Aged at Your Home," *Homiletic and Pastoral Review* 58 (July 1958): 983-84.

10 Vera Marie Tracy, "After Dark: A Hospital Sketch," *Catholic World* 130 (November 1929): 134-39.

11 In "Sick Room Study," *Ave Maria* 54 (6 September 1941): 294, the author imagines the sick person ministering to the priest who comes to call on him or her.

12 Florence White Rogers, "Letters to the Needy," *America* 50 (31 March 1934): 616-17; the quotation about Lourdes is from James Louis Small, "Vignettes of Lourdes," *Ave Maria* 11 (19 June 1920): 771.

13 Two excellent books have explored this romanticism with great subtlety and insight: William M. Halsey, *The Survival of American Innocence: American Catholicism in an Era of Disillusionment, 1920-1940* (Notre Dame,

1980); and Fisher, *Catholic Counterculture*. Fisher's book, in particular, superbly limns the darkness.

14 Ferdinand J. Ward, C.M., "How and Why of Suffering," *Homiletic and Pastoral Review* 58 (February 1958): 498–99.

15 Sister Celestine, "A Sister's Role in Spiritual Care," *Hospital Progress* 33 (October 1952): 75–77.

16 American Catholics were articulating an ancient ambivalence; for a useful overview of the complex understandings of sickness, pain, health, and healing in Catholic cultures, see Darrel W. Amundsen, "The Medieval Catholic Tradition," in *Caring and Curing: Health and Medicine in Western Religious Traditions*, ed. Ronald L. Numbers and Darrel W. Amundsen (New York, 1986), 65–107; and Marvin R. O'Connell, "The Roman Catholic Tradition Since 1945," also in Numbers and Amundsen, eds., *Caring and Curing*, 108–43. About the Tridentine tradition, to which American Catholics were immediate heirs, O'Connell notes, "Priests and people were likely moreover to ascribe a specific suffering to a specific moral lapse, their own or others', a habit they maintained in the face of official ecclesiastical and theological disapproval" (122).

17 Boniface Buckley, C.P., "In Bitter Praise of Pain," *Sign* 24 (May 1945): 528; see also, for example, Rev. James J. Murphy, "Human Suffering," *Homiletic and Pastoral Review* 49 (March 1949): 485–86; and C. C. Martindale, S.J., "Making Use of Pain," *The Priest* 13 (January 1957): 51–54.

18 Hubert N. Hart, "Notes on the Meaning of Pain," *Ave Maria* 177 (April 1953): 50–53.

19 "P. J. C.," "Error and Disease," *Ave Maria* 35 (9 January 1932): 53. Patrick Joseph Carroll, C.S.C., was editor of *Ave Maria* from 1934 to 1952.

20 Dean H. O'Donnell, C.S.C., "Apostolate of the Sick Room," *Ave Maria* 63 (2 March 1946): 263–66.

21 See, for example, Paul Schaeuble, O.S.B., "Lepers and Leprosy," *Homiletic and Pastoral Review* 45 (February 1945): 381–82.

22 On the association between Hansen's disease and immorality, see Gavan Daws, *Holy Man: Father Damien of Molokai* (Honolulu, 1973), 132–34.

23 Alice Blair, "Share Your Fun," *Catholic Women's World* 1 (October 1939): 37.

24 On CUSA, see Mary S. Hessel, "Catholic Action for the Sick by the Sick," *Catholic World* 167 (May 1948): 163–66; Paul Brindel, O.S.B., Oblate, "I Am a Cusan," *Hospital Progress* (September 1957): 32, 34, 173; Anne Tansey, "Catholic Union of Sick Associates," *Ave Maria* 72 (11 November 1950): 622–25; Thomas Shelley, "Find Happiness in CUSA," *Catholic Digest* 22 (March 1958): 24–26; and Joseph LaMontagne, S.S.S., "I Am a Cusan," *The Priest* 11 (September 1956): 776–80.

25 Frank J. Mallett, "Overcoming Handicaps," *Ave Maria* 46 (24 July 1937): 105-7.

26 John P. Doran, "One Way Ticket: A Visit to Molokai," *Catholic World* 171 (April 1950): 30-35. Doran's ticket, incidentally, was round-trip.

27 Thomas Heath, O.P., "From Evil to Good," *Ave Maria* 101 (1965): 16-19.

28 "They Also Serve: A Series of Letters from an Invalid," *Voice of St. Jude* (September 1950): 16-17.

29 See, for example, "One Lesson Taught by the War," *Ave Maria* 15 (4 March 1922): 275-76; Charlotte Wilma Fox, "The Voice of God," *Ave Maria* 35 (30 April 1932): 557-61; Alphonse M. Schwitalla, S.J., "The Influence of the Catholic Hospital in Our Modern Society," *Hospital Progress* 20 (September 1939): 315; Msgr. Patrick O'Boyle, "I Saw the Eyes of Suffering Children," *Voice of St. Jude* (June 1947): 7, 13; Clement H. Crock, "The Mystery of Suffering," *Homiletic and Pastoral Review* 50 (March 1950): 549-51; Jennie Marie Mucker, "Hidden Apostles," *Voice of St. Jude* (February 1954): 10-13; and Owenita Sanderlin, "My Operation," *Voice of St. Jude* (August 1955): 29-31.

30 Mary E. Hoffman, "The Candle Beams," *Ave Maria* 81 (16 April 1955): 16-17.

31 Haffner, "One Day at a Time," 344.

32 For example, Mary Catherine Shuler, "Silver Lining of Convalescence," *Ave Maria* 59 (8 April 1944): 494-96; O'Donnell, "Apostolate of the Sick Room"; Thomas A. Lahey, C.S.C., "A Letter to Shut-Ins," *Ave Maria* 71 (25 February 1950): 245-49; Florence A. Waters, "Religious Communities for the Sick," *Ave Maria* 77 (21 February 1953): 241-43; and Martindale, "Making Use of Pain."

33 Mary O'Connor, "Are You Pain's Puppet?" *Ave Maria* 73 (17 February 1951): 216.

34 "A headache compared with His crown of thorns! Possibly this may make us a little less timorous in asking for 'more'!" (Martindale, "Making Use of Pain," 53).

35 Bruno M. Hagspiel, S.V.D., "A New Hospital Patroness, St. Gemma Galgani," *Hospital Progress* 21 (March 1940): 97-98.

36 "Heroes," *Ave Maria* 46 (11 September 1937): 341.

37 "Pain can bring greatness to us. It can make people great. It need not. We have seen it in some of our sick, making them only discontented till they find life terribly wearisome. But this failure to grow great by suffering is not due to suffering but to the soul," wrote Bede Jarrett, O.P., in "The Problem of Suffering," *Homiletic and Pastoral Review* 34 (December 1933): 260-65; see also Buckley, "Bitter Praise of Pain," 527.

38 See, for example, the peaceful, productive, and well-organized life of leper colonies portrayed in George J. Renneker, S.M., "Gateway to Heaven," *Catholic Digest* 5 (March 1941): 11–13; Marius Risley, "Damien's Spirit in America," *Catholic Digest* 6 (January 1942): 40–45; and James A. Brussel, "Two-Way Door at Carville," *Catholic Digest* 13 (June 1949): 52–54.

39 "Suffering and Imagination," *Ave Maria* 15 (13 May 1922): 596.

40 Doran, "One Way Ticket," 35.

41 Waters, "Religious Communities for the Sick."

42 See, for example, B. J. Cunningham, C.M., "Is One of You Sick?" *Ave Maria* 81 (21 May 1955): 8–11. Docetic Christologies "denied [Jesus'] real humanity and His actual death," according to Williston Walker, as a way of resolving the terrible contradiction between Jesus' earthly existence and belief in his glory. "The simplest solution of the Christological problem may well have seemed to some the denial of His earthly life altogether." See his *A History of the Christian Church* (New York, 1970 [1918]), 51.

43 William P. McCahill, "Christ in the Wounded and the Maimed," *Catholic Mind* 49 (September 1951): 563–69.

44 From an undated prayer card printed by CUSA, 176 W. 8th St., Bayonne, NJ 07002.

45 Waters, "Religious Communities for the Sick," 241.

46 For some other examples of this theme, see Rev. G. Hardesty, "The Maintenance of the Individuality of the Catholic Hospital," *Hospital Progress* 20 (October 1939): 338–39; Murphy, "Human Suffering," 484; Bertin Farrell, C.P., "Why the Suffering?" *Sign* 45 (May 1966): 55. An especially poignant meditation on this theme, written by a woman paralyzed from the waist down since the age of seventeen, is Vivian T. Murphy, "Sickbed Voyage of Discovery," *Catholic Digest* 14 (May 1950): 74–76. The writer tells herself, "You are one of the crosses that have made [your family] good."

47 Mary Agnes Boyle, for example, contrasts her own resignation to and acceptance of her incurable cancer with the way her non-Catholic relatives rebel against and get angry with their diseases, in "The Long Journey," *Ave Maria* 78 (19 September 1953): 10–13. That non-Catholics do not know how to take life on the chin as Catholics do was a commonplace in the devotional press and may have been the echo among their children of the pride of working-class Catholics of the ethnic enclaves.

48 Morrison, "Religion in the Curriculum," 423.

49 See, for example, Hart, "Notes on the Meaning of Pain," 53; and Heath, "From Evil to Good," 18.

50 Jerry Filan's story is told in Shelley, "Find Happiness in CUSA"; and in Tansey, "Catholic Union of Sick Associates," 623.

51 Murphy, "Sickbed Voyage," 76.

52 Dukette, "Salvation in Suffering," 78.

53 Sprenger, "Do It for Mom, Patty," 51.

54 Fisher, *Catholic Counterculture*, 187.

55 See, for example, Robert O'Hara, C.P., "The Good Life," *Sign* 29 (August 1949): 52–53.

56 See Fisher, *Catholic Counterculture*, 94–99. Here he is talking specifically about the appeal of Dorothy Day's dark anarchism for college-educated children of the Catholic ghettos, but I think the point can be generalized, as I argue in the text.

57 I have discussed this at greater length, with an extensive bibliography on changes in the experience of ethnicity among the many different groups making up American Catholicism, in "The Center Out There, In Here, and Everywhere Else: The Nature of Pilgrimage to the Shrine of St. Jude, 1929–1965," *Journal of Social History* 25 (Winter 1991): 213–32. For useful recent deconstructions of the givenness of white ethnic identity, see Richard D. Alba, *Ethnic Identity: The Transformation of White America* (New Haven, 1990); and Mary C. Waters, *Ethnic Options: Choosing Identities in America* (Berkeley, 1990).

58 The best English-language biography of this unusual holy figure is William R. Bonniwell, O.P., *The Life of Blessed Margaret of Castello* (Madison, 1979 [1952]). Bonniwell's book is based on archival sources that date to the fourteenth century. I have discussed this devotion in "The Cult of Saints and the Reimagination of the Space and Time of Sickness in Twentieth-Century American Catholicism," *Literature and Medicine* 8 (1989): 63–77. Margaret's American shrine is at 701 East Gaul St., Philadelphia, PA 19125.

59 See, for example, "Blessed Margaret: The Cross Transfigured, A Saint for Our Time." Pamphlet published by the Dominican nuns, Monastery of Our Lady of the Rosary (Summit, NJ, 1977).

60 I spent 1985–86 in Italy, studying modern Catholic popular religion and exploring both the history of devotion to Blessed Margaret in Umbria and her cult among contemporary Italian handicapped men and women. The Dominican order in the United States and Italy has been extraordinarily generous to me in this research, allowing me access to all the documents relating to Margaret's cult and inviting me to observe their work in promoting her canonization at the Vatican. I especially want to thank A. I. Cataudo, O.P., in Philadelphia, and Innocenzo Venchi, O.P., the order's Postulator General in Rome.

61 Indeed, were Margaret to be canonized, she would be the first saint whose body was not in perfect physical condition at birth, thus effectively sever-

ing the ancient Western link between physical and moral soundness—as her handicapped devout well know.

62 Devotional writers drew a curtain across the sick room. Addressing him- or herself to an imaginary person in severe pain, an anonymous author in *Ave Maria* intoned: "You enact your monotonous drama of pain in such a divine technique of self-suppression, you make us think that, after all, there is joy in suffering, with sunshine, summer and rose bloom behind the half-curtained windows of a sick room" ("Sick Room Study," 294).

63 See, for example, "Visitation of the Sick," *Homiletic and Pastoral Review* 48 (August 1948): 854; and, in the same issue, Donald L. Barry, "Sacraments for the Sick," 824–27; see also "On Visiting Hospitals," *Homiletic and Pastoral Review* 65 (December 1964): 193–94.

64 George A. Mahony, "Our Friend, the Hospital Chaplain," *Homiletic and Pastoral Review* 37 (September 1937): 1260–64.

65 See, for example, Anthony Kraff, C.P.P.S., "The Difference in the Ministry between Hospital and Parish," *Hospital Progress* 38 (November 1957): 83–84. The training and the reputation of hospital chaplains were improving by this time, but Kraff is still conscious of the parish clergy's scorn. "A Hospital Chaplain" of 1930 laments his being compelled to carry a "double burden"—caring for the sick and enduring the scorn of his fellows. He concedes that "until now" it has been "customary to appoint to this position priests who are often semi-patients themselves" (this chaplain was optimistic—the situation persisted for at least another three decades). See "God's Way with Souls," *Hospital Progress* 11 (April 1930): 172–74. A study of the Catholic hospital chaplaincy has yet to be published.

66 Wilkerson, "Patient-Care Spiritual Needs." For a brief history of the National Association of Catholic Chaplains, see Marilyn N. Gustin, with Rev. Msgr. Harrold A. Murray, *The National Association of Catholic Chaplains: A Twenty-Year History (1965–1985)* (Milwaukee, 1985).

67 On the nineteenth century, see Ann Taves, *The Household of Faith: Roman Catholic Devotions in Mid-Nineteenth Century America* (Notre Dame, 1986), 57ff.; for a modern case, see Catherine M. Odell, *Father Solanus: The Story of Solanus Casey, O.F.M., Cap.* (Huntington, IN, 1988). Sister Celestine ("A Sister's Role," 76) reports the case of an older hospital sister in her order who was believed by patients to be a healer. The first positive evaluations of religious healing appeared in the devotional press in the early 1960s, not surprisingly just when the ethos of suffering and pain was being called into question. For an example of both reconsiderations, see Heath, "From Evil to Good," 18–19. Some writers in the 1960s sought to transform that ethos into a motivation for political action and social responsibility;

see, for example, Father Ronald Luka, "The Way of the Cross Today— Through the Streets of Selma and the Trails of Vietnam," *Ave Maria* 101 (10 April 1965): 6–9. For a discussion of the revival of faith healing among Catholic charismatics in the 1970s by a participant in the movement, see Edward D. O'Connor, C.S.C., *The Pentecostal Movement in the Catholic Church* (Notre Dame, 1971). O'Connor's discussion of healing is not completely free of ambivalence; he seems uneasy at times with this manifestation of the Spirit's presence (see, for example, pages 162–64).

68 My sense of this is impressionistic. The subject of immigrant vernacular healing awaits a study of its own.

69 Tracy, "After Dark," 138.

70 Dukette, "Salvation in Suffering," 78.

71 Jarrett, "Problem of Suffering," 264. Ferdinand Ward criticizes the idea, which he says is shared by many Catholics, that sedation is spiritually wrong ("How and Why of Suffering," 499). Gerald Vann, O.P., approved what he considered the heroic Catholic refusal of "anesthetic drugs, twilight sleep, psychotherapy, and so forth," a resistance that he proudly claimed had its "roots in a feeling that the naked will should be left to conquer the rebellions and repulsions of the instincts, so that the reward due to fighting the good fight may not be forfeit." See his "True Balance," *Catholic World* 151 (July 1940): 485–86. Vann went on to caution his readers against the "glorification of suffering" that he had just urged upon them.

72 The simile of turning off Niagara Falls is from Timothy Chiappetta, O.F.M., Cap., "Prayers of the Sick," *The Priest* 11 (June 1956): 526–27. The Catholic Union of the Sick in America was specifically conceived as a means of preventing the "terrific wastage of suffering that takes place when the sick are unaware or indifferent to the truly marvellous opportunities they providentially have at hand," according to Bishop John C. Cody of London, Ontario, as quoted in Brindel, "I Am a Cusan," 173.

73 Margaret Lehr, "The Advantages of a Handicap," *Ave Maria* 69 (4 June 1949): 728.

74 Lahey was a professor of English, journalism, and advertising at Notre Dame and St. Mary's College; from 1929 until 1959 he was associate editor of *Ave Maria*, to which he contributed a popular column, "Bits Out of Life." From 1959 to 1961, he was chaplain of the university infirmary at Notre Dame. According to his obituary, he was known for his "modesty, his quiet kindness and good humor, his zeal and dedication." Father Lahey makes only a brief and, I realize, not particularly flattering appearance in my essay. Since it is not the business of historians to dishonor men and women of the past, I want to emphasize that Lahey's article, in tone

and theology, is characteristic of the way that handicapped people were imagined and addressed in the devotional press rather than being unique to him. The information on his life comes from *The Province Review* 18 (December 1970): 3, which is published by the Holy Cross Fathers of the Indiana province; a copy of his obituary was graciously sent to me by David Schlaver, C.S.C.

75 For an example of the way that persons with disabilities now view the language used by others to describe (and possess) them, see Evan Kemp, Jr.'s criticism of Jerry Lewis's talk about "my children," in Shapiro, *No Pity*, 20–24.

76 Lahey, "Letter to Shut-Ins," 245–46.

77 Ibid., 247.

78 Vincent Crapanzano, *Tuhami: Portrait of a Moroccan* (Chicago, 1980), 140.

MARY GORDON

Father Chuck: A Reading of *Going My Way*
and *The Bells of St. Mary's*, or Why Priests
Made Us Crazy

I was born and raised a Catholic, and at the very least, by Sartre's
definition (you're a Jew if people call you a Jew), I must still be one. I
am also a pro-choice feminist in her mid-forties. I have been divorced.
I have written one op-ed piece that accuses the Pope of anti-Semitism
and another one that calls the Cardinal of New York to task for sexual
hysteria. I have publicly decried a hierarchical, infantalizing, celibate
male clergy. I have testified in the United States Senate, alongside one
cardinal and several bishops, witnessing to the errors and dangers of
their position and urging that their recommendations be ignored. I go
to Mass, but I have walked out of church during sermons, dragging my
children behind me, in protest against what I believed were the heinous
words emanating from the pulpit. Yet recently, when I am speaking to
my best friend about *The Bells of St. Mary's*, something strange happens.
I start out ironic. Then I notice that I am becoming breathless. "And
then he tells her she has TB, but that everything will be all right, and if
she ever needs him she should just dial 'O' for O'Malley." The tears are

streaming down my face. I try to say something else, but I can't go on. I can't stop sobbing.

I suppose that's what the power of the movies is all about, this bleeding from fantasy to reality. But in the Catholic culture in which I grew up, the two movies (*Going My Way* and *The Bells of St. Mary's*) that starred Bing Crosby as Father Chuck O'Malley filtered into the community imagination as no others did. Each Christmas, when my mother and I watched *The Bells,* she said the same thing: "Bing I love. I will always love Bing. But that Ingrid Bergman. Why that bitch thought she had the right to play a nun like that when all the time she was planning to run away with that Italian, I will never know." A friend of mine reports that whenever his aunt was in her cups she would query: "Do you think Barry Fitzgerald's mother ever went back to Ireland? Or did she stay with him in New York?" And another friend, a radical Jesuit, remarked recently that he didn't think there was a priest in America who didn't have Father Chuck in the back of his mind as an ideal.

Catholics weren't the only ones who liked these films, and their success is only partly connected to their cinematic quality, which is considerable. Leo McCarey's screenplays—particularly *Going My Way*— are witty and tightly constructed. The performances he elicited are first rate: Bing Crosby riffs and croons, Ingrid Bergman is radiant, and Barry Fitzgerald creates a comic tour-de-force. Both films were critical and box office successes. *Going My Way,* made in 1944 during the middle of the war, won six Oscars that year: the film won best picture; Crosby won best actor; Fitzgerald got the award for best supporting actor; McCarey won Oscars for both best original story and best screenplay; and "Swinging on a Star" was voted best song. Although its sequel, *The Bells of St. Mary's,* made the following year, didn't win any of the three Oscars for which it was nominated, it was one of the three biggest box-office grossers up to that time, the other two being *Gone with the Wind* and *You're in the Army Now.* How did this happen to two films without violence, glamour, or exotic locale, and most particularly, without sex? What chord did Father Chuck strike in a country where Catholics were a feared and hostilely regarded minority, still barred from the major corridors of power? Why were two movies whose hero was a parish priest so wildly popular?

The figure of the priest is always ambiguous and therefore fascinating. He is male, but desexualized; his vows of celibacy are a kind of self-castration. Unlike most men, he is more gazed upon than gazing, particularly in the days before Vatican II when he said Mass with his back to the congregation: back then, they looked at him and he looked at God. And still he assumes a fetish role usually assigned to women, in that one part of his body is isolated and idealized: a priest's hands, the only ones allowed to touch the host, are venerated. If a priest was a guest in your house, you were supposed to offer him only white linen to dry his hands on. In Europe, there was a long and robust tradition of anticlericalism, an acknowledgment of the darker side of a priest's humanity. But in America, where the tone of the Church was, certainly by the 1940s, distinctly Irish, priests were understood to be asexual and above the lure of money—pure and treasured vessels wearing themselves out for the love of those they served.

This idealized and desexualized figure always presented special problems for Catholic women. The clergy excluded women from their midst and put them into particular and limited roles in relation to themselves. All the approved roles demanded devotion and various degrees of obedience. But most important, everything could be lost if the woman's regard for the priest shifted into the realm of sexual desire. It was assumed that even if she didn't act on her desire, the desire itself was sinful, not a simple sin of the flesh but a gross epistemological offense: she had taken the sacred figure and lodged him in the place of excrement. And yet the priest, at least in part because of his role as the woman's confessor, the person privy to her most secret thoughts, was often the person in her life with whom she was most intimate. Because of the institution of Confession, Catholic women were listened to by men in a way that was highly unusual: in what other context did our culture not only sanction but demand that a woman's inner life be taken seriously by a man? Certainly, Confession prefigured the largely male-dominated position of the psychoanalytic listener, but psychoanalysis is a voluntary relationship, entered into at the discretion of the patient. The sacrament of penance requires by law that each soul be examined and be self-examined. That the outside examiner, the absolver, be male (i.e., a priest) is part of the requirement. What this requires of women, then, is adoration, devotion, constant regard, an intimacy that goes one way only (he knows everything about her, she knows nothing about him), and perhaps, rarely, an uneasy partnership where work and responsibility are unequally (in one way or another) shared. But the line between you as man and me as woman is irrevocably and eternally uncrossable.

Enter Bing Crosby. Enter Hollywood. Enter Father O'Malley, whom we first see walking down the streets of New York in a black suit, Roman collar, and straw hat. This garb is emblematic of his mixed role: the formal, institutional suit and collar; the informal, rakish American boater. He's asked by a group of ball-playing boys to join their game, but fails to catch a ball that's hit to him, and the ball breaks a window. The homeowner is irate. O'Malley offers to pay later, as he hasn't a cent on him; he tries to use his rosary beads for collateral. The homeowner (clearly not a Catholic) is disgusted. When Father O'Malley tries to retrieve the baseball, which has fallen underneath a truck, he is sprayed by a street cleaner and has to arrive at his new parish, St. Dominic's, soaking wet. We first see Father Fitzgibbon, played by Barry Fitzgerald, mugging shamelessly in mock disapproval of O'Malley's appearance in sweat pants and a St. Louis Browns sweatshirt. Everything Father O'Malley does is wrong: he knocks things over; a phone call for him interrupts the conversation. Father Fitzgibbon looks on, freshly appalled every second. The Old World encounters the New, and the Old World is not amused.

As Father O'Malley, Crosby personifies a particularly American, improvisational approach to life that responds to the moment as the moment demands. But because he is playing a Catholic priest, what implicitly underpins this catch-as-catch-can style is the ancient structure of belief he represents by every breath. Father O'Malley's great gift is to see everyone's need and so provide for it. He is infinitely flexible, infinitely equipped with resources. He's been sent to rescue St. Dominic's, which is in dire financial straits because of over-the-hill Father Fitzgibbon's bad management. But O'Malley knows that it would be a blow to Father Fitzgibbon to find this out, so, although he's really in charge of fixing up the mess at St. Dominic's, he behaves in such a way that Father Fitzgibbon will never know he's not still in charge. Because Father Fitzgibbon's age renders him powerless, he is simultaneously infantalized and relegated to the female role in his partnership with Father O'Malley. When Father Fitzgibbon finally learns the score, he walks out of the rectory into the rain, is returned home by a policeman, and then is sung to sleep by Father Chuck, who croons "Tura Loora Loora."

Father O'Malley's flexible vision, which falls always on the other and never on the self, is particularly useful in his encounters with the troubled young. There is the runaway, Jeannie, whom the Irish cop on the beat brings to Father O'Malley for help. Her parents don't understand her; she wants to be a singer. Luckily, there's a piano in the very room where they're speaking; luckily, Father O'Malley knows the song she wants to sing. He gives her advice on her delivery, urges her to slow the tempo and "sing from the heart." This is the only advice he gives her. Down comes Father Fitzgibbon, shocked that his curate is singing at the piano with a young girl. He is full of stock advice: go back to your parents, find the right man. He sends her away. Father O'Malley, still with no access to money, begs the pastor to give her ten dollars so that she'll be all right.

His touch is equally light with the local hoodlums. Just as the war never seriously impinges on anyone's life, street crime in *Going My Way* consists of stealing turkeys. But the kids are still in trouble with the cops. Father O'Malley wants to save them. He offers them a chance to see a baseball game: he used to work out with the St. Louis Browns, and, since they're playing the Yankees, he has access to unlimited passes. Having won the kids' trust with baseball and hot dogs, he determines to turn their criminal instincts around by making them a choir. They all adore him and give up their wicked, wicked ways.

On his way home from an outing with the boys, he runs into Jennie Tuffel, played by Rise Stevens, who is clearly "someone from his past." His coat collar is pulled up, so she can't tell that he's become a priest.

She says she's on her way to work. "Where do you work?" he asks. "Oh, the Metropolitan Opera," she replies. "An extra in the crowd scene?" he asks. "Why no," she carelessly replies, "I'm Carmen."

Jennie invites him to her dressing room. She goes behind a closed door to dress, so again she doesn't see that he's wearing clerical garb. "You haven't told me why you stopped writing, Chuck. You wrote to me in Rome, in Florence, in Naples, Vienna, Budapest. Then I went to Switzerland and found one of your letters in Lucerne. There was a quaint little post office. The moon was so bright I read your letter on the way home. From there I went to South America. There were no more letters, Chuck. What happened, Chuck? What hap"—she opens the door and sees him in his Roman collar. And then, in a line that expresses the sum total of possible relationships between priests and women, she says, beaming, "FATHER Chuck."

She doesn't skip a beat. And this instantaneous understanding that his status as a priest utterly wipes out her claims as a woman is crucial to the iconography of this relationship as it has played itself out in American life. Jennie understands the score; she calls him "Father" for the rest of the movie (unlike the other friend of his past, Tim, played by Frank McHugh, who also happens to have become a priest) and devotes herself to helping his hoodlums-turned-choirboys.

And it's these boys, in cahoots with Father O'Malley, who save the parish. Although he is vague about his past, he reveals that he had had a band in St. Louis (it's important, I think, that although St. Dominic's is in New York, Chuck is from the Midwest) and gave up his ambition to write music for the priesthood. He has written a song, "Going My Way," which his friend Tim tries to sell to some Tin Pan Alley publishers. Jennie offers Carnegie Hall and the Metropolitan Opera Orchestra as backup for herself and the boys singing Chuck's song. But no dice, say the music publishers, "Too high class." After the publishers have supposedly left the theater, just for fun the boys sing the other song Chuck wrote—the up-beat, bouncy, less highbrow "Swinging on a Star": "Would you like to swing on a star / Carry moonbeams home in a jar / And be better off than you are / Or would you rather be a (mule, fish, pig)?" This is what the publishers have in mind, and what they'll pay for the song will completely wipe out St. Dominic's debts, including the mortgage on which the Herbert Hoover–lookalike banker, played by Gene Lockhart, has been ready to foreclose. But Father O'Malley insists that the payment for his song be put in the collection basket so Father Fitzgibbon will think that the sudden swelling of the exchequer is the result of his preaching.

Just as everything seems to be all right, St. Dominic's burns down. But that, too, is all right because the banker's son falls in love with the runaway girl, Jeannie, and, nudged by Father O'Malley, makes an honest woman out of her—just before he goes off to the war (the only mention of which in the whole film occurs here). Near the end, as Father O'Malley is about to leave to save some other parish in trouble, without, of course, even so much as a sigh of regret or wistfulness, all the loose ends seem tied up. But there's one more. Father Fitzgibbon had left his mother in Ireland forty-five years before, and he hasn't seen her since. He said he'd go back when he got a little ahead, but there always seemed someone more in need than he. In the last scene of the film— engraven on the souls of Catholics of a certain age and stripe—Father Fitzgibbon's mother totters in. Now, he looks about a hundred and ten, so you figure she's at least a hundred and thirty. They're both very small (she's incredibly, unglamorously wizened), and they embrace— the priest boy-son and his crone-mother—as O'Malley walks into the sunset, tall, erect, alone.

Father Chuck's next stop is St. Mary's, another parish in trouble. Its school is on the verge of bankruptcy. A wicked old capitalist, Horace Bogardis, wants to tear it down and make a parking lot to serve his new building. But the sisters of St. Mary's are praying for a miracle. Sister Benedict, played by Ingrid Bergman, is in charge.

We see from the beginning that Sister and Father have different worldviews: Sister, an idealist with a foreign accent, is a stickler for standards; Father wants everyone to have fun. On his introduction to the school, he declares a holiday. She's outraged, anticipating the trouble the children will get into. He breaks up a fight in the school yard, congratulating the winner. Sister Benedict takes the side of the loser, Jimmy, who lost because he turned the other cheek on her advice. Father O'Malley tells her that a real man has to fight back. She secretly goes to a sporting goods store and buys a book on boxing (crossing over into a male role), reads it, and teaches young Jimmy how to fight. After her lessons, he stops turning the other cheek and wins. Father O'Malley has seen Sister Benedict pantomiming Jimmy's moves, so he knows something's up.

Meanwhile, we meet Mrs. Gallagher, a single mother, who asks Father O'Malley to help her out. She has a thirteen-year-old daughter, and her husband walked out on her years ago. Mrs. Gallagher wants Father O'Malley to find some place for her daughter, Patsy, to board so she can go to St. Mary's and get away from her mother "before she finds out how I earn my living." Father O'Malley doesn't bat an eye or suggest that she find another line of work; he makes arrangements for Patsy to board with the rectory housekeeper and attend the school.

In *The Bells of St. Mary's*, unlike *Going My Way*, Father O'Malley makes important contacts with women: Sister Benedict, Mrs. Gallagher, and, finally, Patsy herself. He tells her she looks too old for her age and, in a surprisingly invasive gesture, without asking her, he rubs the lipstick off her mouth and pulls the hairpiece from her hair. "What's this?" he asks, laughingly shaking it out. "A rat, Father," she says. "You'll find you can't even have so much as a small mouse here." Gratefully, she laughs with him at the joke of his stripping her of adornments. He allows her to be a little girl, her true self.

Later, Father O'Malley visits Mrs. Gallagher at her apartment, announcing that he has a surprise for her. The surprise turns out to be Mr. Gallagher. Now, although he had abandoned her and her daughter years before, forcing her by this abandonment into a life of prostitution, she can't wait to see him. She just wants to put on a new dress and powder her nose so that he can see her at her best. They sing a song with Father O'Malley and agree to get together again.

Patsy gets off the elevator on her mother's floor to see a man leaving the apartment, embracing her mother and talking about plans to take her away. Visibly upset, she gets back into the elevator without seeing her mother, but the man gets in as well, asking her if she'd like "a stick of gum." We next see Patsy struggling over her exams in Sister Benedict's classroom, and then we see Sister Benedict unhappily grading them. Father O'Malley comes upon her, and she tells him that Patsy has failed and can't graduate. He urges her to pass Patsy:

> *What's passing, Sister?*
> *Seventy-five,* she says.
> *Well, who decided that? Why not make it sixty-five?*
> *Why not just pass everybody?* she responds.
> *Why not?*
> *What about standards?* she asks. *Do you believe in having no standards?*
> *It's better than breaking a child's heart.*

Before this, Father and Sister's banter had faint echoes of the Tracy/Hepburn comic exchanges. But in the debate over passing Patsy, the non-comic issues that also mark the Tracy/Hepburn partnership arise. Central to that duo's doings is Hepburn's inflexibility, her false standards as opposed to Tracy's flexible and truer vision. Every time Sister and Father disagree, Father is right: boys should fight back; Patsy should be allowed to pass. But Sister Benedict refuses to bend, and Father O'Malley leaves, his anguish visible on his mobile and suffering face.

In a series of events too improbable to record here, the tycoon gives Sister Benedict his office building to use as a new school. While directing the moving of furniture, Sister Benedict collapses. The doctor diagnoses TB, but he doesn't tell her—he tells Father O'Malley. In a breathtaking demonstration of medical perceptiveness, he orders Father not to let Sister know about her condition: such knowledge would get her too depressed. Instead, he should make her think she's being sent away to Arizona because she's unfit to deal with children. When Father resists, the doctor suggests that he's a selfish wimp. So he goes along, breaking Sister Benedict's heart. She accepts her fate stoically, however, and asks only that she be allowed to stay until graduation.

On graduation day, Patsy's parents appear together, and Patsy confesses to Sister Benedict that she had deliberately flunked her exams so she'd be left back and allowed to stay with Sister for another year. She says she wants to be a nun. Whereas in *Going My Way* Father O'Malley never reveals why he became a priest, Sister Benedict in *The Bells* waxes lyrical about her vocation. We see her as both emotional and devout when she speaks about the joy of giving up ordinary womanhood for God and, later, when she weeps in prayer, asking God to keep her from being bitter. Father O'Malley neither prays nor speaks of his life; Sister Benedict, the female, is permitted, even required, to be emotive and to narrate her life. We see her as vulnerable in a way that we never see him.

Rising from her knees, she takes her leave of the other sisters, and then of Father O'Malley. Just as she turns away from him, we see a series of emotions—grief, regret, longing—pass over Crosby's face. In a sentence drawn from a hundred romances, he calls after her, "I can't let you go like this." She comes back, meeting his eye. "When the doctor said you were perfect, he was right, but he didn't mean your health." He tells her that she has TB—"just a touch," and she smiles with the kind of ecstatic look that made millions of men and women fall in love with her. We expect, we long for them to fall into each other's arms, but instead they separate, with his promise that if she needs him she can just dial "O" for O'Malley.

The romantic dance between priest and nun is as exquisitely choreographed as the most formal minuet. They are witty and attractive, with a charge between them as man and woman, but no boundaries are ever crossed. Each of them perfectly accepts his or her role. Father O'Malley is always in charge: it would have been possible for him to have her transferred if he had thought she was doing a bad job with the children, while there is nothing she could do to affect his fate, except perhaps to pray that he'd get hit by a car (which would, of course, be a sin and something she would never do). His actions cause her reactions; her actions are met with the distant and laconic stoicism that is the hallmark of a real priest, a real man.

The model that Father Chuck offers is that of an endlessly giving ego, a position made possible not only through the suppression but the complete excision of desire. And not just sexual desire, but the desire for money, power, recognition, kindness, rootedness, gratitude, or praise.

He is the endless source of comfort, the endless granter of wishes, the meeter of needs who seems to need no comfort, to have no needs of his own. Ever suggesting, by his informality, the possibility of intimacy, he is in fact rigorously refusing intimacy. An impermeable shield protects his life from outside contact. Father Chuck makes things happen that change people's lives, but nothing can change him. It is significant that whenever Father Fitzgibbon asks him why he became a priest, the phone rings, and he never gets to answer the question. He is the source of all authority, but he makes no judgments and inspires neither shame nor fear.

Everyone calls him Father, but in fact his role is much more mixed. He's both the ideal father and the ideal mother, nurturing yet with access to power, particularly in the sacred American precincts of show business and sports. Although his aura is maternal, his identity is necessarily and inextricably connected to maleness. He couldn't be what he is, stand where he does, were he not a priest, a male. His maleness is iconic, but it is a particular kind of maleness cut off from the implications of sexual demand. It is part of the nature of his vocation to make no demands, so he gives no ground, no place for anyone to stand. There is no *there* there with Father Chuck. With him, you could be swinging on a star.

JAMES T. FISHER

Clearing the Streets of the
Catholic Lost Generation

During the summer of 1993, I attended the wedding of a close
relative at the Chapel of the Choirs in St. Peter's Basilica, Vatican City.
It was my first trip to Europe. Wandering amidst fervent pilgrims and
clerics, I needed to remind myself that their religion had reigned over
my family and our ancestors, in Ireland and America, for as long as anyone knew. Viewing the corpulent *Santissimo Bambino* of the Ara Coeli
in Rome ("Here," wrote William L. Vance, "the hopelessly 'medieval'
nature of Catholicism was most apparent . . . all concentrated in one
ridiculous and pathetic figure"[1]), I experienced some of the "envious
ambivalence" of the Yankee Nathaniel Hawthorne, whose *Marble Faun*
(1859) had crystallized two centuries of American Protestant brooding
on the eternal "otherness" of Catholicism.

Then I saw Mickey Rourke and remembered how I had remained an
American Catholic through twenty-odd, rather trying years. It wasn't
actually the Mick in person, but a tiny photo booklet entitled *Bellissimi
Superstar Mickey Rourke*, which I spotted alongside more convention-
ally devotional articles in a gift stand on the Via del Conciliazione, in

plain view of St. Peter's Square. The Italians, like the French, idolize Mickey Rourke for all the wrong reasons, which is why *Bellissimi Superstar Mickey Rourke* is full of stills from the ludicrous film *9½ Weeks*.

There are neighborhoods of a certain cast from Worcester to Philadelphia where you can find a man in his thirties who will recite by heart choice portions of the script for *The Pope of Greenwich Village* (1984), Mickey Rourke's signature film and a "cult movie" among people for whom the term has no meaning. This man is Irish-American, but he probably has a few Italian relatives. His parents grew up in a place like Dorchester or Washington Heights or Kensington and moved their family to a liminal suburb in the 1960s, where he attended Catholic schools and developed an attitude problem. He was among the multitude of American Catholics who "left" the Church in the decade following the Second Vatican Council (1962–65), but not because of *Humanae Vitae* (the 1968 encyclical reaffirming the Church's ban on artificial birth control) or changes in the liturgy: he was never that involved in the first place. And yet he became, perhaps without knowing so or even caring, part of a Catholic cultural underground whose populist spirituality rejuvenated life in America and finally offered the promise of making peace with a tradition founded on the faith of immigrants.

"What is Chinese tradition and what is movies?" asks Maxine Hong Kingston in *The Woman Warrior*.[2] This essay is not about films but a reluctant generation of Catholics whose fugitive soul has been sighted in recent years in such unlikely places as Mickey Rourke movies. *The Pope of Greenwich Village*—directed by Stuart Rosenberg and adapted by Vincent Patrick from his 1979 novel—is beloved among Catholics who venerate the idea of the old neighborhood with a twist of hip urbanity, as embodied in the mien of the Irish fashion plate, Mickey Rourke. In the spirit of that ethnic crossover familiar to many of us, Rourke plays Charlie Moran, a half-Irish, half-Italian aspiring restauranteur who has been—in the words of his Italian cousin, Paulie the waiter (played by Eric Roberts)—"serving a sentence" as maître d'hôtel in an undistinguished Manhattan eatery rife with bookies, crooked bartenders, and loan sharks. When Paulie gets them both fired for cheating the house, we begin to discern a pattern in which Charlie's "tribal loyalty" to his irresponsible kinsman dooms his aspirations to a life of dignity and class, as achingly symbolized by his golden WASP girlfriend from Maine, Diane (Darryl Hannah), an aerobics instructor.

Paulie drags Charlie into a "score" designed to finance a wager on a racehorse that he knows to be the secret product of "artificial inspiration"; the horse, whose nominal sire was "some no-name piece of garbage," will go to the post at extravagant odds and will surely win, thanks to its "champion's genes." (In a beautifully ironic scene, Paulie confidently explains to his cousin: "Horses ain't like people, man, they can't make themselves better than they're born." The relish with which Paulie lays out the strategy for his betting coup neatly captures a poignant, largely unrecorded genre of American barroom discourse.) The two men recruit Barney (Kenneth McMillan), an older Irish locksmith from the Bronx, to crack a safe that Paulie alone knows to contain tens of thousands of dollars belonging to Greenwich Village mobster "Bedbug" Eddie Grant (Bert Young); the money is being held there for pick up by Detective Walter "Bunky" Ritter (Jack Kehoe), who is the "bagman" of higher-ups on the take in the New York City Police Department.

Detective Ritter interrupts the burglary in progress and is accidentally killed by a fall through an air shaft; Charlie and Paulie must then evade the wrath of Bedbug Eddie (the capo gladly relinquishes Barney's fate to the hands of his own kind, the police: "Let those Irish hardons take care of themselves!") while awaiting their big day at the races. The film is lovingly attentive to every nuance of New York ethnic difference as we like to remember it; negotiations between the Irish and Italians are choreographed in rituals of eating, drinking, gambling, and naming ("I know you, you're Jinty, right?" says Paulie to an Irish bartender in the Bronx. "It's Ginty." "Same thing.") Unlike the films of, say, Martin Scorsese, *The Pope of Greenwich Village* does not aspire to grandiose truths via its gritty particulars; it is simply a collection of skillfully stylized performances by a host of "ethnic" character actors, including Philip Bosco, Joe Grifasi, and M. Emmet Walsh (and, in one of the film's many subtle touches, an Italian-American ruffian is played by Kevin Breslin, son of Jimmy Breslin, the Irish chronicler of New York street Catholicism).

While every character in the film is clearly a baptized Catholic, with the exception of Charlie's girlfriend, Diane—who wisely flees the scene, carrying a boxful of his stolen mobster loot and their unborn child— the Church remains in the distant background throughout (as Charlie leaves an off-track betting parlor, broke and dejected, he glances ever so quickly at a group of passing nuns on the sidewalk). We witness instead what Robert Orsi has called a "theology of the streets," but where Orsi focused specifically on the activities characterizing the "festas" of Italian Harlem, *The Pope of Greenwich Village* trails a wispy faith across a historical-geographical panoply of immigrant Catholicism.[3] Only when the Irish cops visit the mother of their dead colleague in search of incriminating evidence do we glimpse the ancient source of moral authority that once governed their terrain. After Mrs. Ritter (Geraldine Page, in one of her last and greatest performances) asserts her Irish matriarchal power—"My Walter was tough as a bar of iron [pronounced *eyen*], and he didn't get that from his fathah"—she tells the cops that if they disturb her son's room, she will call her brother, "an old-fashioned parish priest with gray hair," and then summon the media to show how the mother of a dead hero is treated: "The two of us could do a job on the six o'clock news that would have this city in teahs."

The Pope of Greenwich Village coheres by the force of Mickey Rourke's presence. He is both the exemplary lost boy of his Catholic generation and a promising bridge to our newfound past, with his crazy pompadour and his respect for the ways of the streets that we grew up hearing about. Yet, as Charlie Moran, he also conveys a vague desire for something else: he yearns to get off the endlessly revolving wheel of ethnic obligation, which no longer works right anyway; he is a "white man" with no excuses that outsiders would take seriously. In the film's pivotal scene, Diane, Charlie's soon-to-be ex-girlfriend, plaintively asks: "Why are you always one inch away from becoming a good person? . . . You're all caught up in your tribal loyalties, your neighborhood, Paulie." When Charlie answers, "Maybe I don't want to change," Diane gives him a slap on the kisser. "I knew this would happen," he responds, resigned. "Hit me again and see if I change." He gets another whack. Trapped in the knowledge that Diane is right, but not knowing *how* to change (when Diane said earlier that he had outgrown Paulie, a puzzled Charlie replied, "Maybe WASPs outgrow people. Italians outgrow clothes, they don't outgrow people"), Charlie is reduced to the Gesture, coolly donning his sunglasses for the final exit from his dream future.

Rourke's celebrity persona is inevitably represented through historically disembodied images of sweet savagery and self-punishment. Occasionally, as in Kevin Sessums's 1991 *Vanity Fair* profile, "Fighting Irish," Rourke's disturbing appeal is directly attributed to his religiosity:

> Deeply Catholic, Rourke seems to feel guilty about his role as a sex symbol, which reached a crescendo with "9½ Weeks." . . . "After '9½ Weeks' I did every project in the world to go in the opposite direction till it almost put me out of the business. A French interviewer said to me once, 'Look at what you're doing to yourself. Don't you realize what you're doing?' She had tears in her eyes."

Sessums reiterates Rourke's "pride in his Irish-Catholic heritage" in describing his controversial support for the Irish Republican Army (Rourke played an IRA soldier in *A Prayer for the Dying;* he also played Saint Francis of Assisi in *Francesco,* which was never released in the United States) and provides an ethnoreligious interpretation of his late-blooming boxing career: "Like all curious Catholic boys, whose humanity is measured by the length of their guilt, Rourke seems to seek out punishment as if it were a way to purify himself."[4]

Rourke himself has said that he took up boxing to get back "the edge" that he had lost in the days since *The Pope of Greenwich Village,* his "first meaty role." As an Irish-American icon who has "tarnished himself with his own disillusioned touch," Mickey Rourke acts out a script that is nearly as old as the movies themselves. "When it came to playing the tough American, up from the streets," wrote Daniel Patrick Moynihan, "the image was repeatedly that of an Irishman. James Cagney was the quintessential figure: fists cocked, chin out, back straight, bounding along on his heels. But also doomed: at the end of the movie he was dead."[5]

At the end of *The Pope of Greenwich Village*, his manly effort to beat the mob foiled by another of Paulie's stunts, the doomed Charlie Moran tells his cousin: "You know, you've got a serious thinking disorder." The response to this film of many of my acquaintances suggests that he was speaking to a lot of those who—like Charlie and perhaps Mickey Rourke himself—cling to the old street myths rather than face the uncertain prospect of becoming just another post-ethnic white guy in America. What is Irish tradition and what is movies? How truly can a unique Catholic consciousness elude the taunting claims of convention?

As a member of what Milwaukee's Archbishop Rembert Weakland has called the "lost generation" of American Catholics, "this necessarily'll have to be about myself" (to quote Jack Kerouac, the patron saint of so many of us). I am a late product of Irish-American "ghetto Catholicism," a term banned by scholars at least a decade ago because it conjured an experience now deemed mostly illusory. So many of the Catholic and ex-Catholic artists and intellectuals I meet come instead from your typically diverse American background—with a Jewish or Yankee ancestor in the mix, or at least a wealthy, liberal "*Commonweal* Catholic" relative somewhere—that I am often surprised to find, as Moynihan put it, that "there are some of us left."[6]

One of my great-grandfathers emigrated from the west of Ireland just in time to drown while digging the Panama Canal; his widow, who raised their family alone, lived in Brooklyn for seventy more years. Other forebears found work as barkeeps, stevedores, and, finally, civil servants, all within a twenty-mile radius bounded by Newark, Flatbush, and Jamaica Bay. Thanks to World War II, the dream of full employment and even property ownership began to kick in—so far so familiar. Yet for one side of my family, in particular, social and occupational upward mobility has been minimal, evoking the dreaded specter of the once-violent debate among social historians over differential patterns of ascent between ethnic and religious groups. Who needs a wedding in

Rome when there are still twenty-one counties in New Jersey to choose from? Talk about white-ethnic upward mobility all you want; the Irish can still break the theoretical heart of many a social scientist.

I grew up in Will Herberg's America, courtesy of the American Cyanamid Company. In *Protestant-Catholic-Jew* (1955), Herberg showed how the highly localized ethnic loyalties of the prewar "old neighborhoods" gave way to a broader configuration—the "triple melting pot"—which legitimized Catholicism and Judaism as national religions so long as they bolstered what Herberg called "the idolatrous civil religion of America." This was a perfect formula for the social adventure of postwar suburbia, but Herberg could not have foreseen the extent to which Catholics would re-create the old neighborhoods in former cow pastures. My mother still speaks with some pride of having resided in "New England" for eight years, but there was nary a daughter or son of the American Revolution to be found in that Levittown-style Connecticut subdivision, quaintly named "Sheffield Park," where we lived amongst Irish, Italian, and French-Canadian pilgrims from Waterbury, New Haven, and even more exotic locales to the north.[7]

If anything, Catholic suburbia witnessed the final triumph of "Irishization" in the American Catholic Church. The hundreds of new parishes and schools created in the 1950s and 1960s were bound to be led primarily by Irish priests: there were a lot of them, to begin with; they also tended to be well-connected to diocesan administrators and were generally quite pleased to assume a pastorate in the new promised land. Those were heady days for the first-generation, middle-class suburban Irish, when all the world seemed to revolve around their loud, boozy cookouts; their paneled basement rec rooms ("What is it about [the] Irish and paneling?" asks the actor-comedian Denis Leary); their Notre Dame football on the radio in the "era of Ara" Parseghian. (An indelible memory: I'm kicking a football around by myself in a leafy yard, autumn in the mid-1960s, when the booming cry of Van Patrick of the Mutual Network, "Touchdown, Notre Dame!" pours forth from half the kitchens on the block, followed by the roars of our fathers.)

Slowly, it all went sour. While strawberries and thoroughbred racehorses can go bad overnight, the Catholic moment succumbed to an accretion of blows in the wake of a Vatican Council that had generated too many grandiose expectations. The Church pledged to become engaged with "the modern world," yet for every guitar-slinging, ponchoed priest celebrating a folk Mass, there was an old-timer who lost his vocation. Several of the nuns who taught in my junior high school took flight without even returning our homework. The crisis was hardest felt by those of our parents whose lives had been seared by duty to the Church and its sacred mysteries. The stakes were much higher than the right to use birth control; ordinary people wept over the fate of the Mystical Body of Christ and all those who belonged to it.

There were two issues of *Time* magazine that my mother nervously hid from me in the 1960s. One featured a drawing of Hugh Hefner on the cover; the other (whose blasphemy was intensified by its delivery during Holy Week, 1966) simply depicted three words in bold red letters, bordered in black: "Is God Dead?"

My parents grew up in a neatly bounded world where their "difference" from those on the outside was a given; they were obliged neither to proselytize nor to show an undue interest in non-Catholic America. Suddenly, in the late 1960s, elite secularists began to display a fascination with the crisis of the Church: John Kenneth Galbraith remarked that the unraveling of American Catholicism was the most surprising, dramatic social fact of his lifetime, while Daniel Bell opined, "[T]he paradox of the post-conciliar church . . . is that as authority grows progressively weaker, the protest against it intensifies." For the first time in American history, the ordeal of Catholicism not only mirrored that of the broader culture, but recast it in frighteningly vivid colors. The generation gap was most traumatically experienced by Catholics because their young were slipping through the fissures in both family and church, as well as renouncing that most fragile inheritance: the dream that they might make permanent the modest gains of their parents, who, as Richard Rodriguez writes, "were not 'role models,' exactly; they were people . . . making their way in America."[8]

Catholic Americans fought and died in Vietnam in vast disproportion to their representation in the populace. But David Miller, a member of Dorothy Day's radical Catholic Worker movement, became the first American to publicly burn his draft card and serve time in protest against the war. Early on the morning of 9 November 1965, Roger Laporte, a recent graduate of the Jesuits' Le Moyne College and an antiwar follower of Day and Daniel Berrigan, set himself afire outside the United Nations Building in New York. Late on the afternoon of his death, a massive power outage cast New York and much of New England into a darkness that lasted well into the night; in Connecticut we huddled together and drank hot chocolate by candlelight. I don't recall so warm a moment from the decade to follow.

I sometimes nervously joke that the study of history appealed to me as a means for connecting the riots in our house with the riots in the streets of places like Newark, where my great-aunts cooled their heels in fear and anger behind barricaded apartment doors. Finally, the conflagration spread to the Catholic schools, including St. Bridget's Junior High, where a teacher fresh from Holy Cross implored us with this novel suggestion: "Think!" He so impassioned our seventh-grade religion class that he was subsequently confined to teaching social studies, but, as Catholic Worker cofounder Peter Maurin liked to say, he had "blown the dynamite" of Catholic life and thought.

One of the most tired literary conventions in American culture is that body of work authored by "victims" of Catholic schooling, oppressed and terrorized as children only to exact revenge as complaining adults eager to satisfy the demands of the genre. (This is a separate issue from the sexual abuse of children by priests and other religious. I can only report that in five years as an altar boy I came in contact with dozens of clerics, from the holy to the surly, and witnessed not the slightest hint of impropriety, although, it is true, I was never inclined to get friendly with the authorities.) In fact, the swift and sure punishment that was openly meted out to parochial school miscreants like myself only raised the stakes of self-expression and inspired a kind of precocious defiance that teachers had to grudgingly respect, since our faith community was uniquely committed to the pursuit of truth, especially when it hurt. My Catholic school years produced moments of transcendent theater; debates sometimes raged until buses were missed, but nobody complained. Although you might earn a love tap from a French-Canadian nun now and again, there was a more enduring lesson to absorb about the disarming power of words and ideas, especially when they emanated from a source whose origins were elusive and mysterious.

In the early 1970s my family moved back to North Jersey, where I passed up the opportunity to travel two hours each day to attend my father's old parochial high school in Jersey City. In public school I was quickly disappointed to learn that incorrigible students were denied the privilege of sparring openly with the authorities, discovering instead a dizzying array of occupations concerned with ministering to maladjusted youths. My spirited antics often resulted in separation from my peers for sessions with professionals who demonstrated their rather passive concern before referring me to the next station along the therapeutic gauntlet. In the meantime I helped to create an "underground" newspaper, in league with some highly sophisticated, often Jewish students whom I regarded with no little amazement. For guerrilla theater in the halls, I stuck pretty much to the Irish and Italian guys, but that wasn't enough to keep me from being classified with the screwballs and "freethinkers" whom my Jersey relatives viewed with disdain and trepidation.

Those were horrid times for a lot of us of all stripes, but for many older Catholics—clinging valiantly to their toehold in the new middle class while doggedly seeking to preserve some remnant of the ancestral faith—each day brought new assaults on their dignity and self-respect. I had relatives who believed that Archie Bunker was actually created to vindicate their beleaguered existences. (In watching reruns I have come to see their point, Norman Lear's original intent notwithstanding. Were we really supposed to believe that Carroll O'Connor played a working-class WASP from Queens?) These guys had fought the wars; they never expected to grow terrified of their own children.

We often showed our Yale students a documentary on the 1970 student strike in protest of the Black Panthers' trial in New Haven, *Bright College Years*. From my perspective, the film portrays a chilling divide between the stylishly uncouth Yalies, arguing in the common rooms of their residential colleges, and the assorted freaks assembled on the Green, who today's kids erroneously assume were also students. The filmmakers themselves were preoccupied with the meaning of these events for Yale, but the most telling scenes focus on the bitterly angry reactions of older, working-class New Havenites to the freaks, some of them undoubtedly their own children. Meanwhile, back on campus, Yale's chaplain, the Reverend William Sloane Coffin, is shown vigorously defending student radicals to alumni attending a reunion. The film concludes by depicting a ceremony in which President Kingman Brewster—supposedly a liberal adversary of the Old Blues—is treated to a rousing locomotive cheer, as if to suggest that Yale will roll grandly along, with the generations reconciled again, once passions have subsided.

Few of the Irish or Italian kids from New Haven who joined the ragtag youth-culture army later became the subjects of articles about radicals "rejoining the establishment." Like their brothers and cousins who were fighting in Vietnam, they found precious little to return *to*. Lower-middle-class Catholics generally faced a stark choice: you could honor the wishes of your family and your own ambition by toeing the line (like, say, New York Mayor Rudolph Giuliani, just one of many whose own striving "sixties" bore no resemblance to the decade of myth), or you could cast yourself adrift in the knowledge that no one back home gave a damn about "finding yourself."

By the mid-1970s, I was beginning to notice a cultural style that even now is difficult to name. I kept running into people who were interested in the same things I was, similarly imbued with an attitude and mystique that none of us wanted to identify as a product of our religious imagination, especially as our heroes were strictly unchurched, we thought. I had discovered Kerouac and Charlie Parker and John Coltrane on my own, but it was during my first year at a Catholic college that I heard from various disaffected alumni of parochial schools about the likes of Jackson Pollock, Sri Aurobindo, and even Thomas Merton, the Trappist monk whose name never came up in the introductory theology classes that, yes, even in those days, were largely devoted to such "canonical" figures as Malcolm X and Black Elk (who, though nobody knew it at the time, was actually a Catholic missionary and greatly displeased with his treatment at the hands of premature multiculturalists).

The Catholics we read were all Europeans; America, after all, had been strictly mission territory to the Church until 1908.

An experience whose meaning similarly took years to unfold occurred upon the death of my grandfather at the end of 1976. I had dropped out of college for the second time and was living in Hoboken and driving a taxicab in New York; the relatives spoke of me only in connection with their prayers to various patron saints of hopeless causes, lost souls, blown minds. I was hanging around with men who, while waiting in the garage for cab assignments, spoke fervently of their plans to return to Nicaragua and depose the oligarchy. I had no idea what they were talking about, but listened sympathetically because it was en route to their country on a mission of mercy following an earthquake in 1972 that my towering boyhood hero, Roberto Clemente, had been killed.

I did not tell them—or anyone else—that my dingy, unheated room (the landlord had taken his family back to Italy for the winter) had become the site of occasional nighttime visitations by what appeared to be some of the leading figures of Christian history, or that I was undergoing certain experiences that left me in no doubt of something's residing within me (let's call it a soul) that would survive my bodily demise. I was thus inclined to grope my way back to our beginnings. The night of my grandfather's wake, I arrived early in Wood-Ridge, a tidy village poised right atop the Jersey Meadowlands, where the Ku Klux Klan had burned a cross in the 1920s on the churchyard lawn near where my grandfather would be buried. I walked into the public library and started reading James J. Kavanaugh's *A Modern Priest Looks at His Outdated Church* (of a popular genre from the late 1960s), and I remember wondering if all the loud complaining I had done masked a fear of facing what I really believed.

Even thus prepared, the wake was a shattering event. Following the viewing a young priest somewhat nervously announced that, at the request of the family, the contemporary (post–Vatican II) prayers for the dead would be replaced by an "ancient and venerable" ceremony that consisted simply of the recitation of the rosary with certain litanies and benedictions added. In the next few moments I felt the room spin free of its moorings, as dozens of people whom I had tended to see as elderly squares hit a vocal stride that brought forth some collective memory of what we historians like to call the immigrant Church. A plumed honor guard of the Knights of Columbus stood watch as this Catholic call-and-response became a swinging, rocking chorus of the faithful, delighted to proclaim, yes, this is what we believe, always have, always will. (The only experience that came close in later years was a performance by Sun Ra's Intergalactic Arkestra of "This World Is Not Our Home," in which the band paraded through the crowd—their costumes even reminded me a bit of the Knights.)

A lot of ex-Catholic intellectuals exalt in theory the concept of "traditional" cultures, but condemn their own with shame and anger. At the end of the 1970s—by then at Rutgers, which, like many large, northern state universities, houses a Catholic undergraduate majority—I witnessed the flowering of a softer variant on this theme, the beginnings, perhaps, of a postmodernist Catholic sensibility in which certain elements of the subculture were reintroduced to a secular environment. A young woman I knew sparked a near riot one year by dressing up for Halloween in a plaid convent-school uniform. A kid I'd known as an altar boy in Connecticut emerged as the leading spokesman of the punk rock scene in those years; he created the visually striking *Punk* magazine and counseled readers of the *Village Voice:* "Don't go out with Catholic girls," then promptly ignored his own advice.

New Brunswick was rich in characters I admired, reluctant hipsters who had taken flight and been knocked on their collective ass until there was no answer but New Jersey, where refugees from the likes of Holy Spirit of Absecon, Red Bank Catholic, Christian Brothers Academy, and St. Joseph's of Metuchen surreptitiously constituted a free-floating "parish" of their own—Our Lady of the Shadows, say. The liturgies may have been a bit unorthodox, but with Eric Dolphy in the choir and Kerouac at the pulpit our devotions sure sounded great.

They nearly excommunicated me for writing a doctoral dissertation on American Catholic history, as though crossing back into the academic world and bringing our stories with me betrayed some sacred trust. I realized for the first time just how sensitive the issue of religious nonidentity was for my friends, who so assiduously dismissed their heritage, yet inevitably wound up with each other: in barrooms, in marriages, in deep. I sought to vindicate every one of us through the recovery of a usable past, but about all I could come up with were convert intellectuals like Dorothy Day and Thomas Merton, with whom we had absolutely nothing in common. Nobody believed me when I wrote that Jack Kerouac was the most Catholic writer in America.

In defiance and despair I turned to the works of Andrew Greeley for some consoling wisdom. For years Greeley had fought a two-front battle against a recalcitrant, if not inept, Church hierarchy, on the one hand, and the academic establishment, on the other (with special scorn reserved for anxiously "passing" Catholics who bemoaned their inherited anti-intellectualism). Amidst his mountain of diverse, fevered works, Greeley maintained a fairly consistent devotion to a model of Catholic life that was rooted in neighborhoods, featuring a practical liberalism and a realistic appraisal of human frailty. Based largely on an idealized vision of Chicago-Irish history, Greeley's oeuvre bravely challenged the heretofore untested assumptions that equated immigrant Catholicism with urban racism and reactionary politics. Armed not only with massive survey data but with the instincts of a storyteller as well, Greeley continued to raise the stakes until he finally tackled even the myth of Catholic sexual repression.

Yet Greeley was doggedly resistant to the dark side of his Catholic universe. I had no trouble believing his assertions that most Catholic school graduates tended to hold sane attitudes toward sex, race, and religion. But what about the dropouts, castaways, and rebels bred from the same system? Who spoke for those of us who had no piece of the Church to claim as our own, yet were nowhere else at home? At some point it dawned on me that we amounted to a Catholic tradition in our own right. While still in high school I had watched a wiry Shore rat named Bruce Springsteen perform to a half-empty house at New Brunswick's State Theater, and since all I could think of was my new favorite author, I slipped backstage and asked Springsteen about Kerouac; he gave me that grin and said, "Yeah, I know that man."

Springsteen had sung about being alone in the confessional, but it wasn't that so much as it was his ruder theology of the streets — constructing the same kind of sacralized geography as *On The Road* and other Kerouac works that scarcely take God's name in vain. The rock & roll populist-cum-nativist Dave Marsh would allude to "anti-Catholic imagery run rampant" [*sic*] in such Springsteen songs as "If I Were the Priest."[9] But that wasn't the point at all — it was the mystically concrete sensibility that pervaded the music, lending it a profoundly traditional dimension that evoked the religious fidelity to local detail of Kerouac, the bard of Lowell, Massachusetts.

Springsteen's spiritual aesthetic had been prefigured by numerous Jerseyans of his generation, including the poet Michael Lally, born in 1942 to "a family of cops" in South Orange. In a 1967 poem, "You Remember Belmar NJ 1956," Lally linked the sexy, bargain glamour of the Jersey Shore with his own and his Irish buddies' discovery of American popular culture:

> ethnic beaches, ethnic streets
> ethnic hangouts, jetties, kids
>
> . . . .
>
> Crazy Mixed Up Kids with names like
> Sleepy, Face, Skippy, Skootch, Me Too Morrissey
> & Nutsy McConnell imitated themselves and Marlon
> Brando, danced to Frankie Lyman and the Teenagers
> or Little Richard. . . .[10]

I have always believed that the genius of Beat spirituality was rooted in Kerouac's redemption of the popular culture of his 1930s working-class youth from the approbation of neo-scholastic Catholic taste-makers. The British scholar Paul Giles has recently produced an exhaustive interpretation of this uniquely American Catholic sensibility, relying heavily upon David Tracy's argument that Catholics imagine "analogically" and so discern grace incarnate in the things of the world. "Kerouac," Giles writes in *American Catholic Arts and Fictions*,

> spends some time in *On The Road* celebrating the fact that
> Greyhound bus stations analogically resemble each other all over

America. While Whitman, say, might have been moved to describe something similar, in Kerouac we find the poetic emphasis skewed toward celebrating these bus stations in themselves. Kerouac is not so interested in elucidating the abstract shape of an overall design as he is in revealing what he takes to be the "grace" inherent within these mundane objects. To his mind, such "grace" is guaranteed by the way these worldly objects participate in the larger structures of analogy; yet this transubstantiative power ultimately resides not within those ideal structures but within the actual material objects. . . . Unlike Whitman or Emerson, who present themselves as privileged seers prophetically empowered to perceive invisible resemblances, Kerouac styles himself as a surrogate Catholic priest in whose hands sacramental analogy becomes a materialized and worldly event.[11]

Although Giles tends to essentialize Catholic difference, he has boldly recovered the spiritual aesthetic of a variety of artists (from Eugene O'Neill to Frank O'Hara to Martin Scorsese) in whose work "religion operates as a more subliminal force dictating patterns of thought and behavior of which texts (and their authors) are not necessarily aware." The work of the artists among my Jersey apostate generation confirms Giles's distinction between "the concrete, incarnational, and fully embodied [Catholic] mode" and "that more abstract, disembodied 'Protestant' genre of American romance." "Catholic realism," claims Giles, "invests the mundane world itself with spiritual significance."[12]

Giles might also have explained the role of class in many American Catholic arts and fictions. Kids whose parents don't exactly encourage European sojourns or art-appreciation courses tend to develop deeply personal, highly localized aesthetics through which mythological riches are wrung from "the mundane world itself." Mike Young, for example, is a South Jersey artist who attended Holy Cross High School in Delran during the late 1960s, but left without a diploma. His painting *Bob's Conga* (1989) memorializes a long-ago evening spent in a bungalow at Lake Pine, deep in the Jersey Pine Barrens. In the midst of a highly

Figure 1. *Bob's Conga* (1989) by Mike Young. Oil painting on acrylic-primed burlap over canvas. 60" × 50". Photograph courtesy of Marcia Goldner. Reproduced with permission of the artist.

spirited jam session with a variety of found percussion instruments, one of Young's friends cut his hand on a drum made by Mike's brother Bob, who would later calmly ask, "Who bled on my conga?"

In *Bob's Conga* (Figure 1), palm prints are arranged in a swirling, rhythmic pattern against three horizontal bars of different hues, evoking both a variety of aural tones and an array of shrouds redolent of cloth bearing a faint imprint of Christ in his Passion. Young has brilliantly suggested a relationship — characteristically muted and understated — between an incident from local mythology and Christian history. In the painting's upper and lower panels the palm prints are rendered as traces, hinting at both the struggle to attain a voice and the quest for wholeness signaled by their movement toward the center of the canvas.

Bob's Conga also evinces an interest in pre-Christian cave drawings and echoes the influence of American Indian sand paintings on the work of Jackson Pollock. Like other artists of the lost generation of Catholics, Mike Young draws heavily on sources from the American cultural underground as it has evolved since the early 1940s. The powerful attraction of many Catholics to versions of African-American culture has never been explored, but it is a social fact that acquires meaning from its anomalous quality. Since the early 1970s at least, American intellectuals have generally felt quite free to equate ethnic Catholicism with urban racism (a view I heard reiterated at a symposium on Dorothy Day at Loyola College in October 1993, when a scholar, intent on maintaining Day's immunity from the religious culture into which she converted, added to my litany of the virtues of neighborhood Catholicism: "and racist!").

At the same time, critics who routinely linked Kerouac's emulation of African-American cultural forms to slumming primitivism overlooked the step *up* in class embedded in his appropriation of jazz improvisation. Kerouac spent much of his youth in a Lowell ghetto where he learned English as a second language; one of his jazz idols, Miles Davis, the son of a wealthy dentist from East St. Louis, dropped out of Juilliard to study instead with Charlie Parker. It was on a football scholarship that Kerouac went to Columbia, where he felt out of his depth socially and finally dropped out after completing virtually no courses; years later, he fervently wished to be taken seriously as an artist by jazz musicians who often had more formal education than he did. (A number of African-American jazz artists were themselves Catholics. A friend and confessor of Billie Holiday has noted the "strange connection between the very seductive world of nightlife and jazz, and the sort of life that a certain kind of Catholicism can propel you toward."[13])

Catholics who imitated African-American culture could be readily forgiven for not knowing of their own ethnic traditions and for filling the void with an idealized surrogate presumably based on oral and improvisational genres. But as the writer David Bradley has argued: "Every fucking culture known to man, woman and child has an oral tradition. To talk about the African oral tradition and ignore *Beowulf* is to pretend that Negroes are somehow doing something that Celts, Franks—wherever you lived—didn't, and that's ridiculous."[14] Catholic educators in this century were generally under the sway of a neo-Thomist philosophy that derided ethnic particularism while exalting a disembodied European model of "integral" Catholicism.

This tradition may have served the Irish, in particular, as a substitute for a post-famine culture steeped in guilt and shame. It enjoyed its greatest influence, though, among clerics and official Catholic intellectuals. At the level of the parochial schools, where neo-scholasticism was enshrined in the notorious *Baltimore Catechism,* the breakdown occurring in the 1960s propelled kids in every liberating direction. One possible explanation for the fascination of young Irish Americans with black culture in those years is that the edgiest of these characters were often urban transplants from formerly mixed neighborhoods. (Mickey Rourke's "childhood was spent in the streets around what is now one of the infamous Liberty City housing projects in Miami. He spent a lot of time hanging out with young black and Cuban toughs."[15])

Urban Irish-American experience often mirrored the conventional pathography ascribed to black inner-city families. A photograph from the early 1960s shows me in a convertible, surrounded by a half-dozen widowed aunts and unmarried female cousins, the legendary "Honan girls," who transmitted the lore of our family in the absence of those male "characters" who had died well before my time. Despite the folklore of "white flight," many Catholics never left the old neighborhoods, although social scientists and political pundits were loathe to concede that Irish, Italian, and Slavic Catholics comprised a good portion of the Great Society's urban poor. At least one African-American scholar has noted with sympathy the seeming disparity between the morale of black and of Irish urban youth. In *The Good High School: Portraits Of Character and Culture,* Sara Lawrence Lightfoot quotes a social worker in a school near Boston:

> Irish kids screw themselves. . . . They have directed their energy into a negative tradition, shut down their horizons. . . . Are they going to always have these attitudes? We should try to challenge the way they feel . . . help them to see the beauty in other people. . . . I think this is their last chance, and ours, to help them.

By contrast, "the Black kids are spiritually and physically together. They are as one—not just in a hostile way but in a supportive way."[16]

In the 1960s, a Catholic version of the urban noble savage began to emerge, represented most notably in the works of the New York memoirist and poet Jim Carroll. Embraced while still a teenager by the downtown literary bohemians, who cast the young basketball star/heroin addict in the role of angelic, self-destructive jock, Carroll later compared himself to another of the many protégés of the Czech-American Andy Warhol, filmmaker Paul Morrisey: "one of those most dangerous of creatures—a Bronx Irish Catholic who transcended his surroundings just enough, while partially maintaining the essential qualities of his white ghetto upbringing."[17]

Carroll's earliest writings were published in 1978 as *The Basketball Diaries*. Sports have always been crucially important to urban Catholics, providing opportunities not just for athletes, but also for coaches, journalists, promoters, and a variety of characters whose lack of polish and education excluded them from more refined vocations. In the 1960s, sports became the main conduit for interaction between urban Catholics and blacks; by the late 1970s, sports talk was providing grounds for the preliminary stages of reconciliation between different generations of Catholic men, a reconciliation made possible by the profoundly democratic mysticism of the streets and school yards. This development rendered the former basketball coach and broadcaster Al McGuire perhaps the most significant Catholic of his era. Known primarily as a feisty scrapper during a stint with the New York Knickerbockers in the 1950s, McGuire went on to coach at several lesser-known colleges before becoming a legend at Marquette, the Jesuit university in Milwaukee, which he led to an NCAA title in 1977.

As an analyst on collegiate telecasts in the late 1970s and 1980s, McGuire presented his streetwise Irish existentialism to a national audience. He spoke of brawling with players in the locker room; he shared his philosophy of recruiting ("All I said to kids was, 'You're born and you die by yourself' "[18]); and he proclaimed his conviction that no one should consider himself educated until he had driven a cab and tended bar for a year. McGuire was characteristically shy about revealing the profoundly Catholic sources of his worldview. His former broadcast partner, Billy Packer, recalled that he found McGuire difficult to understand until he saw him at an Easter Mass in downtown St. Louis. "I walked in and there was this strange mixture of wealthy people and vagrants. When I went down to take Communion, one of the vagrants was in front of me. I looked at him and it was Al."[19]

I thought of Al McGuire when I heard about the terrible accident in Sacramento involving the professional basketball player Bobby Hurley. I was having lunch in a peculiar Indianapolis Italian chain restaurant of the sort that would be inconceivable in New Jersey. I thought of the dank armories in Jersey City where the Hurleys had sustained and extended the urban-Irish legends of the past, so unlike the pastoral mythology of Hoosier basketball. I also recalled a recent article in *New Jersey Monthly* magazine that extolled the Hurley family's deep neighborhood roots in a town long presumed dead, where characters with nicknames like "The Fa" remember when Bob Hurley, Sr., was himself a promising ballplayer before becoming a coach and adviser to mostly African-American youths. Now one of Hurley's sons lay seriously injured, while another, in the midst of a depression unrelated to his brother's accident, had left the Seton Hall University basketball team.[20]

Moments like these recall the old line: "the point of being Irish is knowing the world will break your heart." Call it fatalism, if you will, but tragedy seems to provoke that practical compassion we have viewed upon so many occasions. I have called the theological dimension of this Irish Catholic temperament "anti-triumphalism" in the absence of a more precise term. One of my earliest memories is of attending Mass with my family at my grandparents' parish in North Jersey and seeing my father faint and slip to the floor. A tough-looking man with a crew cut vaulted over the pew and lifted him up, while his wife rubbed my father's neck and shoulders as he came to. The feeling linked to that memory was revived years later when I interviewed an Irish-American man who had participated in a disastrous communal experiment inspired by the Catholic Worker movement. While he only vaguely recalled the radical separatism of the commune, the man's eyes watered as he remembered local Irish priests, with "hearts big as houses," who had had no use for visionaries but never failed to appear in times of suffering and need.

This is such an elusive spirituality that it is no wonder converts like Dorothy Day and Thomas Merton never quite got it even as they wrote about and preached the virtues of humble Catholicism. The most interesting Catholics have rarely been identified as "religious" precisely because of the reticent quality of their faith. Maybe that's why sports have been so important to keeping the larger traditions alive. Pete Axthelm's *The City Game* (1970) was the first work to identify the meaning of basketball in the urban neighborhood; the book also paid tribute to the worldly wisdom of Al McGuire. Axthelm, who was a graduate of the Marian Fathers' Chaminade High School on Long Island, went on to Yale in the early 1960s and became the sports editor of the *Yale Daily News*. A brilliant student, whose senior essay on the confessional novel was published by Yale University Press, Ax—as he was known to everyone—launched his career in sports journalism as a horseracing writer for the *New York Herald Tribune*. While still at Yale, he had conducted interviews in New York with the likes of Jimmy Breslin and had hung out at the various New Haven joints that were patronized by the same types of non–Ivy League local characters I came to know several decades later.

Axthelm was a great sportswriter, a profligate gambler, and a liberal humanist who is believed to have played a role behind the scenes in the Black Power demonstration on the victory stand at the 1968 Olympics in Mexico City. In the 1970s, Ax became a raconteur on network football and racing telecasts; many felt that he had squandered his literary gifts. After Axthelm's untimely death in 1991, Hunter Thompson wrote that "he was a black priest in a family tradition that openly worshipped gambling and had no regard for money."[21] Yet the editor of a racing paper revealed that Ax had contributed the royalties from his columns to Covenant House, a network of Church-sponsored homes for runaway children. His life and death traced the fault lines of the American Catholic temperament that I have been struggling to describe here. On the one hand, as his friend Andy Beyer wrote, Ax "loved the whole subculture of gamblers, bookies, hustlers, loansharks, touts, crooks, and assorted wiseguys." On the other hand, Mike Weisman, the former executive producer of "NBC Sports" could call Axthelm "our conscience," a man who "put sports in perspective, and would be outraged at injustices." [22]

I guess, in a way, you had to be there: a lot of people are still so uncomfortable with analytical efforts to articulate this highly paradoxical spiritual ethos that it's largely communicated in code. Years ago, one of the circulation supervisors at the Rutgers library took note of the books I had checked out over a period of months; at some point he'd seen enough evidence of my interests in jazz, horseracing, amateur Buddhism, and the literature of the dispossessed to know that it was time to introduce himself: now I am the godfather of his and his wife's first child. Then there was the night when I started talking to an Irish guy in a bar who, I'd heard, was a big fan of the Philadelphia Eagles. Soon I learned that he had compiled a massive journal documenting a year in the life of his team, which I consider one of the more remarkable unpublished works in the literature of American sports. I later discovered that he kept another kind of journal, recording a spiritual adventure of surpassing beauty and turmoil in which I grudgingly recognized much of my own travail. This guy was also the first one I heard recite—with a perfect ear for New York ethnic dialect—large portions of the screenplay for *The Pope of Greenwich Village*. He was far from the last.

The lost generation of Catholics has generally resisted the Church's heartfelt invitation to return to the fold (we have even been offered a "ministry to divorced and alienated Catholics," for which I often feel more than half-qualified). Unlike Greeley's "communal Catholics"— more familiarly known as "cultural Catholics"—this cohort is not interested in asserting its right to pick and choose from among those aspects of a Catholic identity that may gratify post-yuppie needs. So the question may fairly be raised: How can a cultural style be called Catholic if it meets neither the demands of orthodoxy nor the conventions of apostasy?

It is true that these Catholics often seem the least interested in their own experience. The phenomenon I have described has always been paralleled by, and is deeply indebted to, a tradition of hip Jewishness.

No one has better interpreted the genius of Kerouac's spirituality than his friend Allen Ginsberg, who offered a straightforward analysis of Kerouac's critical dismissal: "His sense of soul was rejected . . . by literate people who doubted the reality of soul. . . . The pseudo bohemians wanted sumpin' smarter and more degenerate and terrible."[23] Ginsberg always maintained a protective stance toward Kerouac even when he was assailed by his old friend during his precipitous alcoholic decline, although Ginsberg must have been puzzled as well as saddened by the ritualistic quality of Kerouac's self-destruction. As Wilfrid Sheed wrote, in a 1968 essay on the equally inscrutable Eugene McCarthy, "I have known more [Catholic] promise gone to waste for want of a doting Jewish mother than history will ever hear about."

"You may find," Sheed continued, "that no matter how hard you believe in the secular world and what needs doing there, you will retain this reflex about yourself: I must not use it for my own glory—even if what it needs is my own glory."[24] This tradition of self-abnegation is as deeply rooted in American Catholic culture as its origins are difficult to determine. For me, though, the lost generation of Catholics—for all its Gnostic qualities—enters this tradition precisely through a fidelity, albeit often intuitive, to a profoundly orthodox doctrine, the Mystical Body of Christ. This ancient teaching was revived by European theologians of the 1930s who were seeking an organicist model of the Church that intimately linked its members to Christ while reaffirming the validity of the sacraments and hierarchy.

In the United States, Dorothy Day grew fervently attached to this model during the late 1930s, but as an old-time antinomian she emphasized the mystical personalism implicit in the doctrine, which the Church had always feared. Aside from its role in fostering personal spirituality, Day also sensed that the metaphoric power of Mystical Body imagery could inspire a Catholic rejection of autonomous selfhood—a temperament or attitude whose incarnations were visible in the immigrant neighborhoods she haunted. Street Catholicism has indeed been premised on this insight that the locus of personal authority is to be found outside the private self, whether in the family (or, more broadly, what Robert Orsi, borrowing from Emmanuel LeRoy Ladurie, has called the "domus"), in the neighborhood, or even in sports and other activities that recast the classic mode of American individualism. (Contrast this style with, say, the version of self-possession fostered in the leading boarding schools of New England.)

None of this entirely explains why the Mystical Body seems to draw one toward an experience of self-dispossession—evident in the affinity of Kerouac, Axthelm, and many others for those humble souls whom Day called "ambassadors of Christ"—and to inspire a "preferential option" for the spirituality of the marginal, the broken, the fugitive. Yet where Liberation Theology seeks concrete empowerment of the dispossessed, the Catholicism of the streets is quietist: it seeks not social change but personal affirmation in anonymous gestures of compassion, acceptance, and resignation. I am not arguing that Day promoted this temperament so much as that she, an outsider, named it. Many homegrown Catholics, by contrast, would be loathe to assign a theological value to what seemed to come naturally. I would simply say, as a historian and a certain kind of Catholic, that this metaphor of the Mystical Body, with its consoling promise of self-dissolution, is the key to a profound yet scarcely acknowledged cultural style at the heart of urban American Catholic experience.

And it has gotten a lot of people in trouble. Many of those inclined toward mystical transport discovered mind-altering substances and were drawn into the social milieux in which they prominently figured. Enough has been written about the Irish and alcoholism: it could be argued that there is actually a *Catholic* drinking subculture that subsumes other ethnic groups within a historically Irish model of convivial drinking. One thing about drinking is that, as a legal activity, it offered those of the lost generation who may once have favored other drugs a means of reentering the social orbit of the previously scorned older generation. Together, they have witnessed far too many succumbing to "the long hours that are the open seacocks that scuttle many lives."[25]

The character type I have sketched has recently reemerged in American popular culture, this time in a more self-referential context. The producers of the ABC police drama "NYPD Blue," envisioning for the lead role "a thirty-seven-year-old New York guy who had drifted a lot and been completely weathered by it," cast actor David Caruso in the part. During my plane trip back from Rome in 1993, I saw Caruso in the forgettable movie *Mad Dog and Glory* and thought he resembled one of my own characters. Reading a *New York Times* interview with Caruso confirmed that impression, especially when he recalled his feelings as an eighteen-year-old from Queens, "walking around hearing voices from all the stuff I'd absorbed in the streets. I felt like I had to get out of there, that if I had to take that F train one more time I was going to kill myself."[26]

The *Times* has long had a problem dealing with white ethnicity, and Bruce Newman's interview with Caruso, "A Splash of Red for 'N.Y.P.D. Blue,'" predictably demonstrated an obsessive interest in his red hair. Newman compared him in that department with James Cagney and Spencer Tracy, but avoided the possibly more significant Irish origins they all share. Yet Caruso was quite specific about his debt to Cagney, indicating that at an early age the model provided by the actor was as important to him as the action he observed in the streets. "People say, 'Taking your ethics from a movie star?' Yeah, from the footage. Because the footage spoke to me." Caruso also seemed to understand the historical irony of his television role as a New York cop. His grandmother "'definitely had a civil service job picked out for me,' he says. 'She's always telling me, David, come back and I'll get you on at the fire station. They'll have you. And in a funny way, I'm back there doing that now, sitting in an unmarked car on Queens Boulevard. I guess I was a generation beyond having that as a destiny, but it's spiritually who I am.'"[27]

As Detective John Kelly, Caruso embodies a version of street Catholicism in its maturity: there is a Church in his balanced life (he plays basketball with his confessor), the Church of all those once troubled youths who can perhaps now call their souls their own. Reminiscing about his wild days with a fellow member of the Emerald Society, a fraternity of Irish cops, Kelly knowingly remarks: "Nah, I can't drink like that anymore." The Irish have been derided as "the crybabies of the Western world." James Connolly was probably closer to the mark when he said that an Irishman is born apologizing. Like some law-enforcement answer to Mickey Rourke, Caruso's Detective Kelly offers silence and cunning, if not exile, as commentary on an ethnoreligious tradition that his persona recapitulates and typologically fulfills.

NOTES

1 William L. Vance, *America's Rome* (New Haven, 1989), 2: 8.
2 Maxine Hong Kingston, *The Woman Warrior: Memoirs of a Girlhood among Ghosts* (New York, 1977), 6.
3 See Robert A. Orsi, *The Madonna of 115th Street: Faith and Community in Italian Harlem, 1880–1950* (New Haven, 1985), 219–31.
4 Kevin Sessums, "Fighting Irish," *Vanity Fair* (July 1991): 74–80, 138–41.
5 Nathan Glazer and Daniel Patrick Moynihan, *Beyond the Melting Pot: The Negroes, Puerto Ricans, Jews, Italians, and Irish of New York City* (Cambridge, 1963), 246–47.
6 Ibid., 262.
7 See Will Herberg, "Religion and Culture in Present-Day America," in *Roman Catholicism and the American Way of Life,* ed. Thomas T. McAvoy (Notre Dame, 1960), 15.
8 Daniel Bell, "Religion in the Sixties," in *Religion American Style,* ed. Patrick H. McNamara (New York, 1974), 171; Richard Rodriguez, *Days of Obligation: An Argument with My Mexican Father* (New York, 1992), 63.
9 Dave Marsh, *Born to Run: The Bruce Springsteen Story* (New York, 1981), 60.
10 Michael Lally, *Rocky Dies Yellow* (Berkeley, 1975), 11.
11 Paul Giles, *American Catholic Arts and Fictions: Culture, Ideology, Aesthetics* (Cambridge, 1992), 56.
12 Ibid., 168; see also James Terence Fisher, *The Catholic Counterculture in America, 1933–1962* (Chapel Hill, 1989), 205–47.
13 John White, *Billie Holiday: Her Life and Times* (New York, 1987), 18.
14 Will Nixon, "An Interview with David Bradley," *Poets and Writers* (July/August 1990): 31.
15 Sessums, "Fighting Irish," 141.
16 Sara Lawrence Lightfoot, *The Good High School: Portraits of Character and Culture* (New York, 1983), 163–64.
17 Jim Carroll, *Forced Entries: The Downtown Diaries, 1971–1973* (New York, 1987), 43–45.
18 *New York Times,* 23 February 1993.
19 *Washington Post,* 16 March 1985.

20 Bill Handelman, "Full-Court Family," *New Jersey Monthly* (December 1993): 62–65, 80.

21 Hunter S. Thompson, "Death of a Sportsman," *Esquire* (April 1991): 152.

22 *Washington Post*, 4 February 1991; *Boston Globe*, 5 February 1991.

23 Allen Ginsberg, *Allen Verbatim*, ed. Gordon Ball (New York, 1974), 234.

24 Wilfrid Sheed, "The Politician as Professor," in *The Morning After: Selected Essays and Reviews* (New York, 1971), 129.

25 Jimmy Breslin, *Damon Runyon: A Life* (New York, 1991), 7.

26 *New York Times*, 19 September 1993.

27 Ibid.

FRANK LENTRICCHIA

Making It to Mepkin Abbey

Prayer is pure and perfect, according to the authority of
St. Anthony, when the contemplative no longer realizes
that he is praying or indeed that he exists at all.
— *Thomas Merton*

Occasionally, on the campus of Duke University, where I teach,
I run into Stanley Hauerwas, a man I am drawn to but hardly know.
Stanley is a major force in theological ethics and the commander of the
only unselfconscious foulmouth in the professoriate. I hear they complain about him at his home in the Divinity School. Stanley is lean and
totally focused.

Why did he say, out of nowhere, that I should meet Mike Baxter, of
all people? Maybe because I once told him that I was an ex-Catholic
and considered myself a half-assed ascetic. Stanley would not have paid
attention to "half-assed" and he probably thinks "ex-" can't go in front
of "Catholic." Mike Baxter is a Roman Catholic priest, studying under
Stanley for his Ph.D. Stanley is not a Catholic.

I'd never had an interest in religion, especially the words that go with
religion. Especially the word "God," which I wish people wouldn't use,
even those who believe. Stanley believes. Stanley once told me that the
point of his life was to worship "God." He doesn't speak in quotation
marks. I believed him. Myself, I worship what they call "literature," an-

other word that bothers me. I worship some of it. Most of it is like everything else.

I was surprised (still am) that I wasn't able to resist Stanley's suggestion, that I prolonged the accident of our encounter, and that I let myself give in, even though something in me was truly loathe to give in. Since there is always something in me truly loathe to give in, I am describing a banality, not a crisis. I told Stanley to tell Mike to call me. I couldn't manage it on my own, but of course I didn't admit that to Stanley. About ten days later I heard from Mike Baxter. We would go to dinner.

The first thing that hit me about Mike, startled me a little, was his eyes, but not because they're blue verging on gray. This man's eyes looked like those of a boxer who has just taken a crushing shot, flush on the jaw, and he's about to go, staring into the far distance, glassy. But at the time I didn't think, This guy's about to go. At the time I thought nothing. At the time I was a little scared by the look. The truth is, as soon as Stanley informed me of his existence, I wanted to talk to Mike Baxter. Understand, I had no desire to "meet" him; I was doing research on a touchy subject, maybe a touchy-feely subject. But I didn't tell Stanley that either, and the question was, how would I bring it up to Mike, a total stranger? I wonder what Stanley told him? Why was *he* supposing we were getting together? I'm betting Mike didn't bother to ask himself the question, and I'm betting that he, too, had a reason that had nothing to do with "meeting" me, which he would never tell me, even if I asked, and I never asked.

My reason was this: I wanted Mike's reaction to something that had been happening to me over the last two or three years. "Happening to me" is dull but correct. I told him that these—what?—had always had the same prelude: solitude, perfect quiet in the late morning, the end of a period of work on the writing of the day, an empty house with not even the two cats around, and me gazing aimlessly through the rear windows into the backyard, a dense enclosure of trees and bushes. I'm not sure "prelude" is the word. I'm not sure that I'm not talking about the thing itself. I wonder, at these moments, what I look like. A boxer who has just taken a crushing shot, flush on the jaw? Am I about to go, or have I just returned?

I wasn't seeking the considered judgment of a man of "God." Mike doesn't speak in quotation marks either. What I wanted from Mike was confirmation, I wanted him to supply the significance, to say *yes*. Naturally, I didn't tell him that. And I held back a crucial piece of information, another consistent motif in the prelude, if these were preludes. I never told him that these times occur only after the writing has gone well, in moments of unshakable satisfaction, when I neither regret the past nor strain to peer into the future—concerning writing or anything else. Never mind that the following morning, when I sit down with yesterday's pages, my satisfaction will be shook to death.

I know enough theology to know that hopelessness for the future is the technical definition of despair, the denial of God, the ground of suicide. What I was feeling in those moments was outside hope and its despair. I was inoculated against the past and the future, granted immunity from guilt and disappointment. I found myself floating in carelessness, the ground of nothing at all. I told Mike, mustering my best style of philosophic sophistication, that I wouldn't call what I was trying to tell him about "good," because I couldn't choose it. If the good is good then we must seek the good, else how can we be good? I declared it, triumphantly, beyond good and evil. Mike smiled a small smile.

Not even now can I read the smile. Mike doesn't give you those face contorters, the kind that lay us open to inspection. I had zapped him with a twinkling irony from a safe distance. I could do small smiles. If he were reminded, at that moment, that he was a graduate student and that I was not—he knew who I was all right—then good, we were even, because I knew who he was all right: a priest. What the hell was he giving me back? An ironic retort to my irony? These small smilers think they know our secrets. He was trying to drag me someplace, this punch-drunk man of God. He was trying to get me to say a particular word, and it wasn't "God" or "mysticism," but I prevailed. I didn't say it. Instead, I reached, I drew quickly: "pure consciousness," "sudden immediacies of light," "the landscape moved in closer, like a presence," "the quiet got bigger." I was phrasing; I repressed the subject at hand.

Mike was relaxed, talking easily. He wasn't phrasing, his eyes were looking maybe normal. He was smiling those small smiles. He had something on me, but he was probably okay. Then he fired the silver bullet. During dessert—no one has ever done in a dessert with more careful, unremitting attention—he mentioned that over spring break he had spent some time at a Trappist monastery. Mepkin Abbey, in South Carolina, a five-hour drive from Durham. What you see right away, he said, is that these people are happy. All you have to do is take one look at them and you know. It's obvious.

I recovered myself with a reference to Thomas Merton. Then Mike said a few things about Merton, but I remember only one—his opinion that the famous Merton autobiography, *The Seven Storey Mountain*, the international best-seller, translated into who knows how many languages, the book that brought many to the monasteries in the fifties and sixties, for retreats and forever, this book, Mike said, was, in his opinion, "a little pious."

I hadn't read a word of Merton: another part of the sixties that never happened for me. I didn't mention this to Mike. The only thing I knew about Merton was what everyone knew: that he gave up sex, drinking, and a promising literary career in order to enter Gethsemani Abbey, a Trappist monastery somewhere in Kentucky, back in the days when the rules were severe and you communicated largely through sign language. It turned out he had a major literary career anyway.

The next day I called Mike to tell him that I had made up my mind. What I said to him sounded to me, even then, in the grip of my enthusiasm, like bad writing. This is what I literally said to him: "As soon as you said that you went to the monastery, I knew I wanted to do that, all my life." I called a friend who I like to imagine has always lived in a Trappist monastery, a monk of writing. He said, "Take me with you." He's fifty-four. I called another friend—all his life, a monk of rock and roll. He said, "That's so brilliant, man." He's about to turn forty and I have been feeding him visions of the horror ever since he made it to thirty-nine. I'm fifty. About the happiness of those monks of God—it's obvious—I said nothing to Mike.

I walked past the security checkpoint and picked out a man in the small crowd waiting for arriving passengers. Long-sleeved black shirt, buttoned to the collar; gray pants, black shoes, and glasses; dramatic widow's peak, salt-and-pepper wavy hair, brushed back hard; cheek-bones startling in their prominence. Older than me. Stern. Who else could it be? I was still maybe fifteen yards away. I darted a self-conscious glance to my left, De Niro–like, freeing myself for a split second, then back on him. He knew who I was. He said, "Frank," but the voice didn't match: too young, too easy, like a boy, not yet a teenager, asking if you (yourself not yet a teenager) could come out and play. They had sent Leonard Cunningham to the airport to get me.

In the van I came to the conclusion that I was being taken for some-one else. Leonard Cunningham thought I was a lot younger; he thought I was a prospect who had come to look the place over. Leonard Cun-ningham was giving me his philosophy of entry, a warning. His views were strong, no doubt he had let the abbot himself know, more than once. Never mind that Mepkin Abbey had no novices, that it hadn't had any for some time, that the median age there is sixty-four. People weren't choosing the life and Mepkin Abbey was dying.

A man needs to have a sense of accomplishment before he comes, said Father Cunningham. Otherwise he leaves after a short while. I asked him what he meant by "a short while." He said five to ten years. I had to clear up the confusion; I was imagining myself inside his misconception, going all the way; I was terrorizing myself. So I re-vealed my occupation, my purposes, my age. "You carry it beautifully," he said. I took brief but major pleasure in the compliment, then con-centrated, mercilessly, on the aggravating little pronoun. "You're look-ing at sixty-eight years of humanity," he said. He had been a monk for thirty-one.

About halfway there we stopped at a self-service gas station. A small man in a big, grimy American model of the seventies pulled around to another pump. The panic of imagining myself as Brother Frank, a monk at Mepkin Abbey, was being replaced by something else, a hundred times worse. I was grotesque, an alien on my own planet. The windows of the van were rolled up. What was a self-service gas station or a big grimy American model of the seventies? Things were falling away. Leonard Cunningham got back into the van and we drove on and I was asking him where he was from and he was saying "I'm a black man from Charleston." He's lighter than me. I made some guesses that I kept to myself. I was cold. Leonard Cunningham was beginning to look black and I didn't know where I was supposed to be.

A few weeks before I flew down to South Carolina, I bought several of Merton's books. I got through only the first twenty or so pages of *The Seven Storey Mountain;* the details of the secular life promised to be endless, the route to Gethsemani a boring prospect. I wanted the thing itself but was too conscientious to cut to the chase. Merton's contemplative books—Mike loaned me one the night we had dinner, making the extravagant claim that he "knew" I would like it—these books were short and lyrically knotty and uncluttered by mundane autobiography. I ate them up. Books about becoming empty; books about the struggle to defeat distraction; about letting go so that happiness in the form of God could enter and fill you up. One's "happiness" (a word worse than "God" or "literature") is always the lurking subject, if not at hand, then close at hand.

Merton was good at describing the agony in stony places but I suspect he held back on the lonely pleasures of his ravishment. I wondered about his constant return to the theme of community, the importance of the liturgy. In *The Rule of St. Benedict,* the law of monastic life for over a thousand years, it says that the punishment of a grave fault in a monk is exclusion from the common table. "No one shall speak or meet with him. He shall work alone. . . ." The punishment assumes the desirability of community and the pain of isolation. But didn't "monk" derive from a Greek word meaning one who lives alone? Not only had Merton chosen the monastic life, in his later years he requested complete solitude. He became a hermit. The man was protesting too much. He didn't want us to know how good it was, going all the way. He was guilty.

I knew I had one thing in common with Merton. We wrote books, we worked alone. In his "Author's Note" to *Seeds of Contemplation,* he had written, in the first sentence, no less: "This is the kind of book that writes itself almost automatically in a monastery." It was easy to crack the code; I knew why he had been seduced.

As we rolled through the gates of Mepkin Abbey, it was clear that I had not convinced Leonard Cunningham that I wasn't a prospect. He said, "In this place, a writer can cut his own course."

When you pass through you lose the familiar: the rural quiet you encounter at Mepkin Abbey is a thingish presence, the texture of all that can be experienced. You are disturbed by an infringing strangeness but you like it. You feel a hounding pressure which does not respect your peripheries—your famous need for strict autonomy. But you do not mind being dominated, robbed, or even, should it come to that, obliterated.

To pass through the gates is to move into "another intensity," a spreading flatland park of live oaks that dips suddenly into the waters of the Cooper, which run beside it for about three miles: brown and broad; imperceptible in its flow and impenetrable at its surface; a river reflecting light with a glare of such subtle sleight of hand that if you stand at the river's edge and a largemouth bass jumps close to you (this happened), before your eyes, all you will know is the huge dark sound of its belly-thunking reentry, and the deep rippling circles, traces of a thing which in southern lakes and rivers surpasses its defining form and becomes a tall tale. You miss the vision but have the experience.

But Mepkin Abbey is not a story about the flickering Big One that gets away. The story is true, but the point of Mepkin Abbey is that there is no story adequate to what occurred during those three days in late April of 1991. Mepkin Abbey welcomes no storyteller; it will not yield to sly narrative method, or maybe any other kind of method. At Mepkin Abbey, nothing happens.

We passed through—in early evening the gates would be closed and bolted—and pulled up to the guest dormitory: maximum accommodation, four retreatants. There were four of us, but I never saw anyone else enter or leave the premises. I heard muffled alarm clocks at 3:00 A.M., that's all. Leonard Cunningham showed me to the door and then that ebullient spirit of the highway said good-bye, turned and left, disappeared. I felt, at the time, that he left me too abruptly, even though I knew, at the time, that he hadn't.

I walked into an impression of strong alignments, an interior offering the pleasures appropriate to the perfect line and perfect angle. Structure and stillness. Is plane geometry an erotics for the ascetically inclined? Furniture embodying the idea of unobtrusiveness. In this place it would be difficult to recall decorative clutter. A simple crucifix over the bed. A room designed against distraction, for the better concentration on essential things. A mediator's base. I was in my room; the panic at the gas station was someone else's memory.

Two texts, placed on the small table, await me. Messages. A Bible, which I thumb but do not read, and a sheet of paper listing the undeviating schedule of the liturgical day, the ritual shaping of time toward the elegance of a Euclidean form, the sanctification of everyday life. At Mepkin Abbey they work against the trivial eventfulness of time, there being only one event, but the liturgy is not performed by angels. My primary intuition at Mepkin Abbey is of contemplation and its loss, and the work to recover, which is prayer. Prayer, says Merton, is the desire to pray.

If Merton is right, I have been praying for a long time. If what he says is true about writing contemplative books in a monastery, he knows exactly what sort of prospect he can seduce. Bad enough he has to write the phrase "writes itself"—I imagine myself a medium of the God of Writing who never revises. Cruelly, Merton finds it necessary to double my imagined pleasure. He has to say "almost automatically." I know how the qualifying "almost" plays into his hands. I know what he's implying: he's letting me think that I will be spared some self, granted an observation post, indulged sufficient self-consciousness to be the happy registrar of my happy experience at the happy scene of writing.

I will not be required to surrender totally. Is this Merton's coded message? That the self can be preserved in a monastery? Will I be able, there, to stand on the border of self and no self? Is Mepkin Abbey the place, and is my room the room in which perfection finds "access to the page"? And I would survive to tell all and write prefaces to the world in which I, too, would say, "This is the kind of book that writes itself almost automatically in a monastery."

From my room at Mepkin Abbey I walk to the Cooper twice daily, once in late morning at eleven, and once in late afternoon at four, undeviatingly: my little addition to the liturgical life. So that I can loiter in the small and unpretentious graveyard where lie Henry R. and Clare Boothe Luce, and several of their relatives.

The quiet of Mepkin Abbey is at least partially a gift of the secular life that Henry R. Luce drove to economic perfection in his labors as publishing magnate. He was a major force in the Republican Party, she a major American convert to Catholicism who, in 1949, gave some 3,500 acres of their low country estate and antebellum rice plantation to those dedicated to creating a counterculture — a Trappist monastery being the only place in the world, said Merton on the day he died, in 1968, where communism works.

The tombstones have an unobstructed view down the slope to the river. Off to one side there is a black wrought-iron bench, which eased my low back pain, and which I would pull in front of the Luces, so that, my back to them, I could enjoy an unobstructed view of the river.

Once I saw a small heron stalk the edges of a backset. Another time a car moved slowly down the winding gravel road that passes about thirty yards off and dead-ends in a cul-de-sac. The car turned through the cul-de-sac and went back. Disappointed visitors to the Abbey, who came and left without leaving the car. Never saw me. Good they didn't leave the car. Women are welcome here. To make their retreats in a Trappist monastery. They have a special husband-and-wife cottage. Are they assuming abstention? The rhythm method? Are men now making retreats at convents? Across the river, about halfway, a powerful outboard, not that loud, dragging a water-skier, gone in five seconds. Luce should have bought the river.

I'm giving the impression that these little distractions preoccupied me. Mostly I sat there pleased with myself that I didn't care if I couldn't pray, or read the Bible, or have a serious memory, or a serious anything. That heron stalking the edge of the backset, walking away from me, head cocked, death eye staring fatally down into the shallows, I saw him several times. That was good. I was just loafing, I was "inviting my soul."

Boredom must be a familiar and welcome enemy at Mepkin Abbey, God's sly gift, the severe and necessary test of craft. Monasteries are places dedicated to banishing the distractions that keep us from facing up to what we are revealed to be in the times of our boredom. In the condition of true boredom, we have nothing left but ourselves. In the condition of true boredom, we are permitted perfect focus on the sound of our inner voice, in single-toned monologue, repeating itself. We become an emptiness no presence can fill. The monks face up to it; they have the craft; they have a 1,500-year tradition of discipline on their side. At Mepkin Abbey, I know nothing.

Leonard Cunningham told me they have 40,000 chickens, for the eggs. On my second morning, when I wasn't happily registering anything, when I felt private and autonomous, the chicken houses of Mepkin Abbey rescued me from the boredom which I could not distinguish from myself. Retreatants must not, however, wander over alone. The monks have put up a sign on the road to the farm saying so. Go ye to the church on your own, but go ye not to the farm. Expensive and dangerous machines; assembly lines; men at work whose distraction might be costly, and not just financially.

The monks who work the egg farm make real what the Luces made possible, Mepkin Abbey's exile society. The chicken houses sustain the community's spare material needs and its counterculture of monasticism. If the chicken houses should fail, these men go back to the parishes, to be who they are not. I needed a guide to the chicken houses and Father Aelred, the cantor—educated at the University of Virginia, a cherub out of the Italian Renaissance, far younger than me—agreed to take me over. A man I could imagine confessing to, and, a day later, in a sense, I did.

Bless me, Father, for I have sinned. O my God, I am heartily sorry for having offended Thee, and I detest all my sins. The pains of Hell. When I was less than a teenager, confession was coming out of church on a late Saturday afternoon having made a perfect Act of Contrition and having done my penance without a grudge and knowing with complete joy that should I be struck and killed by an automobile before I reached home I would go directly to Heaven, because God would find my soul beautiful. Now, at fifty, I think confession is telling who you are to someone who will not judge you a failure because you fail. To confess, to periodically relinquish privacy, to renounce solitude as an end in itself. It seemed a rehearsal for friendship; a discipline for community.

On the way to the chicken houses I asked Father Aelred to tell me what the Sacrament of Reconciliation was. I had seen the phrase in a brochure for retreatants given to me by Mike Baxter. If you wish to see a priest about a spiritual problem. If you wish to take the Sacrament of Reconciliation. "You knew it as confession," he said; he didn't add, "and that tells me how long you've been away." I said nothing. Reconciliation is not my problem; I've never been separated. I needed to confess. Not the sins, the sins are banal. The telling itself, last rites of absolution performed by and for the terminally hidden. "The terminally hidden": Truth or narcissism? Truth as narcissism? Those Brando movies of the fifties, which I took in in the fifties, exacting their price, now in my fifties? I am reluctant to confess, and a writer I admire tells me why. The confession may well be a plagiarism, marked by obvious suppressions.

Reading is the masturbation of my middle years. "My middle years" is a phrase of infinite hope. I read too much. Bless me, Father, for I have sinned.

The shocking thing about the chicken houses of Mepkin Abbey is that they are an extension of the aesthetic of Mepkin Abbey. The monks can cause plane geometry to prevail even in a chicken house. It is a miracle of some magnitude that a place that has a natural right to violent stench has only a barely intolerable one. The chicken houses are actually clean.

Father Aelred was giving me the news about the chicken houses and the news was exceptionally good. The Mepkin Abbey egg is famous in South Carolina. The military bases demand it. The chickens are maximally productive; the chickens of Mepkin Abbey are happy. The egg farm will not fail because the farmers of Mepkin Abbey practice their art cunningly. Father Aelred is too modest to say that it doesn't hurt the business that the people know who cultivate those eggs. The romantic aura is intense; the people are swept away.

With the exception of the abbot, the cantor, the guestmaster, and the very old, all the monks work the farm, but no more than a morning stint, four hours. Those with special skills in gardening, carpentry, automobile mechanics, and other arts pull less than a full shift. The afternoons are free for the pursuit of what monks pursue. Henry Luce would have been proud of this smashing venture in capital. Someone Luce abhorred said that in an economically just world we would work in the mornings and be free to pursue what we would pursue in the afternoons. Merton is right again, but there is one thing I will not do: I will not read his autobiography.

The schedule for retreatants says, *Rise 3:00 A.M.*, but I set my alarm for two-forty-five. Punctuality is my one undisputed virtue. The church is a five-minute walk. Time to shower and shave, but I take no chances. Cold water and toothpaste provide the required shock. I dress and walk fast and get there at three o'clock, twenty minutes before the praying of the first canonical hour. Two or three monks are already there.

The church is a long and narrow rectangle: at the far end the altar, at the other, the entrance, where, split by an aisle, there is a row of chairs for retreatants and day visitors. In front of this row a pew where a few monks sit, the ancient and the infirm. The choiring monks occupy the special pews facing each other on each of the long sides, about halfway between the entrance and the altar. Two pews on each side, each broken its entire length by small partitions that mark off individual spaces.

I sit invariably on the left side. I should chant and sing with the left side only, but it takes me a day to learn this. For the first day I chant and sing with both sides. The ancient and bent monks sitting near me are charitable; they find the places in the texts for me; they do not tell me to sing only with the left side. I must amuse them. Another enthusiastic retreatant. Tries to get here before us, chants all the time. Father Aelred sits alone, between the halves of the choir, in front of the retreatants, back to me, guitar in hand, poised, waiting for the knock that will announce *Vigils, 3:20*. It comes and he intones the first phrase in his warm and liquid tenor.

Vigils. We have come to the Lord's house; we are a gathering, keeping the watch with our nocturnal devotions while the world sleeps. We are diminished images of the angels, who need no sleep. We wait and watch for the light of the world.

I chant and sing with the monks, working hard to stay with the meaning of the texts, but the message is no match for the music. I lose the meaning so much the better to assume the music, the vocal timbres and ranges, which now, free of signification, enjoy an unimpeded path to me, their dominion.

4:00: Vigils end, Mass. I take the eucharist, actual bread, wine red and robust, burning its way down. I like the burning. Body and blood. I am not unreconciled, but I am unconfessed. Mortal sin. Why are adults standing in a circle? I am part of the circle, thinking about the circle. I will do it again, body and blood, next day, and a few hours before I must leave I will request to see Father Aelred, in guilt, who says, "Sometimes you have to work outside the system. You know the meaning later. It depends on what you do from here." I take him literally. "From here": Mepkin Abbey as the matrix of my future action, a burden I do not wish to contemplate.

4:45. Mass ends, lights are extinguished, and in the full dark, in the night's advancing chill, we begin the twenty-five-minute thanksgiving meditation. I am not ungrateful but I do not give thanks. I have no meditative subject, I attempt no directed thought, but the pictures come nevertheless, across an abyss, unsummoned but not unwelcome, of wife, children, parents, and friends. The unavoidables. I see them all as snapshots of fresh-faced classmates in a high school yearbook who do not deserve their fate. Their distance from me in this darkness is absolute but not terrifying. I think that they have escaped. I do not want to say that they have escaped from me. I try to gather these pictures to myself, these breathless faces, but they stay outside, like the dead.

5:20. The period of meditation is over, and we head directly to the dining hall where breakfast, like all meals at Mepkin Abbey, is taken in silence. Like dinner, which follows midday prayer at twelve-fifteen, breakfast is contiguous with a period of concentration and worship in church. We are not in church but I cannot tell the difference in mood or intention. Eating together—the monks and retreatants are separated by a folding partition, except for dinner, when I can eat and watch the monks at the same time—this, too, is liturgical. I'm hungry; I take communion again, this time without a twinge of guilt. Why do we require dinner conversation? In this silence, the surfaces of things give sufficient pleasure.

The partition is folded back and a six-foot lean man walks in wearing an apron and carrying a platter of scrambled eggs. Because at breakfast and supper I cannot enter the monks' dining hall to serve myself, he is here to serve me. He introduces himself in a voice just above a whisper as Brother Christian. He says something witty that I can't remember. I learn later that he was the abbot before the present abbot. The one before him, the first abbot of Mepkin Abbey, sits near me in church and finds my place in the texts. Another servant.

Brother Christian has the body of a miler. He used to be a canon lawyer. His wit doesn't subtract from his dour aspect, and I believe the man cannot lose an argument. He looks at my empty plate, points to his platter, and asks if I'd like "another shot." At my last vespers he will pass me a folded-up article from the *National Review* highly critical of my profession. I like his phrase "another shot" applied to scrambled eggs. I think he likes it too.

In my room I set my alarm for six-thirty. It is still dark. In the church, at *7:00*, we celebrate *Lauds:* morning song, praise for the rising sun.

Mepkin Abbey wishes to confer upon me freedom to give everything to concentration, in a monastic time zone dedicated to intention pursued without impediment, to the eye fixed unwaveringly on the object. My failures during the praying of the liturgical hours are therefore obvious and easy to recall. My patience and my charity, unlike my punctuality, are not among my undisputed virtues, and they are pressed quickly to their limits: by the visiting soprano who, consistently, holds on to the last note of the last phrase, into the silence, a cloying sweetness of tone, just hanging there; by the possible novice, there to look and be looked over, a bass with a tin ear, who stands next to me for a day and assaults my pitch at every service. I imagine the two of us monks, assigned places in the choir next to one another, till death do us part. Water torture, a musical death sentence, and I know that I could not do it. To request a change of station would hurt him; I must request transfer to another abbey, Gethsemani. (I meet with our abbot, Father Francis. He tells me that my request for transfer requires a special dispensation from Rome. My case is doubtful, he says. I ask, respectfully, But why? In the kindest possible manner, Father Francis tells me that my case is trivial, that he will not put it forward.) And I am hurtled into boredom by readings from the Bible not done with keen attention to the aesthetic values of rhythm and sound. Unless they come across as beautiful performances of great writing, poetry, not conversation, I cannot, and do not, listen. Sensuous beauty is the first temptation, which I never refuse.

Thoughts of failure, the hubris of solitude, managed at a safe distance, in the reflective space of composition. At *Vespers* and *Compline*, the day's closing canonical hours, where the contemplation of the day should take place, and the sins of the word, deed, and the heart need to be reviewed, I do not contemplate and I do not review. "For the examination of past actions is a great help against falling into similar faults again." I must heed Scripture, but I do not heed Scripture: "Do not let the sun go down on your anger and give no opportunity to the devil. . . . Let all bitterness and wrath and anger be put away from you, with all malice, and be kind to one another, tenderhearted, forgiving one another, as God in Christ forgave you, for we are members of one another."

Vespers, evensong, *6:00 P.M.*; *Compline,* complete, the last of the canonical hours, *7:35 P.M.* I let the sun go down without self-examination; I do not ask forgiveness; I cannot feel myself a member. My kindness and tenderheartedness are without object, unless, perhaps, I am the object. Unless, perhaps, I forgive myself. The light falls and we must pray for protection against the night, but I do not pray for protection against the night because I do not feel the lurking threat. Compline is my treasured hour. The light falls and I feel whole. Let what will come, come. Compline, complete.

8:00 P.M. Retire.

Waiting for my flight back, I sit in a nearly deserted boarding area, thinking about reentry, thinking about taking Mepkin Abbey back with me. I worry that Mepkin Abbey will break apart in the earth's atmosphere, burn up, become nothing. And then things go back to normal. Then I'm home.

Five months later, I run across this passage in Merton: "When a man enters a monastery he has to stand before the community, and formally respond to a ritual question: *Quid petis?* 'What do you ask?' His answer is not that he seeks a happy life, or escape from anxiety, or freedom from sin, or moral perfection, or the summit of contemplation. The answer is that he seeks *mercy.*" I try to, but cannot imagine what the secular world would have to become for that ritual to obtain, for it to be one of ours.

PAUL GILES

The Intertextual Politics of Cultural Catholicism: Tiepolo, Madonna, Scorsese

Our identity is not only something pregiven, but also, and
simultaneously, our own project. We cannot pick and choose our
own traditions, but we can be aware that it is up to us *how* we
continue them . . . every continuation of tradition is selective,
and precisely this selectivity must pass today through the filter of
critique, of a self-conscious appropriation of history.
—*Jürgen Habermas*

You know that
We are living in a material world
—*Madonna*, "Material Girl"

Recent discussions of cultural ethnicity and religion within the
American context have frequently found themselves torn asunder somewhere between the Scylla of essentialism and the Charybdis of perfor-
mativity. The essentialist approach involves a reification of particular
psychological or sociological characteristics in an attempt to identify
them exclusively with some particular grouping. In a 1992 interview
with *Italian Americana,* for instance, Camille Paglia claims that her own
kind of "combination of the contemplative and hard work" is "very
Italian," an idea that would make John Foxe turn in his grave.[1] No less
misleading, however, is the notion of ethnicity as a purely discretionary
phenomenon, a self-conscious invention of fictional identity through
costume, speech, or manners, typically re-created ironically through
parody or pastiche. Such are the "postmodern modes of ethnicity,"
claims Vivian Sobchack, and certainly it is possible to see the relevance
of this category to the particular kind of cultural product Sobchack

discusses: films such as Norman Jewison's *Moonstruck* (1987), and so on.[2] Sobchack's theoretical model owes much to the opposition between *descent* and *consent* in Werner Sollors's influential book, *Beyond Ethnicity* (1986), in which *descent* connotes ancestral heritage, and *consent* connotes a more voluntary or contractual allegiance predicated on radically demystified modes of ethnicity.[3] But if Sollors's view of *descent* verges toward an archaic form of reification, the kind of essentialism espoused by Paglia, then this notion of *consent* that Sobchack and others promote would appear to dissolve the burdens of ethnic and religious consciousness within a transposed melting pot celebrating the free and quintessentially American individual. In this sense, the reconstruction of ethnicity in terms of mutable "postmodern" identities would testify, in the most traditional manner, to an American power of unfettered liberty and romantic self-invention.

It may be one thing for an actress like Cher to assume a discretionary Italian identity in a film like *Moonstruck*, however, and quite another for Saul Bellow, for instance, to take on the discretionary mask of an Italian Catholic novelist, or Martin Scorsese to turn into a filmmaker of the Scandinavian school. As Habermas says, we cannot pick and choose our cultural traditions, but we can choose what we make of them by subjecting such traditions to rigorous and self-conscious forms of critique.[4] This interrogative stance is necessary because ideas of ethnic or religious identity, as such, have no more or less meaning than questions of personal identity in any other sphere. To ask about the reality or meaning of ethnic and religious background within the consciousness of any given character is immediately to become enmeshed in metaphysical dilemmas about the authenticity of the subject and the ontological coherence, or incoherence, of the self. This is why autobiography, the traditional genre for expressions of ethnic and religious difference, is generally an unsatisfactory medium for this kind of intellectual debate, because it tends to refer conceptual questions inward, to the upbringing of the writer or subsequent issues of personal belief, rather than outward to the more complex business of how such variations become disseminated and inflected within the larger, amorphous structures of culture and society. This subjectivist romanticizing of the differential self also helps to account for a frequently tedious intertwining of ethnic discourse with ethical or pedagogical concerns: Gregory Jay, for instance, has written recently of a need to dissociate multiculturalism from identity politics by emphasizing how the "exploration of otherness and cultural identity" should achieve a sense of "strangeness" that problematizes "the history of how my assumed mode of being came into existence." Such a "pedagogy of disorientation," as Jay calls it, may be admirable in itself, but its impetus once again involves affiliating a recognition of difference with the liberal project of openness to the other.[5]

My argument is, however, that by concentrating more on externalized reflections and subliminal manifestations of ethnic and religious difference, it may become possible to shift the terms of the argument away from individual beliefs and personal conscience toward the more material signs of cultural antagonism, those areas within worldly texts where hegemonic and alternative assumptions fail to coincide. To call this a "political" use of ethnicity is not necessarily to demand that it fulfill an oppositional function: it is rather to distinguish ethnicity from its more familiar appearance within ethical situations, where the debate is centered around the integrity of the private soul rather than the disruptive contingencies of a public world. From this perspective, ethnicity necessarily appears not only within channels of hybridity but also within forms of displacement and even disguise. This is one reason why attempting to recognize secularized modes of Catholicism (for instance) within cultural texts appears to be such a tantalizing and difficult business. We need to rescue ethnicity from any lingering associations with pastoral simplicity, what Sollors calls the idealization of "a privileged 'in-group' vantage point," betokening a nostalgic claim for some "authentic" knowledge of any given community; we also need to insist on how ethnoreligious discourse is at its most illuminating and significant when it interrelates with the finished article, the fully grown, worldly product.[6] But this is to make life considerably harder for the scholar; it would appear much more problematic to discuss Catholic influences on Donald Barthelme's fiction, for instance, than on Mary Gordon's. Even if one senses Catholicism as a ghostly undercurrent in Barthelme's fiction, it is far from easy to disentangle this particular chain of signifiers from among the many others circulating around Barthelme's dense and elliptical texts. By transforming themselves into realms of the unconscious—both a textual and a psychological unconscious—the shades of ethnic and religious inheritance typically exile themselves to the margins of cultural works, comprising what Julia Kristeva calls the "blind boundaries" of any given text.[7]

This is why the conceptual significance of ethnic and religious discourse can be recuperated only in formal terms. The focus for this kind of criticism should be not so much what is said, but how it is articulated. One particularly helpful line of approach here is what Ella Shohat calls the principle of "ethnicities-in-relation," the playing of ethnic discourses off against each other so as to analyze how they function "intertextually through distortion, exaggeration, inversion or elaboration of a preexisting text."[8] The usefulness of this lies in its recognition of how any given enunciation within the field organizes itself formally in relation to the *langue* of its signifying system. In this way, it becomes possible to reconceive ethnicity as style, understanding style not merely in the sense of a willful aesthetic performance, but (more crucially) as a strategic arrangement whereby the rhetoric of the text marks itself out as different from how it would be in the absence of implicit ethnic or religious discourses. To reconsider ethnicity through the mirror of intertextual style is to refuse the imposition of an essentialist grid that would simply flatten texts into structural ideologies, while at the same time acknowledging how the unbearable lightness of idiosyncratic genius must always negotiate with a more amorphous matrix of darker and heavier cultural forces.

I want to discuss how this cultural Catholicism manifests itself as aesthetic style in the work of an Italian painter, an American popular artist, and, at greater length, an Italian American filmmaker. My earliest example is taken from the world of eighteenth-century Venetian art. Domenico Tiepolo was the son of Giambattista Tiepolo, the more famous Venetian painter renowned for his relatively conventional, devotional themes. Domenico, by contrast, garnered a reputation for more ironic or realistic, even low-life, landscapes; he painted acrobats and carnivals, sliding at times into the scatological or the slapstick. In

Figure 1. Domenico Tiepolo, *The Institution of the Eucharist* (1753),
reproduced by permission of the Statens Museum for Kunst, Copenhagen.

his 1753 painting *The Institution of the Eucharist* (Figure 1), we see
a perfect example of cultural Catholicism as intertextual style.[9] The
incongruous manifestation of God as flesh within the material world,
the theme and title of this work, is highlighted visually by the unorthodox low viewpoint that serves to make this scene of the Last Supper
appear just slightly ludicrous. The backsides of two apostles comprise
the most prominent feature in the center of the canvas, introducing
a deflating perspective that formally recapitulates an emphasis on the
grossly corporeal nature of the human body toward which Tiepolo is
implicitly drawing the spectator's attention. Thus Tiepolo projects his
religious aesthetics within a mode of intertextual dialogue, reimagining
more orthodox Venetian tableaux within a kind of surreal parody. The
iconography of his text can be traced within the system of a signifying
chain in terms of where it conforms to, or deviates from, a specific set of
cultural assumptions. This is not, of course, to claim that earlier forms
of Venetian painting lacked religious content; it is simply to point out
how the particular kind of theological issue Tiepolo is addressing works

in with his predilection for the carnivalesque, so that religious culture here becomes reimagined as aesthetic style.

To suggest that ethnic or religious discourses only have critical significance when conceived aesthetically is not to relapse into the free-floating, performative idiom. Tiepolo paints as he does, not simply because he "chooses" to do so, but because his artistic style self-consciously intersects with all the other cultural, historical, and psychological freight that, as Habermas notes, circumscribes the self's continuation of any given tradition. Ethnic and religious valence, in other words, resides neither in the "soul" nor in the volitional powers of the artist, but in the interstices of the text. It is not an interiorized but an externalized phenomenon, a series of signs that can be interpreted by the observer only in relation to other kinds of worldly events. By rotating the axis of ethnicity from the ethical to the aesthetic, we refuse that self-authenticating essentialism that would reify particular customs into some kind of firm moral code. Rather than connoting an inherent category in itself, ethnicity comes to appear as a way of signifying contingent differences within the material world. From this angle, it becomes possible to appropriate the unstable, tantalizing qualities of ethnoreligious discourse as necessary elements within parallel aesthetic frameworks, rather than, as in the older theoretical models, attempting hermeneutically to decipher ethnic or religious foundations "behind" the veils of textual appearance.

An equally provocative interplay between the sublime and the ridiculous manifests itself in my second example of cultural Catholicism as intertextual parody, the work of Madonna, whose aggressively desacralizing materialism plunders the American liberal conscience by turning its soul into flesh. Once again, it seems counterproductive to discuss Madonna by simply positioning her within a system of "Italian pagan Catholicism," in Camille Paglia's words; it would be more illuminating to consider Madonna's work in concrete terms, through an analysis of how it interacts and jars with the values and assumptions of American society.[10] Without addressing the Madonna phenomenon in detail here, it seems pertinent that many of her most celebrated productions have involved overt parodies and transformations of more established institutions and the images associated with them. The Catholic Church itself, of course, is travestied in the gleefully blasphemous song "Like a Prayer," but the singer also (for instance) reconfigures stereotypes of the Hollywood blonde in her famous video of "Vogue." Parody, as we know from Linda Hutcheon and other theorists, is a double-edged language, which both pays tribute to, and also ironically dissociates itself from, the primary text to which it runs parallel; and in the "Vogue" video we see Madonna both glamorizing and demystifying the legend of the charismatic Hollywood star so as to create a space for her own reinvention of this trope in terms of a more populist mentality.[11] Madonna revises the otherworldly projections of cinematic hagiography, moving in and out of a series of poses imitating Rita Hayworth, Marilyn Monroe, and others. Through these chameleonic gestures her text renders these icons radically provisional, casting them as fabricated mythologies that appear easily recreated from outside charmed Hollywood circles. This accords with the general theme of the song, which concerns how aesthetic constructs should be seen as a mass, democratic operation. Anyone, claims Madonna's "Vogue," can "strike a pose" and turn into a Monroe lookalike: "There's nothing to it." (Note the clever pun there: "nothing to it," it's easy; but also "nothing to it," it's hollow, insubstantial.) With the "truth" or otherwise of this contention I am not concerned here; what is of more interest is how this democratizing of iconography can be affiliated with a discourse of Catholicism, in its most desublimated and culturally heterogeneous form. In the "Vogue" video, an ordinary material girl is seen to be "transubstantiated," as it were, into the realm of secular saints. Likewise, within the Madonna world generally, the performer's religious heritage becomes transformed into a materialized Catholicity, a putative universalism that embraces all and excludes none.

In this way, Madonna deploys parody so as to both disenfranchise and universalize American institutions, to divest them of their substantive power by transforming them into mere simulacra of themselves. For many people, the most discomforting aspect of Madonna is her capacity to mirror some of the most cherished American values—fame, money, success, self-promotion—while at the same time reflecting them in a hyperbolic, surreal, and disturbingly alien manner. The effect uncannily resembles what we see in reactions to the work of Andy Warhol, who similarly holds up a blank glass to the cherished idols of modern America, depriving them of any privileged "aura" or moral spirit. Instead, Warhol, like Madonna, flattens his icons out materialistically, while turning them into emblems of communal ownership. It is noticeable that much recent cultural criticism has been uncomfortable with Madonna, just as it used to flounder around positivistically with Warhol, because in both cases there has been a widespread failure to appreciate the subtext of religious discourse, in however secularized a form, within their works of popular culture. In *Madonnarama*, a recent collection of essays discussing the star's work, there is only one brief reference to her ethnic and religious background, and no attempt at all to relate her texts to the work of others similarly negotiating a displaced Catholic idiom.[12] Instead, many of the contributors nag away at the old question of whether Madonna's output is truly feminist and subversive, or whether she has sold out to the empire of commerce—the same tired antithesis that dogged Warhol criticism for so many years. There is a marked reluctance to extend the terms of analysis outward, to position the individual talent within a broader cultural, ethnic, and religious tradition.

Religious influences, in particular, have become a blind spot within contemporary critical analysis. For the most part, the cultural discourse of religion seems stuck between a rock and a hard place: between a romantic idealization of separatist identities on the one hand, and political criticism's hardheaded erasure of metaphysical propensities on the other. It would, perhaps, be more valuable to develop a criticism that would treat ethnic and religious discourse as nodes within a conceptual matrix that also includes the pressures of class, gender, and race. It would be important also to recognize how the less obvious—sometimes hidden—implications of these discourses come to impact texts in complex aesthetic ways, often through styles of parody or surrealistic distortion that set up rebarbative tensions among different discursive practices and ideologies.

For my most extended example of religious ethnicity as intertextual practice, I have chosen to focus on three distinctive films by Martin Scorsese: *GoodFellas* (1990), *Cape Fear* (1991), and *The Age of Innocence* (1993).[13] These later works offer a particularly good opportunity to study the ludic displacements of ethnic consciousness, because the director has to some extent been moving away from the ethnic center of Little Italy that framed many of his celebrated earlier narratives. In a 1991 interview, Scorsese remarked on how he wanted "to be able to try some different things, rather than staying with exactly the same stories or same types of characters." He also said he saw *GoodFellas*, which revolves around the lives of New York gangsters, as "the end of the trilogy" whose earlier components include *Mean Streets* and *Raging Bull*.[14]

GoodFellas is interesting for the scholar of American ethnicity, because it represents organized crime as a family concern, linked inextricably to community and good fellowship. By portraying the Mob through the narrative perspective of a small-town hoodlum, Henry Hill (Ray Liotta), Scorsese achieves a flat, documentary-like tone that seems to normalize these illegal activities without either condoning or condemning them. Partly because he is not of pure Italian blood, Hill always remains to some extent an outsider in this underworld; similarly, the style of Scorsese's film works through a double-edged discourse that does not simply observe or empathize with this environment, but rather plays its assumptions off against those of the wider American world. For instance, after Hill's first criminal conviction, he is greeted outside the courthouse by Jimmy Conway (Robert De Niro), who rushes Hill off to a party—a "graduation present," as he describes it—to celebrate the young man's breaking of "the cherry." The point here is to provide a parodic counterpoint, to show this community of mobsters setting up an alternative familial structure that darkly shadows normative American values. Again, when chief gangster "Uncle Paulie" Cicero (Paul Sorvino) is sent to the federal penitentiary, he promptly establishes a surrogate ethnic community inside the jail, presiding over the daily rituals of Italian cuisine and buying off any prison guards who threaten to obstruct his gastronomic pleasures. "We owned the joint," boasts Henry Hill, describing how for these gangsters prison appears almost as a source of pastoral comfort.

Thus *GoodFellas* depicts the easy infiltration and appropriation of national institutions by Italian American racketeers who are, on the whole, also good family men preserving a fierce loyalty to their ethnic clans. Near the beginning of the film, Henry Hill calls the protection business a "police department for wiseguys, for people who couldn't go to the cops," and he talks of how this system of tribute works just as it used to back in the old country, only now of course they were doing it in America. This, continues Hill, is what the FBI could not understand: to this particular community, the police represent not the compulsions of law as opposed to the attractions of corruption, still less the powers of good confronting evil, but rather a particular kind of ethnic option. For these Italian Americans, the "morality" associated with the American justice system connotes a specific ideological outlook, not any universally valid or binding force.

In this way, Scorses uses the images of Italian Americana to establish a series of dialogues and crosscurrents that suggest how these mobsters are engaged in an unconscious parody of orthodox civic life. Appropriately enough, David Ehrenstein quotes Scorsese as saying his "attitude as a film director has always been . . . provocation": "I want to provoke the audience. Like in *GoodFellas*. What these people do is morally wrong, but the film doesn't say that. These guys are really just working stiffs. They understand that if you cross a certain line it's death. But that's 'business.' And it *is* business. In that world it's normal behavior."[15] Scorsese's representations here of interactions between Italian American ethnicity and more established social forms provoke his audience into considering how models of good fellowship operate, and how they can manifest themselves in circumstances that most people find alien and repulsive. By showing how good and evil, community and crime, are heterogeneously intertwined, the film undermines any ethnocentric or universalist claims to abstract law and truth. The film's unstable and parodic style is nicely epitomized right at the end, as the closing credits run over a soundtrack of Sid Vicious singing "My Way," in his inimitable punk parody of the standard version made famous by Frank Sinatra.

Within this parodic structure, ethnicity emerges as a form of intertextuality, a playing with and against inherited traditions so as to demonstrate the divergent assumptions that go with different forms of cultural identity. Ethnicity therefore becomes not an idealized category in itself, but rather a defamiliarizing gesture, a self-conscious bracketing of inherited customs or aesthetic patterns. Scorsese spoke in 1993 about the pleasure he takes in reworking particular film genres—"it's no fun without the rules of the game," as he put it—and it is not difficult to see an analogy between these formal codes of film genre and the formal, overdetermined systems of ethnic society that Scorsese is working with.[16] In both situations, Scorsese's tendency is to start with specific codes or formal parameters and then to problematize them, so that his films establish a series of narrative tensions between what might be expected and what actually happens. He used this technique particularly effectively in *New York, New York* (1977), which offers a grimmer, iconoclastic rereading of the spectacular tradition of Hollywood musicals; but in his more recent work such intertextual dexterity has been developed both as the condition of ethnic consciousness and the site of religious difference.

A similarly double-edged style manifests itself in *Cape Fear* (1991), Scorsese's reworking of a 1962 thriller directed by J. Lee Thompson. In the earlier film, Sam Bowden (Gregory Peck) appears as a relatively uncomplicated moral hero who ultimately manages to ward off the threat of Robert Mitchum's Max Cady. In Thompson's version, Bowden was the upright prosecutor who put Cady away; in Scorsese's revision, however, Cady has emerged from a fourteen-year spell in prison to seek vengeance on the man who was his defense attorney. Scorsese's Sam Bowden is said to have concealed a crucial report concerning the promiscuity of Cady's victim in the rape and battery case out of his, Bowden's, own certainty that Cady was in fact guilty as charged. Hence Scorsese's Bowden, played by Nick Nolte, emerges as

far more morally ambiguous than the earlier Gregory Peck character, an ambiguity heightened by the mood of potential transgression
that constantly hovers around the margins of his very proper middle-
class household. When, for instance, Leigh Bowden, played by Jessica
Lange, mentions casually to Sam as they're getting ready for bed some
aspects of incest, necrophilia, and bestiality that have arisen in a recent legal case, he breathlessly asks her to "do that again," to repeat her
wicked words for his own erotic entertainment. Leigh herself wants to
hear about the incidents of "rape and aggravated sexual battery" that
her husband encounters in his professional capacity, and, initially at
least, she appears to welcome the idea of some sinister intruder as a relief from marital boredom. In *GoodFellas,* Karen Hill (Lorraine Bracco)
uneasily admits she finds herself excited by guns, and though of course
the persona of Leigh in *Cape Fear* is much more understated, still we
find the psychological ambiguity associated with her character anticipating the disruptive themes of sexual violence and perversion that
make up an increasingly uncomfortable subtext in Scorsese's reworking
of the narrative. Cady (Robert De Niro) joking drunkenly to Lori Davis
(Illeana Douglas) about how he hacked his wife into fifty-two pieces
is one example of this; Cady handcuffing Lori to the bed is another.
Most disturbing of all, however, is the way Bowden quizzes his daughter Danielle (Juliette Lewis) about what happened between her and
Cady when the latter tracked her down at school. Danielle appears in
only her underwear during this scene, and Bowden's questions—along
the lines of "Did he touch you?"—seem to veer at times more toward
the prurient than the protective.

It is this boundary that Scorsese's texts are always probing, the ways
in which the ethical parameters of conventional society mask elements
of hypocrisy and self-deception, how the pressures of conformity can
never quite stifle the allure of the forbidden. My point would be that
Scorsese's brand of outsiderhood emerges more strongly through its
intertextual relationship with Thompson's earlier work, where the traditional WASP assumptions were held firmly in place. From this angle,
we can see that Scorsese's treatment of *Cape Fear* is simultaneously
an homage to Thompson's film, and a parodic reconfiguration of it

through the lens of the director's own Italian American, Catholic sensibility. The self-consciousness of this relationship is epitomized by the way Gregory Peck, Robert Mitchum, and Martin Balsam, the stars of the earlier movie, all play cameo roles in Scorsese's picture, just as Elmer Bernstein's music is also a direct reworking of Bernard Herrmann's original score. The knowledgeable film critic J. Hoberman was consequently moved to call Scorsese's film "a choreographed hall-of-mirrors, an orchestrated echo chamber," which in one sense it is; but it would be unrealistic, if not altogether misconceived, to demand that a cinema audience of the 1990s be intimately conversant with a film made back in 1962, even if this kind of detailed comparison would merit study.[17] The importance of this "hall-of-mirrors" lies not so much in the film's technical details as in how its intertextual processes function thematically: Scorsese's *Cape Fear* both conforms to its generic prototype and also, at key points, deviates from that standard model. Scorsese uses Thompson's narrative derivatively, setting up certain hermeneutic expectations, but the brilliance of this new work lies in the way he flaunts and eventually overturns the internal logic of that conventional structure.

In Scorsese's reinterpretation, the crucial character becomes not the hero but the villain. De Niro's Max Cady is cast as a dark agent of redemption, a negative image empowered paradoxically to reveal what a Catholic mentality would see as the sins of pride and lust, that are almost, but not quite, concealed by Bowden's comfortable WASP environment. At one point, Cady says to Danielle that he doesn't hate her father at all: "Oh no. I pray for him. I'm here to help him. I mean, we all make mistakes, Danielle. You and I have. But at least we try to admit it, don't we? But your daddy, he don't. Every man carries a circle of hell around his head, like a halo. Your daddy too. Every man, *every* man, has to go through hell to reach his paradise. You know what paradise is? Salvation." De Niro's character bears less resemblance to the Max Cady of Thompson's 1962 film than to the rogues and outcasts in the stories of Flannery O'Connor. The narrative function of many of O'Connor's central figures—Hazel Motes in *Wise Blood*, the Misfit in "A Good

Man Is Hard to Find"—is to expose those complacencies locked into the materialistic patterns of life in Georgia, and De Niro's dislocating charisma performs much the same task within Scorsese's modernized version of the same environment.

This is not, of course, to suggest that Scorsese's film endorses or validates Cady's crazed beliefs. Fired with the apocalyptic zeal of his backwoods Pentecostal sect, the outlaw delivers his Nietzschean aphorisms about the power of the superman, and duly receives his infernal comeuppance when Danielle douses him with flames in the final, climactic scene on the boat. In a rigorously theological and allegorical interpretation of this film, Robert Casillo associates Cady with a "satanic principle," betokening a widespread "confusion and subversion of values"; such a reading, however, turns on the assumption within this film of a clear "moral standpoint," the positing of a metanarrative closure that Scorsese's aesthetic refraction of religious discourse tends to resist.[18] The film follows Catholic instincts rather than Catholic dogma, deliberately positioning itself on the edges of decorum so as to interrogate the moral limits as well as the generic boundaries of conventional, humanistic American discourse. The mood here recalls Scorsese's discussion of *Raging Bull* back in 1980, when he suggested that the boxer, Jake La Motta, might be "on a higher spiritual level, in a way, as a fighter": "He works on an almost primitive level, almost an animal level, and therefore he must think in a different way, he must be aware of certain things spiritually that we aren't, because our minds are too cluttered with intellectual ideas and too much emotionalism."[19] Scorsese's notion of the "animal level" being "spiritually" preferable to an excessive intellectualism—a familiar idea also within O'Connor's fiction—involves the ludic reformulation of a tenet in traditional Catholic theology. In Catholic thought, the concept of "angelism," the proposition that human beings can or should aspire to the disembodied condition of angels, is held to be more dangerous to the spirit than certain more venial kinds of worldly transgression. Toward the end of *Cape Fear*, Cady tells Sam Bowden, "Tonight you're going to learn to be an animal. To live like an animal and to die like one." While Bowden does not actually die, such a transformation into animalistic status is exactly what befalls him, as his smug sense of individual dignity is brought low by the need to defend himself against Cady's naked violence.

Apart from this theological subtext or subconsciousness, we also see class and ethnic components emerging within these climactic scenes. At the moment in the plot when Cady has murdered Bowden's private detective, creating a gruesome bloodbath in the attorney's pristine home, the director told Nick Nolte and Jessica Lange to go crazy, to shed their civilized inhibitions and act as if they were demented. After reducing the Bowdens to nervous wrecks, Scorsese later boasted to everyone on the set: "Finally I got these WASPs to act like Italians!"[20] Perhaps this was a throwaway line from Scorsese, but it does hint at the significant conflict within this film between the values of Protestantism and Catholicism, understanding those terms in a cultural and secular rather than narrowly religious sense. Scorsese introduces his ethnic and religious subtext to defamiliarize the Bowdens' genteel world; his use of X-ray shots throughout the film acts as a synecdoche of this process, in the way it puts the Bowdens' domestic landscape into reverse, as it were, building in a kind of two-way mirror that implies the arbitrary nature of their culture. Like a Jesuit inquisitor, Scorsese x-rays the Bowdens' assumptions of self-reliance, showing how easily they might be reversed; indeed, the film ends on this note of estrangement, with Danielle intoning, "Things won't ever be the way they were before he came." Thus Cady's brutalities work permanently to subvert the foundations of this community, to expose its half-suppressed lusts and vanities to the gaze of otherworldly judgment.

Though *Cape Fear* generally received favorable reviews, Terence Rafferty, writing in the *New Yorker*, described Scorsese's film as "a disgrace: an ugly, incoherent, dishonest piece of work," whose "sordid" nature aspires to the "consecration of something debased and profane."[21] Rafferty's reaction is interesting—particularly his complaint about the film's "profane," "corrupt," and "perverse" aspects—because it does bring into focus the ways in which Scorsese's cinema is often genuinely disturbing, especially for viewers more at ease with the kind of Protestant cultural world in which dualisms of good and evil, the light and the dark, are kept safely apart. In J. Lee Thompson's *Cape Fear*, it is easy to distinguish the heroes from the villains; in Scorsese's *Cape Fear*, by contrast, these moral qualities get all intermingled and confused, as the upstanding lawyer falls into temptation while a violent murderer apparently opens up the potential for a state of grace.

The Age of Innocence, released in 1993, offers another view of WASP social mores being reexamined through the lens of Scorsese's Italian American style of Catholicism. Just as *Cape Fear* plays knowingly on its own intertextual status through the echoes and mirrors that relate it back to Thompson's earlier work, so Scorsese's *Age of Innocence* foregrounds its revisionist perspective by the use of voiceover narration, a strategy that emphasizes that the events on screen are being narrated retrospectively and must therefore be susceptible to reinterpretation. Hence the temporal past—New York in the 1870s, which provides the setting for Edith Wharton's novel—becomes aligned implicitly with the anteriority of Wharton's own text, published in 1920, thereby introducing a gap between event and enunciation that Scorsese exploits so as to reorganize his narrative along different ethnic lines. The idiom of Scorsese's film is designed to exploit its belated quality: Wharton's belatedness in relation to old New York becomes a parallel to Scorsese's belatedness in relation to the ethical codes that shape Wharton's novel. The emphasis in both cases falls on distance, estrangement, and a rearrangement of perspective.

Scorsese's genius, then, is to appropriate *The Age of Innocence* as his own story, thereby shedding new and unfamiliar light on Wharton's classic novel. As several reviewers noted, it is not too difficult to draw parallels between the rigid conventions of old New York society and the world of rules, regulations, codes, and rituals portrayed by Scorsese in his earlier films set in the New York underworld. As Andrew Delbanco nicely put it in the *New Republic*, "There is a gangsterish quality to Wharton's old New York social clique, which, when someone steps out of line, proves as expert at shunning, expulsion and other forms of social murder as any of Scorsese's mobsters."[22] Some critics, though, found Scorsese's nervous camerawork too flashy to do justice to the understated, euphemistic atmosphere of Wharton's culture. John

Updike, for instance, writing in the *New Yorker*, complained that "from the opulent, giddy look of Scorsese's panning shots, we might be at one of Caligula's orgies."[23] But Updike's outlook is nostalgic: his preference would be to bridge the chasm between primary text and its transmission across time, a divide that Scorsese intertextually exploits so as to imbue Wharton's narrative with other kinds of cultural meaning.

The pattern of Wharton's text is to establish a relatively clear dichotomy between the integrity of the heart and the corruptions of society. While not unsympathetic toward May's trusting naïveté, the novel becomes satirically scornful in its depiction of her enthusiasm for the vacant set pieces of New York social life, which May approaches "with the beaming readiness of which her mother had set her the example in conjugal affairs." Consequently, Wharton represents Newland Archer and the Countess Olenska—and May Archer as well, to some extent—as victims of the stultifying mechanisms of social convention within this supposedly privileged "little world."[24] Updike, faithful to Wharton's interiorized, novelistic spirit, wrote that the only section of the film he saw as really successful is when Scorsese abjures social tableaux to concentrate more on the book's psychological aspects, as when Newland realizes his wife has scared off the countess with a premature claim of pregnancy: "the audience was still . . . The terse dialogue is almost exactly Wharton's; after two hours of visually powerful false flourishes, authentic power arrives from the heart of the novel—from the heart, ultimately, of the little girl to whom her father seemed lonely and unfulfilled and her mother cool and implacably conventional."[25]

Without wishing to deny the emotional force of this scene, I would suggest that Updike's general critique of the film is based on inappropriate premises. For while Wharton posits a clear antagonism between the lovers and society, Scorsese, by contrast, chooses to emphasize how their passion itself arises inextricably out of the repressive codes and customs of this New York milieu. Scorsese has said one of the things that interested him about Wharton's novel was what he identified as its mood of "repressed emotion, forced restraint, and obsession"—psychological traits he has frequently explored in other contexts, as for instance with the character of Travis Bickle in *Taxi Driver.*[26] In *The Age of*

Innocence, however, these repressions and obsessions become modulated formally into sequences of signs and symbols: when Newland Archer dispatches yellow roses to the countess and then lilies of the valley to his fiancée, the screen is filled first by an eruption of yellow, then by a more benevolent white that dissolves into a shot of Newland escorting May through a white aviary. Hence the emotions of the characters and the themes of the narrative are signified cinematically through abstract forms of iconography; but such iconographic styles are represented by Scorsese as being also the axis on which this New York society turns. Within this world, to send particular kinds of flowers from particular florists involves semiotic gestures, coded signs of romance, that indicate how these relationships necessarily work themselves out within a cycle of performative ritual. Whereas Wharton scorns the corruptions of ritual, Scorsese luxuriates in them: whether at the New York opera, or in the Louvre, or during the archery tournament at Newport, Scorsese shows how Newland and May—especially the more conventional May—blend in with these patterned environments. During one of their ritualistic dinner parties in New York, Scorsese frames the participants within two symmetrical candlesticks, as if they were celebrants at some secular altar.

In this way, we can see that Scorsese is less concerned than Wharton with a nonconformist conscience or romantic modes of protest. Wharton places the personal relationship between Newland Archer and the countess at the center of her novel; at the center of Scorsese's film, however, is ritual, with the individual lovers emerging paradoxically as products of the very circumstances from which they wish to secede. The power of their desires is fueled, as so often in Scorsese's films, by the director's scenarios of "repressed emotion" and "forced restraint"; his characters typically are most excited by what they cannot get. This is why, as Lizzie Francke acutely observed, the female characters in this film tend to be "fetishized as works of art, glittering objects of desire . . . significantly, Archer kisses Ellen's feet as his first expression of devotion towards her, a moment reminiscent of the erotically charged scene in *The Last Temptation of Christ* in which Christ washes the feet of Mary Magdalene."[27] Wharton's culture of social indicators and oblique hieroglyphics becomes transformed, in Scorsese's vision, into a situation where passion is defined less by the heart than by icons, fetishes, and obsessions. To the mortification of John Updike, Scorsese in his *Age of Innocence* recreates the world of *Raging Bull* all over again.

The argument that Scorsese has simply travestied Wharton's novel is too simplistic. At least one reviewer, Gabriele Annan in the *New York Review of Books,* expressed a preference for Scorsese's impersonal detachment over Wharton's more engaged satire.[28] My purpose here, though, is simply to outline how these are both interesting texts coming from very different cultural and ethnic perspectives. I am not, of course, trying to claim that there is anything "Catholic" about Scorsese's films in a theological or devotional sense; but I am suggesting that his Italian American style of Catholicism helps move his works in a cultural direction radically different from that of Wharton's *Age of Innocence* or Thompson's version of *Cape Fear.* I would suggest moreover that such ethnic and religious differences manifest themselves most compellingly within this intertextual or parodic form, in which implicit dialogues become established between conventional or generic expectations and various forms of narrative deviance. The attempt to describe religious ethnicity as embodying some kind of idealized or essentialist quality is no longer feasible for any number of theoretical reasons; nor can we simply extrapolate an understanding of the "minority" status of particular texts from the reified conceptions associated with archetypes or essentialisms. The burden of my argument, however, is that it may become possible to consider these questions of religious ethnicity in narrative through more subtle kinds of analysis concerned with thematic discontinuities, ironic or parodic styles of defamiliarization, and other forms of structural difference.

NOTES

1 Christine Bevilacqua, "Interviews: Camille Paglia and Sandra Gilbert," *Italian Americana* 11. no. 1 (fall/winter 1992): 76.
2 Vivian Sobchack, "Postmodern Modes of Ethnicity," in *Unspeakable Images: Ethnicity and the American Cinema,* ed. Lester D. Friedman (Urbana, 1991), 342.

3 Werner Sollors, *Beyond Ethnicity: Consent and Descent in American Culture* (New York, 1986), 5.

4 Peter Dews, ed., *Autonomy and Solidarity: Interviews with Jürgen Habermas*, rev. ed. (London, 1992), 243.

5 Gregory Jay, "Taking Multiculturalism Personally: Ethnos and Ethos in the Classroom," *American Literary History* 6, no. 4 (winter 1994): 627–28.

6 Werner Sollors, introduction to *The Invention of Ethnicity*, ed. Werner Sollors (New York, 1989), xix–xx.

7 Julia Kristeva, *Desire in Language: A Semiotic Approach to Literature and Art*, ed. Leon S. Roudiez (New York, 1980), 124.

8 Ella Shohat, "Ethnicities-in-Relation: Toward a Multicultural Reading of American Cinema," in Friedman, *Unspeakable Images*, 238.

9 Jane Martineau and Andrew Robison, eds., *Art in the Eighteenth Century: The Glory of Venice* (New Haven, 1994), 338.

10 Camille Paglia, *Sex, Art, and American Culture* (New York, 1992), 251.

11 Linda Hutcheon, *A Theory of Parody: The Teachings of Twentieth-Century Art Forms* (New York, 1985), 61.

12 Lisa Frank and Paul Smith, eds., *Madonnarama: Essays on Sex and Popular Culture* (Pittsburgh, 1993). The brief reference to Madonna's "ever flowing reservoir of Catholic guilt" appears in the essay by John Champagne, "Stabat Madonna" (115). The best discussion to date of Madonna's religious parodies can be found in Barbara Bradby, "Like a Virgin-Mother?: Materialism and Maternalism in the Songs of Madonna," *Cultural Studies* 6, no. 1 (January 1992): 73–96. Bradby demonstrates in detail how the album *Like a Prayer* embodies a parodic "materialization of the story of the Virgin Mary" (90).

13 These three films appeared too recently for me to consider in the Scorsese section of my book *American Catholic Arts and Fictions: Culture, Ideology, Aesthetics* (Cambridge, 1992), 335–50.

14 Roger Ebert and Gene Siskel, *The Future of the Movies: Interviews with Martin Scorsese, Steven Spielberg, and George Lucas* (Kansas City, 1991), 10.

15 David Ehrenstein, *The Scorsese Picture: The Art and Life of Martin Scorsese* (New York, 1992), 70.

16 Henry Allen, "Marty, Meet Edith," *Washington Post*, 19 September 1993, G7.

17 J. Hoberman, "Sacred and Profane," *Sight and Sound*, n.s., 1, no. 10 (February 1992): 11.

18 Robert Casillo, "School for Skandalon: Scorsese and Girard at Cape Fear," *Italian Americana* 12, no. 2 (summer 1994): 225, 214, 221.

19 Mary Pat Kelly, *Martin Scorsese: The First Decade* (Pleasantville, N.Y., 1980), 32.

20 Ehrenstein, *Scorsese Picture*, 189.

21 Terence Rafferty, "Mud," *New Yorker,* 2 December 1991, 156, 158.

22 Andrew Delbanco, "Missed Manners," *New Republic,* 25 October 1993, 34.

23 John Updike, "Reworking Wharton," *New Yorker,* 4 October 1993, 210.

24 Edith Wharton, *The Age of Innocence* (1920; rpt. London, 1966), 275, 258.

25 Updike, "Reworking Wharton," 211.

26 Francine Prose, "In 'The Age of Innocence,' Eternal Questions," *New York Times,* 12 September 1993, H29.

27 Lizzie Francke, "Screen Dreams of Beautiful Women," *Observer Review,* 16 January 1994, 15.

28 Gabriele Annan, "A Night at the Opera," *New York Review of Books,* 4 November 1993, 3-4.

PATRICK ALLITT

The Bitter Victory: Catholic Conservative
Intellectuals in America, 1988–1993

Communist regimes collapsed throughout Eastern Europe in
1989, ending a forty-four-year period of political and religious persecution. America's Catholic conservatives rejoiced. Ralph McInerny, a
Notre Dame philosopher, declared, "In Germany, in Czechoslovakia,
Hungary, Rumania, to say nothing of Poland, the people, having put
down their tyrants, go to their churches. What an enormous *Te Deum*
has gone up during these past months. Is it fanciful to look to these
newly liberated people for the renewal envisaged by the Second Vatican Council? Their ferocious faith, tested by half a century and more
of tyranny, shames us."[1]

Anti-Communism had been central to the Catholic conservatives'
outlook throughout the Cold War; what would they do without it? Was
America's status as the world's one remaining superpower something
to celebrate or to regret? After his moment of celebration, McInerny
warned: "There are those who see what is happening in Eastern Europe
as the desire for what is most loathsome in our own society." Political
freedom, a great good in itself, had been abused in the West, especially

by a sexual revolution "that is undoing the country because it symbolizes the belief that we can make up the rules, we can define what human nature is, we can defy the God who made us."[2] In the same vein, the Catholic convert and priest George Rutler pointed out what was for conservatives a familiar paradox: "Oppression [in Eastern Europe] has been the health of the church because at the heart of the faith is the Cross or, in other words, suffering. In the West we have lost the Cross through indolence."[3] To Catholic conservatives, 1989 was a year pregnant with new possibilities but fraught with new hazards. To enjoy the fruits of victory, America had to regain the spiritual superiority that had entitled it to prevail.

The conservatives were not a homogeneous group. Among them were an aging group of "paleoconservatives," veteran Cold Warriors and anti-welfare free marketeers; a middle-aged group of hawkish "neoconservatives," many of them former radicals, who now supported democratic capitalism and had strong connections with the Jewish right; and a variegated crowd of Catholic traditionalists, young and old, who feared that America's capitalist-hedonist culture was undermining its religious and moral traditions. Members of all three groups yearned to restore an America which, they believed, had once shown due reverence to the family, traditional morality, and the Christian faith. To them America's moral decay found its fullest expression in the one-and-a-half million abortions performed each year. Between 1988 and 1993, the years that marked the end of the Cold War and the beginning of the New World Order, they made common cause with like-minded Protestant and Jewish conservatives against foreign and domestic threats. Interreligious tensions, much reduced in recent decades, could still flare up, however, as conservative conflicts over the Gulf War showed.

Iraq invaded Kuwait in the summer of 1990. American Catholics disagreed over how the United States should react. When the United Nations set 15 January 1991 as its deadline for Iraqi withdrawal from Kuwait, Archbishops Mahoney and Pilarczyk of the National Conference of Catholic Bishops urged on President Bush a policy of sustained sanctions instead of military force. Their recommendation won the support of two leading Catholic journals, *America* and *Commonweal*.[4]

Nevertheless, most Catholic conservatives favored a counterattack on Iraq. Michael Novak (b. 1933), a leading Catholic neoconservative, argued that by advocating sanctions the bishops were condemning Kuwait to permanent—or at least prolonged—enslavement by a barbarous invader. In an article pointedly entitled "Peace in Our Time," Novak compared the bishops' response to British Prime Minister Neville Chamberlain's appeasement of Hitler in 1938. If Saddam Hussein were another Hitler, as his genocidal persecution of the Kurds already suggested, the bishops would "not escape moral responsibility simply because they spoke in the name of peace. There is a form of peace that is unjust and immoral, and subject to universal moral condemnation."[5] George Weigel (b. 1951), a neoconservative Catholic foreign policy expert, agreed with Novak, adding, as the Gulf War began, that the Americans had shown exemplary scruples over countering Saddam Hussein's aggression. Far from being reckless and warlike (as some Catholic liberals alleged), America had undergone a searching moral debate between the August 1990 invasion of Kuwait and the air strikes of 16 January 1991. "Has there ever been so reluctant a superpower as the United States? Has there ever been a great power, at the pinnacle of world politics and economics, that put itself through such rigors of self-examination before committing its citizens to battle?" Weigel, gratified by the moral rigor of this debate, concluded that the Catholic just-war theory remained relevant and that the allied offensive met its criteria.[6]

A prominent Catholic paleoconservative, Patrick Buchanan (b. 1938), opposed American participation in the Gulf War. Once the Soviet threat had abated, Buchanan favored a return to the old Republican Party policy of isolationism and alleged that Jewish, rather than American, interests would be served by intervention. On a TV talk show, he declared: "There are only two groups that are beating the drums for war in the Middle East—the Israeli Defense Ministry and its amen corner in the United States." A few days later he called Congress "Israeli-occupied territory" and, when asked to identify members of the "amen corner," listed A. M. Rosenthal, Richard Perle, Charles Krauthammer, and Henry Kissinger, all Jews. If America went to war, Buchanan asserted, the fighting would be done by "kids with names like McAllister,

Murphy, Gonzales, and Leroy Brown." Another Catholic paleoconservative, Joseph Sobran, also favored isolationism and made provocatively anti-Semitic comments during the crisis.[7]

Jewish conservatives, such as *Commentary* editor Norman Podhoretz, were horrified by Buchanan's and Sobran's remarks.[8] William F. Buckley, Jr. (b. 1925), a prominent Catholic conservative, recognized the danger of a Catholic/Jewish rift in the conservative movement and wrote a long condemnation of anti-Semitism for the *National Review*. But in criticizing Buchanan and Sobran, Buckley also criticized what seemed to him to be the overreaction of Jewish commentators like Rosenthal, who argued in several columns during the 1992 primaries (in which Buchanan ran as an anti-Bush Republican) that a vote for Buchanan was a vote for anti-Semitism.[9] The *National Review*, said Rosenthal, "once the healthy pride of American conservative intellectualism, now is wan and pockmarked with the disease [of anti-Semitism]." Buckley denied the charge, pointing out that most people who voted for Buchanan in the Republican primaries knew nothing of the affair and did so simply as a way of protesting against Bush.[10]

Meanwhile, the *National Review*, under Catholic editor John O'Sullivan, actually endorsed Buchanan for president despite the anti-Semitism affair. A group of prominent neoconservatives, including Novak, Weigel, and Richard Neuhaus (b. 1936), responded with a letter of protest to the *National Review*, arguing that "conservatives, defending our civilization's ideals, must defend the highest possible standards for public life" and that endorsing Buchanan "sets a bad moral precedent for the future of American politics and the conservative movement." Deeply involved in ecumenical work with Jewish neoconservatives, they felt more strongly about the issue than Buckley and, as he said, passed "far sterner judgments against my targets than I thought reasonable." Buckley had a foot in both conservative camps, "paleo-" and "neo-," which led to his being criticized by both sides. From the paleoconservative side came the libertarian economist Murray Rothbard, who used the rhetoric of anti-Catholicism to denounce Buckley as "the prince of excommunication, the self-appointed pope of the conservative movement" whose "papal bull, his 40,000 word Christmas encyclical to the conservative movement," had betrayed Buchanan.[11]

Rothbard's sarcasm aside, Buckley was by then the grand old man of the American conservative movement.[12] His forensic skill, urbanity, and air of relaxed intelligence made him a great public-relations asset to the political right. Buckley had always spoken up for the Catholic faith and been a conscientious churchgoer, though he had never felt himself constrained by papal or episcopal declarations that seemed to him inopportune.[13] His political ideas had Catholic roots as well. Buckley argued, for example, that the family, not the individual, was the basic unit of society and that the role of the state was to foster conditions in which families could prosper, even, if necessary, by restricting individual rights. Society, in his view, was an organism whose different and complementary parts — men and women, parents and children — cooperated, each in its particular way. Individualistic and contract-based models of society were, he believed, theoretically and practically pernicious. Furthermore, he voiced the traditional Catholic view that government, while it should be limited, is natural and necessary, rejecting the libertarian conservative claim that the state is no better than a parasite on honest citizens' work. With respect to education, Buckley favored the "voucher" system in order to maximize parental choice, and he argued that religion should be reintroduced into schools and other civic arenas. "Whatever else is responsible for the breakup of the family," he wrote, "it is inescapably the case that the official prejudice against religion in education has played a large, perhaps even a decisive role. . . . Conservatives should be adamant about the need for the reappearance of Judaeo-Christianity in the public square."[14]

Buckley, anti-Communist from the beginning and once a champion of McCarthyism, described the end of the Cold War as a "bitter victory," which had been too long delayed for lack of political will. American presidents and diplomats from the 1940s through the 1970s had settled for a "no-win" policy of coexistence with the Soviet Union rather than pressing their advantages. "It was above all Ronald Reagan who turned the tide so that the [prison] sentence of the Eastern Europeans came to an end after forty-four years. He did this by building up the military, by conceiving of Star Wars, by introducing Cruise and Pershing Missiles into Europe against the howls and screams of the left; and by giving the Afghans the materiel necessary to stop an invading Russian army."[15] Pleased to see the immediate military threat receding as the 1980s ended, Buckley nevertheless warned in his "Agenda for the Nineties" that America could not now abandon its military commitments. To the contrary, the events of the last decade had vindicated U.S. strength and showed that America must continue to create state-of-the-art forces against all possible threats. He supported Desert Storm.

In *Gratitude* (1990), Buckley proposed a national service scheme for eighteen-year-olds as part of his plan to nurture American moral integrity. Much of this service could be civic rather than military now that the Cold War had been won. It would, he said, be of immense benefit, both to the needy citizens whom such volunteers would help (Alzheimer's patients, for example) and to the national service workers themselves. Having done their stint in the national interest, young Americans would feel a greater attachment to their nation and civilization. "Service is twice ennobling; it acknowledges that which deserves veneration and satisfies the hunger of those who cannot be satisfied save by a gesture of requital." By contrast, "the failure to express gratitude through disinterested social exertion brings on the coarsening of the sensibilities, a drying out of the wellsprings of civic and personal virtue." Service would be voluntary rather than compulsory because "the state should not be given the authority to exact from unwilling citizens work they are not disposed to do, especially under the general rubric of charity." But the state *should* establish a system of incentives and sanctions, making eighteen-year-olds *want* to serve. (Tax credits were a possible carrot, while the denial of driver's licenses to those who did not volunteer was a possible stick.) Veterans of national service programs should in any event be recognized as "first-class citizens" because "a society that strives after the enhancement of the commonly recognized virtues must encourage, not discourage, civic distinctions. . . . The example set by the more virtuous citizen is a force for good."[16] Despite citations of Thomas Aquinas in his moral argument, Buckley was careful, as always, not to write solely for a Catholic audience.

The *National Review*, which Buckley founded in 1955, had never been a solely Catholic magazine. In its thirty-five-year existence, it had aimed to speak for a principled but realistic political conservatism, including people of all faiths (and of none) in building a viable movement. Nevertheless, many regular contributors besides Buckley were Catholics, including Dartmouth English professor Jeffrey Hart, columnists Russell Kirk and Michael Novak, philosophers Frederick Wilhelmsen and Thomas Molnar, and, more recently, journalists Joseph Sobran and John O'Sullivan. Catholic affairs always got a careful, albeit ecumenical, hearing in its pages. When Pope John Paul II (a hero to conservatives) issued his encyclical letter *Centesimus Annus* (1991), for example, the *National Review* published a special interpretive supplement, including commentary not only by Catholics (Robert Sirico, Michael Novak), but also by Jews (Jacob Neusner, Milton Friedman) and Protestants (Richard Land, Gerhart Niemeyer).[17]

Unlike Buckley, who was a conservative from the beginning, many Catholic neoconservatives had a radical past. Novak, a regular contributor to the *National Review,* and for a time its religious affairs editor, was a case in point. A former seminarian, he had supported the reforms of the Second Vatican Council (1962–65) and had played the role of a Catholic Young Turk through the 1960s and early 1970s.[18] He turned to neoconservatism in the late 1970s after a series of disillusioning experiences with radicals and then wrote a blazing defense of the American economic system, *The Spirit of Democratic Capitalism* (1982), which became one of the handbooks of the "Reagan Revolution." Just and equitable societies, said Novak, depended not only on good mechanisms of distribution, but also on good methods of wealth production, and no system had been as productive as capitalism, especially when linked to political democracy, including free speech and due process. This wealth enabled more people to achieve higher levels of basic human dignity and was religiously defensible. Capitalism, as Novak described it, was based not on selfishness but on family feeling and the urge to assure one's family a prosperous future. Novak, like Buckley, saw the family as the basic unit of society. He too argued that the great American experiment in liberty had been safeguarded by the people's Christianity, which reminded them that politics is an object of provisional, not ultimate, concern.[19]

Describing himself as a "Catholic Whig" rather than a conservative, Novak placed himself in a line of descent from Thomas Aquinas through Alexis de Tocqueville and Lord Acton to Jacques Maritain and Karol Wojtyla (Pope John Paul II).[20] These Catholic Whigs had shared not merely a religious faith, but a distinct social vision in which hope and rationality were tempered by the knowledge of sin and tragedy. "They were concerned with the shape that whole societies should assume, in order to do justice to the moral personality of human persons. All had a sharp sense of the contingencies, ironies, and tragedies of human history," said Novak, in language reminiscent of the mid-twentieth-century Protestant thinker Reinhold Niebuhr, whom he greatly admired. But, Novak added, "Catholic Whigs share with all other progressives a certain hope in the capacities of human beings for approaching ever more closely to 'the building up in history of the kingdom of God.'"[21] He wanted to allay the charge that he was a mere stand-pat conservative and to show that he was advocating a democratic capitalist avenue to true human "liberation," which Liberation Theology and other variants of socialism could not rival.

In 1982, Novak and Ralph McInerny founded *Catholicism and Crisis* (later *Crisis*), which mixed Catholic orthodoxy with arguments for capitalism and realpolitik. It updated the hardheaded political insights of Niebuhr, the dominant liberal Protestant theologian of America's midcentury decades, and urged that the struggle against Communism in the 1980s was as necessary as that against Nazism in the late 1930s and 1940s.[22] Novak led the lay opposition to the National Conference of Catholic Bishops' pastoral letters on nuclear weapons (1983) and on U.S. economic policy (1986), arguing against the bishops' positions and in favor of nuclear deterrence and democratic capitalism.[23] The bishops' letter on the economy appealed for distributive justice and denounced America's vast inequalities of wealth, but had too little to say about what Novak considered the all-important issue of wealth production.[24]

Novak joined in the Catholic rejoicing at the fall of Communism between 1989 and 1991, but he too warned that the utopian frame of mind, of which Communism was just the most vicious manifestation, was not yet extinct. If the institutions of democratic capitalism could be nurtured among the ruins of Communism, said Novak, the world would enter the 1990s "with higher hopes for liberty, justice, and peace than it has known for any of the last six decades. . . . If you liked the 1980s, as *Crisis* assuredly did (especially the glorious democratic revolutions of 1989), you should love the 1990s."[25] Most *Crisis* articles were less upbeat. Reacting to social and cultural problems, they decried the breakdown of the nuclear family, sexually and violently explicit films and television, turbulence among U.S. Catholics, and the Church's perennial temptation to join, rather than fight against, the Zeitgeist. The enfeebled Church, noted one characteristic editorial, "is at its best when it challenges and resists the shibboleths of convention, not when it goes with the flow. We're never so proud of our bishops as when they show themselves willing to pay the price for speaking the truth."[26]

Novak and his collaborators wanted religious faith avowed in public life; they favored the Judaeo-Christian religions, but took seriously the claims of others. Accordingly, *Crisis* argued that British Muslims were justified in demanding the suppression of Salman Rushdie's *Satanic Verses* (1989) because its depiction of Muhammad engaged in homosexual acts affronted their religion. "This pattern of secularist mockery is getting out of hand. . . . Have the procedural claims of liberalism . . . become a pretext for inverting totemic symbols in society, so that hounding heretics is now unfashionable but trashing sacred symbols is cool? Civility requires more than that, in pluralist societies. 'Tolerance' should include respect."[27] In the following months, Cardinal John O'Connor of New York condemned both *The Satanic Verses* and the death sentence that Iran's Ayatollah Khomeini imposed on Rushdie, a position endorsed by *Crisis* but criticized by nearly all the secular media, which took it for granted that free speech outweighed religious considerations.[28]

Novak was too busy as a writer and lecturer to edit *Crisis*, but in

Dinesh D'Souza he found an effective deputy.[29] D'Souza (b. 1961) came from an Indian Catholic family with origins in Portuguese Goa. Raised by Jesuits, he visited the United States in 1978 as a high school exchange student, then stayed on for college at Dartmouth. After a stint in student journalism at the controversial *Dartmouth Review*, he published a biography of fundamentalist leader Jerry Falwell in 1984. "I was raised Catholic," wrote D'Souza, "and hardly receptive to the anti-Catholic fundamentalist tradition." But he was struck by Falwell's influence over the 1980 election and gradually came to realize that Falwell "presides over what I call 'moral fundamentalism' in America," which is "wider and deeper than any religious orthodoxy." Falwell was "the strongest and perhaps most articulate defender of this tradition," and "his promotion of citizen involvement in politics and government is healthy for our democracy."[30] This sympathetic portrait across what had once been a deep Catholic/Protestant rift was one of many signs in the 1980s that political rather than doctrinal questions were aligning and separating groups of Christians.

D'Souza became a national figure when he published *Illiberal Education* (1991), a swashbuckling indictment of "political correctness" on American university campuses. It skewered what D'Souza saw as the hypocrisy of America's major universities on questions of race and gender. In his view, affirmative action programs had undermined rather than advanced the cherished principle of equal opportunity. The search for positive role models for minority groups perverted academic integrity; a rhetoric of tolerance and inclusiveness violated real freedom of speech; and university administrators submitted to groups that depicted themselves as persecuted minorities deserving of special rights and benefits. Meanwhile, academic standards, the real business of universities, were sinking inexorably. D'Souza reminded readers that, "as a first-generation immigrant," he felt "a special kinship with minority students" and believed that "the university is the right location for them to undertake their project of self-discovery." The new campus revolution, however, was harming rather than helping immigrants' and minorities' chances for success.[31] D'Souza's provocative attack on the universities was grist for Novak's mill. Standardbearer for an earlier group of immigrants (and author of *The Rise of the Unmeltable Ethnics* [1972]), Novak believed fervently in equal opportunity, no special favors, and academic meritocracy. He had been verbally mauled by student radicals during his unhappy tenure as a college dean in the early 1970s, and D'Souza's vision of campus folly must have confirmed his bad memories.[32]

George Weigel, another ex-seminarian and a close ally of Novak, first drew widespread media attention with *Tranquillitas Ordinis* (1987), a history of Catholic teaching on war and peace written in reaction to the nuclear weapons debate of the 1980s.[33] Weigel believed that the bishops had caved in to the Catholic left and abandoned a long Catholic tradition of close reasoning on questions of war and peace. To recover this heritage, he argued, the bishops must learn to be attentive to political events and the structure of regimes and not be distracted by the magnitude of the weapons.[34] Weigel saw the revolutions of 1989 as a vindication of his thesis because "the peace [that] seems to be breaking out over most of east central Europe has little or nothing to do with the relative numbers of nuclear weapons, tanks, tactical aircraft, or ground forces, and everything to do with the transformation of the regimes in Poland, Hungary, Czechoslovakia . . . and East Germany."[35] While Novak's characteristic argument was that the Church was insufficiently open to new developments like democratic capitalism, Weigel made the more conservative, or restorationist, claim that the Church had rashly abandoned its own venerable wisdom and must now seek it anew.

As president of the Ethics and Public Policy Center in Washington, DC, Weigel presented himself as a moderate with sane centrist positions. He disassociated himself from both the Catholic left, as represented by the *National Catholic Reporter*, and the traditionalist right, as represented by *The Wanderer*, treating these two journals as extremist mirror images of one another.[36] He particularly admired John Courtney Murray, S.J. (1904–1967), the influential Jesuit who had argued in the 1940s and 1950s that the U.S. Constitution was directly descended from the Catholic natural law tradition. As Murray told it, the Constitution, with its principles of limited government, was not indebted to Locke or Rousseau but, ironically, to a much older tradition of Catholic humanism.[37] In the late 1980s and early 1990s, Weigel tried to rejuvenate what he called "The Murray Project," based on natural law, limited government, and regulated capitalism, and to insist that this tradition could best address contemporary American political and civil life.[38]

Richard John Neuhaus, like Novak and Weigel an influential neoconservative Catholic, was the son of Canadian Lutherans and had followed his father into the Lutheran clergy in the mid-1950s.[39] Working as a pastor in the black slums of Bedford-Stuyvesant during the 1960s, Neuhaus became a civil rights and antiwar activist, and he was a McCarthy delegate to the Chicago Democratic convention in 1968. Even in his radical days, however, he saw opposition to abortion as the "progressive" position because it saved human lives.[40] Without sacrificing his zeal for social justice, Neuhaus became convinced in the 1970s that the American left used the wrong methods and had the wrong animus. In *The Naked Public Square* (1984), the book that marked his emergence as a major neoconservative theorist, he argued that America was doomed if its citizens no longer shared and acted upon a common faith and the same basic moral principles. Without a transcendent goal in the "public square," idolatry, either of the state or of some other secular substitute, was almost inevitable. Communism provided the most terrifying example.[41]

Given the ebbing vitality of "mainline" Protestant churches, Neuhaus looked to the Catholic Church to lead a moral-religious revival: "This . . . should be the moment in which the Roman Catholic Church in the United States assumes its rightful role in the culture-forming task of constructing a religiously informed public philosophy for the American experiment in ordered liberty."[42] That was a surprising idea, coming from a Lutheran minister, but the paradox was resolved by his conversion to Catholicism in September 1990. "I am grateful for my thirty years as a [Lutheran] pastor," he said in an open letter to his brethren of both faiths. "There is nothing in that ministry that I would repudiate, except my many sins and shortcomings. My becoming a priest in the Roman Catholic Church will be the completion and right ordering of what was begun thirty years ago. Nothing that was good is rejected, all is fulfilled."[43] McInerny, who published Neuhaus's letter in *Crisis,* welcomed him into the Catholic fold, but said that in light of the Church's woeful disarray he felt "a bit like the purser on the *Titanic*"; "converts," he mused, "must have the sense of boarding a sinking ship."[44]

In the year of his conversion, Neuhaus established *First Things*, a monthly journal of religion and politics. In its inaugural issue, he and his editorial board, which included many Protestant and Jewish neoconservatives, announced that the journal's pages would be open to conservatives and liberals alike, so long as they were "persuaded" or were "open to being persuaded, of the importance of religion to public life, and of public life to religion."[45] Despite this gesture, *First Things* soon took on a sharply conservative tone, especially on "family" issues and abortion. Neuhaus was careful to remain ecumenical, publishing articles by his longtime Lutheran friend, Peter Berger, as well as those by Jewish writers (David Novak and Hadley Arkes) and Protestants (Stanley Hauerwas and George Marsden).[46]

Novak, Weigel, and Neuhaus, coming from these eclectic backgrounds, brought energy, publicity, and skill to Catholic neoconservatism, along with the support of several Washington and New York think tanks. All three were prolific authors, and all appeared regularly in the national media as experts on Catholicism and conservatism. But the trio encountered challengers as well as champions among American Catholics. They were, for a start, bitterly disliked by Catholic liberals, the most influential and articulate group in the Catholic universities, who accused them (often justly) of exaggeration. For example, David Hollenbach, a prominent Jesuit liberal, wrote that Weigel's book on just-war theory was marred by tendentious polemics. "Only by a one-sided reading of tradition . . . and contemporary realities" had Weigel been able to support his claims, said Hollenbach, and Weigel's "charge that [American Catholics] have abandoned the lineaments of the Catholic tradition on the morality of international politics in both peace and war is . . . flatly wrong."[47] Nor did all Catholic conservatives find Novak, Neuhaus, and Weigel easy to stomach. David Schindler, editor of the orthodox *Communio*, for example, condemned all three for subordinating their religion to their political views (as he saw it) and for trying to sanctify a liberal capitalism that had evolved in the face of Catholic opposition. Citing the first encyclical letter by John Paul II,

Redemptor Hominis, which emphasized that "the redeemer of man, Jesus Christ, is the center of the cosmos and history," Schindler argued that Novak, Neuhaus, and Weigel had come to espouse an impoverished notion of humanity, bereft of its divine center. As Catholics, he said, all three should demonstrate a "Christian as distinct from a liberal understanding of love." In practice, the "ontological self-centeredness" of American liberalism, which the neoconservatives did little to challenge, "makes [its] morality . . . vulnerable when it comes to the hard cases, such as abortion, euthanasia, [and] care for the elderly." Novak, Weigel, and Neuhaus were just as opposed to abortion as he was, to be sure, but Schindler saw abortion as "more than a moral problem," as, "in its primary structural meaning, a religious-ontological problem."[48]

The Wanderer, The Remnant, Fidelity, Thirty Days, Coelum et Terra, and the *New Oxford Review,* other orthodox Catholic journals, also reflected the fear that the neoconservative trio made too many religious concessions to their political agenda. The *New Oxford Review,* edited by former Berkeley radical and Catholic convert Dale Vree, blended rigorous Catholic orthodoxy with a diverse array of social-political views. Vree recently stated that his chief aim was to be "Catholic *sans phrase.* . . . We are concerned for the purity of the faith and we don't want syncretism—getting the faith mixed up and entangled with extraneous interests and causes which then distort the truth," as the capitalist apologists sometimes seemed to do.[49] Still more outspoken against the Novak/Weigel/Neuhaus synthesis (or syncretism) was the Catholic traditionalist Thomas Molnar (b. 1923), a Hungarian who has lived in the United States since 1945: "In my view, this [Catholic neoconservatism] is equivalent to the Liberation Theology of South America, which fortunately is dead. . . . To start now creating another economically based theology is a minor disaster. If nothing else, these people should have the tact to not commit the Church to another economic doctrine." Elaborating, Molnar offered a sweeping *conservative* condemnation of capitalism:

> As far as its merits are concerned, capitalism is just another ideology, which in the history books of the future will take its place

next to Marxism. In fact Marxism may come off better than capitalism. . . . It is the way of man freely to engage in commercial and industrial exchange transactions, but as soon as it is made into a doctrine, not to say a dogma, it becomes an error. The free market is like breathing, okay in its place, but if air is made the be-all and end-all it is at best ludicrous.[50]

Molnar believed that the Church should scrupulously avoid committing itself to economic or political doctrines, while accommodating itself to any conditions that permitted freedom of worship and upheld human dignity.

One group of ostentatiously orthodox Catholics that was convinced of its ability to thrive in a capitalist environment was Opus Dei.[51] Founded in Spain in 1928 by Monsignor Josemaría Escrivá de Balaguer, it won the support of successive popes and gained the status of a Personal Prelature from Pope John Paul II in 1982. A lay organization, Opus Dei tried to sanctify the work of everyday life rather than sequestering religion as a Sundays-only business, and it won rich and powerful lay supporters in Iberia and the Americas. One sympathetic commentator speculated that the group (and such like-minded organizations as the Italian Communion and Liberation and the Mexican Legionaries of Christ) was destined to bear the Church into a new, post–Vatican II era, just as the (then) new order of Jesuits had led the Church to new strengths after the shock of the Reformation.[52] An unsympathetic commentator, on the other hand, described the members of Opus Dei as "Catholic fundamentalists," deplored their secretiveness, and noted that they relied on "a literal, ahistorical and nonhermeneutical reading of papal or curial pronouncements" and acted as spies for the Vatican, reporting all priests, theologians, and bishops who deviated from the most rigid orthodoxy. The distinguished Catholic sociologist Andrew Greeley added that Opus Dei was "a devious, antidemocratic, reactionary, semi-fascist institution, desperately hungry for absolute power in the Church."[53]

One of Opus Dei's leading American spokesmen was the urbane Father Charles John McCloskey, a former Wall Street stockbroker who generated controversy on several Ivy League campuses in the late 1980s and early 1990s for his insistence on orthodoxy and for preaching against the moral dangers of contemporary campus life.[54] He infuriated Columbia University's Catholic chaplain, Paul Dinter, in 1986 by handing out pro-life literature at Columbia's Catholic Center. Dinter, who described Opus Dei as "moralistic and repressive" and accused it of "cult-like recruitment and indoctrination [and] degradation of sexuality and women," tried to get McCloskey banned from campus.[55] After a stint at Yale, McCloskey moved on to Princeton, where Opus Dei bought a large house near the campus in 1989. There he generated more friction by preaching the orthodox injunction to premarital chastity, by deploring the sexual revolution, and by drawing up a list of Princeton courses that Catholic students might find particularly useful. To this list he appended a note: "Remember, everything depends on the outlook of the teacher giving the course. The latter may seem quite interesting and stimulating, but if it is given by an anti-Christian, its impact is counterproductive."[56] Under pressure from liberal Catholic students and faculty, who accused Opus Dei of fascism and McCloskey of thought control, Princeton's chaplain, Vincent Keane, dismissed McCloskey from his position at the Aquinas Center (Catholic chaplaincy to the university) in the spring of 1990. Undeterred, McCloskey continued to work with Opus Dei students and to seek new recruits.[57]

McCloskey saw himself as teaching the orthodox Church magisterium; he denied that Opus Dei had any political axe to grind, but like all Catholic conservatives he found the defeat of Communism "very exciting." With the Cold War over, he predicted that the new conflict "between atheist and agnostic secular humanism facing Catholic Christianity" would come into sharper focus. Catholics should understand that secular humanism was "just as deadly an enemy to the dignity of man as was Communism." He noted that while many American Catholic universities had been "corrupted" by liberalism, a handful—the University of Steubenville and the University of Dallas, for example—remained orthodox and that the most traditional seminaries—Mount St. Mary's in Emmitsburg, Maryland, and St. Charles Borromeo in Philadelphia, for example—were full of enthusiastic young seminarians. Whereas Catholic neoconservatives in public life, such as Novak, Weigel, and Neuhaus, were meticulous about interreligious civilities, McCloskey was frank about what he considered the weaknesses of Protestantism: "[I]ts ahistorical outlook, lack of tradition, and absence of authority do not leave it as a truly viable alternative for educated Christians."[58]

When it came to fighting against abortion, however, the most wrenching moral issue of the era, many Catholic conservatives were willing to make common cause with Protestants. Randall Terry, the evangelical Protestant who founded Operation Rescue, learned his blockade techniques from Catholic pro-life activist Joe Scheidler, a former Benedictine monk. Scheidler organized anti-abortion sit-ins in Chicago during the early 1980s and wrote a "how-to" book on disrupting the work of abortion clinics. Among the methods he advocated were injections of glue in the locks of abortion clinic doors and "lock and block," during which activists placed old cars or concrete blocks against clinic entrances and bound themselves to these obstructions with heavy chains and "kryptonite" locks. Terry also learned such strategies from Catholic activist Juli Loesch Wiley, a former union organizer with Cesar Chavez, who used demonstration methods similar to those of the civil rights movement twenty years before.[59]

In the 1970s and early 1980s, Catholic pro-life militants had found Protestants reluctant to join them because of their apolitical traditions, including St. Paul's exhortation in Romans 13 against breaking civil laws. That reluctance dwindled in the 1980s as more fundamentalists became involved in direct pro-life action.[60] In May 1988, Terry led the first major Operation Rescue demonstrations outside New York City abortion clinics, trying to block clients' access and offering them "sidewalk counseling" on alternatives to abortion. By prior agreement, Catholic demonstrators did not use the rosary in their prayers and Protestants did not pray "in tongues," lest either group offend the other. Among the Catholic protesters arrested in New York were the Auxiliary Bishop of New York, Austin Vaughn, and New York Giants tight end Mark Bavaro. Two months later, at the Democratic convention in Atlanta, Operation Rescue won national press coverage for its confrontational style and its technique of packing the jails with protesters who refused to give their names.[61]

Catholic men and women were equally involved in the anti-abortion cause, with women playing important roles as pro-life activists and theorists. Among the conservative Catholic women writing on the issue for *Crisis, National Review, First Things,* and the main anti-abortion journal, *Human Life Review,* were Ellen Wilson-Fielding, a pro-life columnist; Mary Meehan, a Washington freelance journalist; Janet Smith, Professor of Theology at the University of Dallas; and Joyce Little, Professor of Theology at the University of St. Thomas, Houston. Voicing the common pro-life conviction that abortion kills a child at its most defenseless moment, Little declared in a 1989 article:

> The real horror of abortion . . . is that it violates trust, and does so at the deepest level possible in this "created world of persons" in which the most basic form of entrusting lies precisely in the mother-child relationship. In so doing, it poisons all human relationships, for, to put it very simply and very bluntly, if we cannot trust mothers, to whom God himself has entrusted all children, whom can we trust?[62]

Pro-life activists' favorite analogies with abortion were slavery and the Holocaust. Just as the *Dred Scott* ruling of 1857 had denied personhood to a whole category of people because of their race, activists argued, so had *Roe v. Wade* denied personhood to another category because of their age.[63] America's annual rate of 1.5 million abortions since *Roe v. Wade* had already caused a larger number of deaths than Hitler's Final Solution, and, as with Hitler's victims, the aborted children were personally blameless.[64] New developments in embryology and ultrasound technology were making it increasingly clear that a human life was created at conception.

The most uncompromising Catholic pro-lifer was Joan Andrews (b. 1948), who was repeatedly arrested at clinic demonstrations.[65] Prosecuted in 1986 for trying to destroy a suction machine in a Pensacola, Florida, clinic, Andrews faced a five-year prison sentence because she refused to promise to stop picketing the clinic. Denying the legitimacy of her imprisonment, Andrews then refused to cooperate in any way with prison authorities. She would not even walk, but instead went limp and had to be carried from place to place. Noncooperation led to her incarceration in a tough women's prison, Broward Correctional Institution in Pembroke Pines, Florida, where she suffered strip searches and then solitary confinement, in which she ultimately spent two and a half years, being denied permission to leave her cell even for Sunday Mass. She sustained herself with prayer, writing in 1987: "I don't know what I'd do without the great blessing of prayer. . . . How I love my rosary, the wonderful devotionals people have sent me, and our rescue hymns and Marian hymns."[66]

Throughout her ordeal, Andrews's case got little attention from the national media (the *New York Times*, the *Washington Post*, *Time*, and *Newsweek*), whose editorial position was uniformly pro-choice. Due to the efforts of Atlanta businessman Peter Lennox, a fundamentalist Protestant, however, a massive letter-writing campaign was mounted to bombard Florida's governor on Andrews's behalf, as were a spate of pro-life demonstrations in the state capital, Tallahassee. The state government finally bowed to the adverse publicity generated by Andrews's supporters and released her in October 1988. She went at once to Pittsburgh, to be sentenced in another clinic-raid conviction, but was let off with three years' probation, after which she began a speaking tour with Operation Rescue and joined clinic sit-ins in Canada and Spain, her determination apparently undiminished.[67] Andrews's autobiography, *I Will Never Forget You*, shows her to be an artless, single-minded, ascetic personality, willing to suffer any penalty, including, apparently, death, on behalf of unborn children.

Pro-lifers and pro-choicers both watched the Supreme Court closely in the late 1980s and early 1990s, knowing that it was more likely than Congress to change the legal situation. A succession of appointments by Presidents Reagan and Bush whittled down the Court's pro-choice majority of recent decades, and its decision in *Webster v. Reproductive Health Services* (1989) bore witness to its more conservative complexion. The justices upheld a Missouri law that prohibited the use of state-funded facilities for abortions and required testing for fetal viability before an abortion at twenty weeks. Without reversing *Roe v. Wade,* the Court returned the issue to the fifty states to regulate abortion as each deemed appropriate. Catholic conservatives were as pleased by the decision as pro-choicers were dismayed. Columnist Joseph Sobran, an unflagging pro-lifer and the most prolific contributor to the *Human Life Review,* called the decision "a great victory for the anti-abortion side," though he and other activists noted that much work remained to be done in overturning *Roe.*[68] Three years later, the Court decided a Pennsylvania abortion-law case, *Planned Parenthood v. Casey,* but, while again accepting certain state-imposed restrictions, declined to overturn the *Roe* precedent. Catholic pro-lifers took this decision to be a reversal because three of the most recent Court appointees, Justices Sandra Day O'Connor, David Souter, and Anthony Kennedy, voted to uphold the substance of *Roe.*[69]

While U.S. Catholic conservatives were united in condemning abortion, they differed on the issue of contraception. The Vatican had never permitted artificial contraception, insisting that sex was directed toward procreation and that to deliberately thwart this direction while enjoying the physical delights of sex would deny God's gift and violate natural law. Since the early 1960s, however, some American Catholics, including conservatives, had taken seriously the threat of overpopulation. John T. Noonan, Jr., a prominent jurist, along with Buckley, intimated the desirability of contraceptives, and between 1968 and the late 1980s Novak had openly dissented from the official Church teaching.[70] Other Catholic conservatives continued to see contraceptives as morally wrong, however, and to defend the Church's teaching. James McFadden, a contributor to the *National Review* and editor of the *Human Life Review* since 1974, called contraception "the John the Baptist to the Antichrist of abortion." A couple whose contraceptives failed, McFadden argued, would be mentally disposed toward abortion because they had never admitted to themselves that they were performing a procreative act in the first place.[71] By 1990, Novak was coming around to that view himself. His journal, *Crisis,* carried a justification for the anti-contraception teaching by John Haas, a Catholic convert and professor. In his Protestant youth, said Haas, he had learned that responsible family planning was good. At first, after his conversion, he had found it hard to abandon that view and had simply bowed to Church authority. But now he understood and assented inwardly to the teaching. In Haas's view, three good things flowed from sex: carnal pleasure, friendship, and children, and the greatest of these was children. "Ultimately what explains the sexual differentiation of our natures as male and female is the child toward which our sexuality is ordered." He added that the problem with contraception was "that it invariably treats the procreative good, the child, as though it were an evil." Haas ended with the wry admission that the sight of his own eight children led neighbors to reflect on the English translation of his Dutch name: "rabbit."[72]

Nevertheless, Catholic agitation against permissive abortion laws was not matched by appeals for anti-contraception legislation. The last legal obstacle to the distribution of contraceptives had been removed by the Supreme Court in *Griswold v. Connecticut* (1965), and even those Catholics who were personally opposed to contraception seemed willing to admit that efforts to restore anti-contraception laws would be quixotic. As for the overpopulation issue, Catholic conservatives looked for evidence that environmental alarmists had exaggerated the hazards. Michael Fumento, a freelance conservative writer, claimed that the ratio of food to people in the world at the start of the 1990s was more favorable than ever before and that famines, such as the one in Somalia, were more the result of tyrannical political forces using starvation as a weapon than genuine Malthusian crises.[73]

About homosexuality, another fiercely contested moral issue of the era, Catholic conservatives were dismayed. The Vatican laid down a strict prohibition on homosexual *acts,* while admitting that certain people have a homosexual disposition. "On the Pastoral Care of Homosexual Persons," a 1986 letter, stated that homosexual sex "is not a complementary union able to transmit life; and so it thwarts the call to a life of that form of self-giving which the Gospel says is the essence of Christian living." The Vatican admitted that individual gay people were "often generous and giving of themselves," but insisted that homosexuality was objectively "self-indulgent" because it placed an individual preference before God's plan.[74] Sobran spoke for many Catholic conservatives when he described homosexuality with disgust, as both morally vicious and hygienically unsanitary:

> It should go without saying (and it has to, because progressive opinion doesn't want to talk about it) that anal intercourse is about as unsanitary a practice as can be imagined (though it is edged out by ingesting feces, another common homosexual practice). Long before AIDS was detected, gonorrhea and hepatitis B had become epidemic among homosexuals. . . . It stands to reason that the promiscuous practice of a filthy (and how this plain word jars our progressive sensibilities!) deed should spread diseases rapidly and intensively.[75]

Sobran and other Catholic commentators were indignant that "progressive opinion places a taboo against blaming homosexuals for AIDS" and that public officials who, for example, opposed condom distribution were themselves being blamed for the disease's spread.[76] Another commentator shared Sobran's outrage: "In the course of breaking the law and offending common morality, groups of persons bring down upon themselves a dire plague which now threatens the populace as a whole. Public officials are then accused of bigotry and of furthering the disease when they hesitate to foster the actions which gave rise to the problem in the first place."[77]

Catholic conservatives often used natural law arguments against homosexuality. Robert George (b. 1955), a natural law theorist and professor of politics at Princeton, opposed extensions of the constitutional privacy doctrine to cover homosexual acts. Homosexual acts, like abortions, he argued, were naturally and intrinsically evil, so laws against them, far from infringing anyone's rights, would protect all citizens alike:

> To the extent that the law embodies a legislative concern to prevent individuals from demeaning, degrading, or destroying themselves, it treats [every individual's] welfare as just as important as everyone else's. In seeking to uphold public morals, it favors the moral well-being of each and every member of the public. No one's

interest in living a worthy and dignified life is singled out as more or less important.[78]

This natural law approach, the antithesis of both the liberal and the libertarian view on homosexuality, was assured of a continued public hearing when President Bush, before leaving office in January 1993, appointed George to the U.S. Civil Rights Commission as one of his "midnight" appointees.

Gay activists considered the Catholic Church a tough opponent; gay demonstrations sometimes targeted Catholic services. On 10 December 1989, for example, more than a thousand activists surrounded St. Patrick's Cathedral, chanting anti-Catholic slogans and expressing the hope that Cardinal O'Connor would go to his eternal reward *immediately*. One contingent of demonstrators entered the cathedral during Mass; some chained themselves to the pews, others spat on the consecrated Host, and in the ensuing scuffles one hundred and eleven people were arrested.[79]

The rise of AIDS in the 1980s intensified the homosexuality debate. Condom-distribution programs and "safe sex" education in schools, both of which were liberal proposals to combat the epidemic, seemed hopelessly wrongheaded to Catholic conservatives, first, because they connived at sinful vices and, second, because they maintained the fiction that sex "safely" separated from procreation was a realistic possibility. Conservatives also pointed out the irony that, before AIDS, condoms had been criticized as an inadequate form of contraception because of their relatively high failure rate, yet they were now being proposed as a sure safeguard not against new life, but against death.[80] Premarital chastity was the preferred solution, and conservatives denied that this alternative was unattainable: social and sexual fashions have changed before, they reasoned, and they can do so again. Once a stigma is attached to premarital and extramarital sex or to homosexuality, its incidence will decline, especially if the moral lesson is fortified by the law, with its own potent educative function.[81]

Michael Fumento's *The Myth of Heterosexual AIDS* (1990) fueled the conservative counterattack by showing that gay activists had exaggerated the threat of AIDS to the general population. Unfortunately, said Fumento, some Catholic conservatives, such as "drug czar" William Bennett, were taking advantage of the AIDS scare to preach against premarital sex, hoping to instill a mortal, if not a moral, fear.[82] Fumento made a plea for scientific accuracy and moral probity: "[D]ishonesty underlies the entire moralistic scheme to exaggerate the heterosexual AIDS problem. That it is a course chock full of deception should constitute the first of our objections to using AIDS as a whip to enforce an otherwise honorable and morally correct concept—that of chastity until marriage."[83] Fumento, who described himself as a Burkean conservative, worked in the Office of Civil Rights under the Reagan administration in the mid-to-late 1980s before his criticism of *conservative* uses of the AIDS scare led to his dismissal. In 1990, the controversy swirling around his book, including threats, boycotts of bookstores, and "disinformation" campaigns by AIDS activists, also cost him his subsequent job as an editorial writer at the Denver *Rocky Mountain News*.[84]

The contentious politics of sexuality and the wider "cultural wars" of the 1980s and 1990s seemed, to Catholic conservatives, evidence of America's tragic moral decline, one which even conservative administrations seemed powerless to halt. Whatever their doubts about George Bush, they all interpreted Bill Clinton's victory in November 1992 as a defeat for conservatism. They were dismayed by Clinton's plan, announced in the opening days of his administration, to permit avowed homosexuals to serve in the armed forces, and they saw the new president's sympathies over a wide range of social issues not as evidence of a fresh start, but rather as a reversion to the liberal utopianism they had long detested. They took some comfort from the fact that when Pope John Paul II met President Clinton in August 1993, the Denver crowd of nearly 200,000 who watched the meeting on large-screen monitors cheered lustily for the Pope but booed the President.[85]

Their euphoria at the end of the Cold War had already been tinged with dismay at the state of America in 1989, and the clouds appeared to be getting darker as the new administration took office. In view of the Church's growing difficulties, especially in the United States, they worried that their beloved John Paul II might not be militant enough. He was sometimes reluctant to face down challengers, wrote D'Souza, editor of *Crisis,* and was "glacially slow in dealing with institutional problems that have metastasized through the church, reaching scandalous proportions in some areas."[86] Another Catholic conservative argued that the moral decline had reached a point where "it is impossible in our day to own 'conservative' convictions without a certain amount of intellectual aggression, that is, without an unconservative temperament," because in the 1990s "orthodoxy is an insurgency movement." He depicted Catholic conservatives as radical outsiders attacking a fortress of dissent, where "feminists, liberationists and deconstructionists . . . are dozing on the battlements."[87] Ironically, the Catholic left was just as adept at depicting itself as the "outsider," and each group seemed to take pleasure in situating itself against what it portrayed as a monolithic, dishonorable foe. It might be wise to take both sets of rhetorical claims with a pinch of salt and to see this sparring as a characteristically American method of claiming the moral high ground.

Still, the conservatives had much to lament. Parts of Eastern Europe and the former Soviet Union, far from enjoying a second spring of peace and freedom, quickly deteriorated into a battleground of rival ethnic, religious, and national claims. Even in the politically more stable areas, it was material prosperity rather than religious freedom that seemed most attractive to much of the population. Romania celebrated the overthrow of its tyrant by legalizing abortion. At home, Catholic conservatives made little progress in their fight against abortion, against homosexuality, against the breakup of families, and against the radical secularization of the "public square." Only the most equivocal, least "religious" of their objectives, security for liberal capitalism, seemed assured, and the grinding economic recession of the early 1990s cast a shadow over even that.

NOTES

1 Ralph McInerny, "Te Deum Laudamus," *Crisis* 8 (February 1990): 2–3.
2 Ibid., 3.

3 William Grace, "The World According to George Rutler," *Crisis* 8 (March 1990): 16.

4 Editorial, "The Road Taken," *America* 164 (2 February 1991): 75; Editorial, "Patience and Resolve," *Commonweal* 118 (11 January 1991): 3-4.

5 Michael Novak, "Peace in Our Time," *Crisis* 9 (January 1991): 2-4.

6 George Weigel, "A War about America," *Commonweal* 118 (22 February 1991): 121.

7 William F. Buckley, Jr., *In Search of Anti-Semitism* (New York, 1992), 26-28. See this book for a detailed history of the controversy.

8 Norman Podhoretz, "A Statement on the Persian Gulf Crisis," *Commentary* 90 (November 1990): 17-20; and "Enter the Peace Party," *Commentary* 91 (January 1991): 17-21.

9 On the Buchanan candidacy, see Robin Toner, "Buchanan, Urging New Nationalism, Joins '92 Race," *New York Times*, 11 December 1991, B12.

10 Buckley, *Anti-Semitism*, 169.

11 Ibid., 171, 173, 155.

12 The following summary is based on John Judis, *William F. Buckley, Patron Saint of the Conservatives* (New York, 1988). See also Patrick Allitt, *Catholic Intellectuals and Conservative Politics in America: 1950–1985* (Ithaca, 1993).

13 Buckley openly deplored some papal statements. When, for example, Pope John Paul II issued his encyclical letter *Sollicitudo Rei Socialis* in March 1988, criticizing Western materialism almost as harshly as Communist totalitarianism, Buckley retorted that the letter betrayed a thought process "so mystifyingly antihistorical as to jeopardize the credibility of any thought accompanying it," adding that this encyclical would make the pope "a lot of enemies of exactly the kind he does not need." See his "Papal Misfire," quoted in Richard P. McBrien, *Report on the Church: Catholicism After Vatican II* (San Francisco, 1992), 153-54.

14 William F. Buckley, Jr., "Agenda for the Nineties," *National Review* 42 (19 February 1990): 37.

15 William F. Buckley, Jr., "Bitter Victory," *National Review* 42 (5 February 1990): 62.

16 William F. Buckley, Jr., *Gratitude: Reflections on What We Owe to Our Country* (New York, 1990), xvi-xvii, 25, 114, 73.

17 Special supplement on *Centesimus Annus, National Review* 43 (24 June 1991).

18 Allitt, *Catholic Intellectuals*, 243-88.

19 Michael Novak, *The Spirit of Democratic Capitalism* (New York, 1982).

20 Michael Novak, "Thomas Aquinas, The First Whig," *Crisis* 8 (October 1990): 31–38.

21 Michael Novak, "The Catholic Whig Tradition," *Crisis* 7 (September 1989): 2–3.

22 Acton (pseud.), "The Present Crisis," *Catholicism and Crisis* 1 (November 1982): 1–2.

23 Michael Novak, *Moral Clarity in the Nuclear Age* (Nashville, 1983); and *Toward the Future: Catholic Social Thought and the US Economy* (New York, 1984).

24 National Conference of Catholic Bishops, *Economic Justice for All: Catholic Social Teaching and the US Economy* (Washington, DC, 1986).

25 Michael Novak, "You'll Love the Nineties," *Crisis* 8 (January 1990): 2–3.

26 Editorial, "In Defense of Bishops," *Crisis* 8 (January 1990): 5.

27 Editorial, "The Last Temptation of Mohammed," *Crisis* (January 1989): 4. The title refers to the controversial Martin Scorsese film *The Last Temptation of Christ* (1988), in which Jesus was shown in a sex scene.

28 See "Miscellany," *Crisis* 7 (April 1989): 8.

29 This section is based in part on a telephone interview with Dinesh D'Souza, 18 October 1993.

30 Dinesh D'Souza, *Falwell: Before the Millennium* (Chicago, 1984), 9, 12, 195.

31 Dinesh D'Souza, *Illiberal Education* (New York, 1991), 23.

32 Novak was dean of students at the State University of New York, Old Westbury, in the late 1960s and early 1970s. See Allitt, *Catholic Intellectuals,* 271.

33 This section is based in part on a telephone interview with George Weigel, 6 October 1993.

34 George Weigel, *Tranquillitas Ordinis: The Present Failure and Future Promise of American Catholic Thought on War and Peace* (New York, 1987).

35 George Weigel, *Freedom and Its Discontents: Catholicism Confronts Modernity* (Washington, DC, 1991), 61.

36 George Weigel, *Catholicism and the Renewal of American Democracy* (Mahwah, NY, 1989), 47–69, 70–82.

37 John Courtney Murray, S.J., *We Hold These Truths: Catholic Reflections on the American Proposition* (New York, 1960).

38 See, for example, George Weigel, "The Future of the John Courtney Murray Project," in *John Courtney Murray and the American Civil Conversation,* ed. Robert P. Hunt and Kenneth L. Grasso (Grand Rapids, 1992), 273–96.

39 Joan Frawley Desmond, "Our Moment," *Crisis* 6 (February 1988): 25–29.

40 Richard Neuhaus, "The Dangerous Assumptions," *Commonweal* 86 (30 June 1967): 408–13.

41 Richard Neuhaus, *The Naked Public Square: Religion and Democracy in America* (Grand Rapids, 1984).

42 Richard Neuhaus, *The Catholic Moment: The Paradox of the Church in the Postmodern World* (San Francisco, 1987), 283.

43 Richard Neuhaus, "I Can Do No Other," *Crisis* 8 (October 1990): 5.

44 Ralph McInerny, "Richard's New House," *Crisis* 8 (October 1990): 2.

45 Editorial, "Putting First Things First," *First Things* 1 (March 1990): 7.

46 On this cross-religious development in America, see Robert Wuthnow, *The Restructuring of American Religion: Society and Faith Since World War II* (Princeton, 1988).

47 David Hollenbach, "War and Peace in American Catholic Thought: A Heritage Abandoned?" *Theological Studies* 48 (December 1987): 711–26.

48 David Schindler, "Christology and the Church's 'Worldly' Mission: Response to Michael Novak," *Communio* 19 (Spring 1992): 164–78; see also Mark Lowery, "The Schindler-Weigel Debate: An Appraisal," *Communio* 18 (Fall 1991): 425–38.

49 Telephone interview with Dale Vree, 6 May 1993.

50 Interview with Thomas Molnar, 10 May 1993, Ridgewood, NJ.

51 The following passage is based largely on Paul Longo, "Escrivá's Opus Dei: From Secular Association to Personal Prelature," *American Benedictine Review* 40 (June 1989): 190–203.

52 Charles Helms, "The Future that Works," *Crisis* 8 (November 1990): 30–33.

53 John A. Coleman, "Who Are the Catholic Fundamentalists?" *Commonweal* 116 (27 January 1989): 42–47. Greeley is quoted in John A. Coleman, "Author Replies," *Commonweal* 116 (6 October 1989): 543.

54 Patricia Lefevere, "Campus Ministers Assess Opus Dei's Campus Role," *National Catholic Reporter*, 2 December 1988, 18–19.

55 Paul Dinter, "Catholics at Columbia," *Commonweal* 115 (8 April 1988): 204; and "Author Replies," *Commonweal* 115 (3 June 1988): 351.

56 James Hitchcock, "Condoms, Coercion, and Christianity: A Princeton Tale," *Academic Questions* (Winter 1990–91): 48.

57 Interview with C. J. McCloskey, 3 May 1993, Princeton, NJ.

58 C. J. McCloskey III, "Good Guys Finish First," *Crisis* 8 (December 1990): 14–16; see also C. J. McCloskey, "Choosing a College," *Crisis* 11 (October 1993): 42–44.

59 Garry Wills, "Evangels of Abortion," *New York Review of Books* (15 June 1989): 15, 18–21.

60 Monica Migliorino, "Abortion Battles Ahead," *Crisis* 7 (September 1989): 15–22.

61 Mary Meehan, "On the Road with the Rescue Movement," *Human Life Review* 15 (Summer 1989): 7–23.

62 Joyce Little, "The Gender Gap," *Crisis* 7 (January 1989): 33.

63 See, for example, Michael Fumento, "Beauregard's Manifesto," *Crisis* 8 (February 1990): 25–27, a satire on the pro-choice position and on that of such politicians as New York Governor Mario Cuomo who said they were personally opposed to abortion, but favored the pro-choice position in American politics.

64 See, for example, Richard J. Neuhaus, "The Way They Were, The Way We Are: Bioethics and the Holocaust," *Human Life Review* 16 (Spring 1990): 47–62.

65 The following account of Joan Andrews is based on her autobiography, *I Will Never Forget You* (Harrison, NY, 1989); and on Mary Meehan, "Joan Andrews and Friends," *Human Life Review* 14 (Spring 1988): 7–24.

66 Nat Hentoff, "The Prisoner Who Cannot Be Broken," *Human Life Review* 14 (Fall 1988): 102–6. Hentoff, cofounder of the *Village Voice*, was one of the few non-Catholic Americans from the political left to sympathize with the pro-life cause. He argues here that Florida violated Andrews's First Amendment right to the free exercise of her religion.

67 Meehan, "On the Road."

68 Joseph Sobran, "After *Webster,* What?" *Human Life Review* 15 (Fall 1989): 2.

69 Mary Ann Glendon, "U.S. Abortion Law: Still the Most Permissive of the Liberal Democracies," *Human Life Review* 18 (Fall 1992): 102–4.

70 Allitt, *Catholic Intellectuals*, 163–203.

71 Interview with James McFadden, 12 October 1987, New York City.

72 John M. Haas, "Straight Talk about Contraception," *Crisis* 7 (February 1989): 32–38.

73 Michael Fumento, "The Profits of Doom," *Crisis* 9 (February 1991): 14–18.

74 Bruce Williams, O.P., "Homosexuality: The New Vatican Statement," *Theological Studies* 48 (June 1987): 259–77.

75 Joseph Sobran, "AIDS and Social Progress," *Human Life Review* 13 (Fall 1987): 9–10.

76 Ibid., 11.

77 R. V. Young, "Safe Sex and the AIDS Martyrs," *Human Life Review* 15 (Fall 1989): 81.

78 Robert P. George, "Individual Rights, Collective Interests, Public Law, and American Politics," in *Natural Law*, ed. John Finnis (New York, 1991), 2: 105.

79 Robert Hutchinson, "Seven Trample on Consecrated Host," *Thirty Days* 3 (January 1990): 20–23.

80 Sobran, "AIDS and Social Progress," 7.

81 See, for example, Robert Destro, Joseph Schmitz, and Robert Crnkovich, "Federalism: Reconciling a 'Human Life' and 'States' Rights' Approach to the Legal Protection of the Unborn," *Human Life Review* 15 (Spring 1989): 77–90.

82 Michael Fumento, *The Myth of Heterosexual AIDS* (New York, 1990).

83 Michael Fumento, "Heterosexual AIDS?" *Crisis* 6 (October 1988): 34–35.

84 Telephone interview with Michael Fumento, 5 October 1993.

85 Editorial, "Papal States," *National Review* 45 (6 September 1993): 18–19.

86 Dinesh D'Souza, "A House Divided," *Crisis* 10 (December 1992): 19–22.

87 Chrysostom (pseud.), "Conservatives against the Status Quo," *Crisis* 11 (January 1993): 3–4.

ANDREW SULLIVAN

Virtually Normal

> In everyone there sleeps
> A sense of life lived according to love.
> To some it means the difference they could make
> By loving others, but across most it sweeps
> As all they might have been had they been loved.
> That nothing cures.
> — Philip Larkin, "Faith Healing"

I can remember the first time what, for the sake of argument, I will call my sexuality came into direct conflict with what, for the sake of argument, I will call my faith. It was time for Communion in my local parish church, Our Lady and St. Peter's, a small but dignified building crammed between an Indian restaurant and a stationery shop, opposite a public restroom, on the main street of a smallish town south of London called East Grinstead. I must have been around fifteen or so. Every time I received Communion, I attempted, following my mother's instructions, to offer up the sacrament for some current problem or need: my mother's health, an upcoming exam, the starving in Bangladesh, or whatever. Most of these requests had to do with either something abstract and distant, like a cure for cancer, or something extremely tangible, like a better part in the school play. Like much else in my faith-life, they were routine and yet not completely drained of sincerity. But rarely did they address something that really affected my inner life, something that could unsettle the comfort of my precocious adolescence. The closest they got to self-criticism was in the abstract:

my pride, my selfishness, the faults my parents and friends had identified in me and that I had taken somewhat to heart. But this time, as
I filed up to the Communion rail to face mild-mannered Father Sim-
mons for the umpteenth time, something else intervened. Please, I remember asking almost offhandedly of God, after a quick recital of my
other failings, help me with *that*.

I didn't have a name for it, since it was, to all intents and purposes,
nameless. I don't think I had ever heard it mentioned at home, except
once when my mother referred to someone who had behaved inappro-
priately on my father's town rugby team. (He had been dealt with, she
reported darkly.) At school, the subject was everywhere and nowhere:
at the root of countless jokes and double entendres, but never actual-
ized as a reality or as something that could affect anyone we knew. But
this ubiquity and abstraction brought home the most important point:
uniquely among failings or sins, homosexuality was so abominable that
it could not even be mentioned. The occasions when it was actually
discussed were so rare that they stand out even now in my mind: our
Latin teacher's stating that homosexuality was obviously wrong since it
meant "sticking your dick in the wrong hole"; the graffiti in the public restroom in Reigate High Street (the town where I attended high
school): "My mother made me a homosexual," followed closely by, "If I
gave her the wool, would she make me one too?" Although my friends
and family never stinted in pointing out other faults or inadequacies
on my part, this, I knew, would never be directly confronted. So when
it emerged as an irresistible, overwhelming fact of my existence, and
when it first seeped into my life of dutiful prayer and worship, it could
be referred to only in the inarticulate void of that Sunday evening before Communion.

From the beginning, however—and this is something many outside
the Church can find hard to understand—my sexuality was part of my
faith-life, not a revolt against it. Looking back, I realize that that moment at the Communion rail was the first time I had actually addressed
the subject of homosexuality explicitly in front of anyone; and I had
brought it to God in the moments before the most intimate act of sacramental Communion. Because it was something I was deeply ashamed

of, I felt obliged to confront it; but because it was also something inextricable, even then, from the core of my existence, it felt natural to enlist God's help rather than his judgment in grappling with it. There was, of course, considerable tension in this balance of alliance and rejection; but there was also something quite natural about it, an accurate reflection of any human being's compromised relationship with what he or she hazards to be the divine.

To the outsider, faith often seems a kind of cataclysmic intervention, a Damascene moment of revelation and transformation, and no doubt, for a few, this is indeed the experience. But this view of faith is often, it seems to me, a way to salve the unease of a faithless life by constructing the alternative as something so alien to actual experience that it is safely beyond reach. Faith for me has never been like that. The moments of genuine intervention and spiritual clarity have been minuscule in number and, when they have occurred, hard to discern and harder still to understand. The rest has been a humdrum process of ritual and exasperation, interspersed by occasional, unsolicited moments of grace. In the midst of this uncertainty, the sacraments, especially that of Communion, have always been for me the only truly reliable elements of direction, concrete instantiations of another order, tangible ways in which to express the ineffable. Which is why, perhaps, it was at Communion that the subject reared its confusing, shaming presence.

The two experiences came together in other ways too. Like faith, one's sexuality is not simply a choice, it informs a whole way of being; but like faith, it involves choices — the choice to affirm or deny the central part of one's being, the choice to live a life that does not deny but confronts reality, the choice to persist in the adventure of one's own existential journey, despite its destination's being uncertain and its hazards unknown. It is, like faith, deeply mysterious, emerging clearly one day, only to disappear the next, taking different forms — of passion, of lust, of intimacy, of warmth, of fear — fluctuating between something simply sexual and something far more complex, more integral and integrated. And like faith, it points toward something other and more powerful than the self. The physical communion with the other in sexual life hints at the same kind of transcendence as the physical

Communion with the Other that lies at the heart of the sacramental Catholic vision.

So when I came to be asked, later in life, how I could be gay and Catholic, I could answer only that I simply was. What to others appeared a complete contradiction was, in reality, the existence of these two inextricably connected, yet sometimes parallel, experiences of the world. It was not that my sexuality was involuntary and my faith chosen and that therefore my sexuality posed a problem for my faith; nor was it that my faith was involuntary and my sexuality chosen so that my faith posed a problem for my sexuality. It was that both were chosen and unchosen continuously throughout my life, as parts of the same search for something larger. As I grew older, they became part of me, inseparable from my understanding of myself and of my relationship with God. My faith existed at the foundation of how I saw the world; my sexuality grew to be inseparable from how I felt the world. The two informed each other and had a dialogue with each other. They were, to borrow an Oakeshottian term, modes of experience, and my life was premised upon both of them.

I am aware that this formulation of the problem is theologically flawed. Faith, after all, is not a sensibility; in the Catholic sense, it is a statement about reality, about truth, that is not simply negated by experience; it is a statement about revelation, not sentiment. And there is little doubt about what the authority of the Church teaches about the sexual expression of a homosexual orientation. But I can respond only that this was not how the problem first presented itself. The immediate problem was not how to make what I *did* conform with what the Church taught me (until my early twenties, I did very little that could be regarded as objectively sinful with regard to sexuality), but how to make who I *was* conform with what the Church taught me. This was a much more difficult proposition. It did not conform to a simple contradiction between self and God, as that afternoon in the Communion line attested. It entailed trying to understand how my crushes and passions, my emotional longings for human contact, my stumbling attempts to relate love to life, could be so inimical to the Gospel of Christ and his

Church, how they could be so unmentionable among people I loved and trusted.

So I resorted to what many young homosexuals and lesbians resort to. I found a way to expunge love from life, to construct an existence and a personal trajectory that could somehow explain this absence, and to pray and hope that what seemed so natural and overwhelming could somehow be dealt with. I studied hard and created a studious identity that could explain away my refusal to socialize; I developed intense intellectual friendships that bordered on the emotional, but I kept them restrained in a carapace of artificiality to prevent passion from breaking out. I adhered to a hopelessly pessimistic view of the world, which could help explain my own refusal to take part in life's amusements and pleasures. I threw myself into amateur theater, not simply to give vent to feelings I could vent nowhere else, but to fill up the empty evenings and cavernous weekends that a love-free life can contain. And I constructed fantasies of future exploits, of ambitious dreams that could somehow absorb the adolescent emotions that could not be directed toward real human contact.

No doubt some of this behavior was part of any adolescent's panic at the prospect of adulthood, or was a function of my particular psychological makeup and background. But looking back, it seems unlikely that this pattern had nothing whatsoever to do with my being gay. It had one other twist: it sparked an intense religiosity that could provide me with the spiritual resources I needed to fortify my barren emotional landscape. So my sexuality and my faith entered into a progressive, circular, and tightening dialectic: my faith propelled me away from my emotional and sexual longing, and the deprivation this created required me to resort even more dogmatically to my faith. And as my faith had to find increasing power to restrain all the hormonal and emotional turbulence of adolescence, it had to take on a dramatically caricatured shape, aloof and dogmatic, ritualistic and awesome. As time passed, a theological conservatism became the essential complement to a sexual and emotional crisis. And as the crisis deepened, the theological conservatism became more pronounced.

There was just one problem: the actual content of the faith I adhered to, that I had respect for, that was still a central feature of my life, was a faith centered on the dignity of human beings, on their need for and salvation by the love of God and others. Even in the most structured and barren moments of my Catholic observance, this message was unavoidable. The Jesus of the Gospels, I heard each week at Mass, railed against people exactly like the person I seemed to be becoming: loveless, fastidious, intermittently bitter and pompous, liable to vent my frustration and unhappiness on others who had no responsibility for either. I had grown steadily apart from my parents and family and had constructed friendships on the condition that they contain no threatening emotional intimacy. Although I had prayed and observed the tenets of the faith, I had had no overwhelming spiritual transformation that could have allowed me to overcome this encroaching personal and emotional barrenness, no moment of revelation that had made it bearable or understandable. My faith was what it had always been: imperfect and unavoidable. I could not abandon God; and he would not, it seemed, abandon me. But he seemed paradoxically to be leading me into the kind of loveless desert that the Church and the Jesus of the Gospels had long lamented and decried. It was a desert that, I came later to discover, was not exclusive to me.

In a remarkable document entitled "Declaration on Certain Questions Concerning Sexual Ethics," issued by the Vatican in 1975 and released in the United States the following year, the Sacred Congregation for the Doctrine of the Faith made the following statement regarding the vexed issue of homosexuality: "A distinction is drawn, and it seems with some reason, between homosexuals whose tendency comes from a false education, from a lack of normal sexual development, from habit, from bad example, or from other similar causes, and is transitory or at least not incurable; and homosexuals who are definitively such because of some kind of innate instinct or a pathological constitution judged to be incurable."

The Church was responding, it seems, to the growing sociological and psychological evidence that, for a small minority of people, homosexuality is unchosen, is constitutive of their emotional and sexual identity, and is unalterable. In the context of a broad declaration on a whole range of sexual ethics, this statement was something of a minor digression (twice as much space was devoted to the "grave moral disorder" of masturbation); and it certainly didn't mean a liberalization of doctrine with regard to the morality of homosexual acts. "Homosexual acts are intrinsically disordered and can in no case be approved of," the declaration unequivocally affirmed.

Still, the concession complicated things somewhat. Before 1975, the modern Church had held a coherent and simple view of the morality of homosexual acts. It maintained that homosexuals as such did not exist; rather, it believed that everyone was a heterosexual and that homosexual acts were acts chosen by heterosexuals, out of depravity, curiosity, predisposition, or under the influence of bad moral guidance. Such acts were an abuse of the essential heterosexual orientation of all humanity; they were condemned because they failed to link sexual activity with a binding commitment between a man and a woman in a marriage, a marriage that was permanently open to the possibility of begetting children. Homosexual sex was condemned in exactly the same way and for exactly the same reasons as premarital heterosexual sex, adultery, or contracepted sex: it failed to provide the essential conjugal and procreative context for sexual relations.

The reasoning behind this argument rested on natural law. Natural law teaching, drawing on Aristotelian and Thomist tradition, argued that the sexual nature of man was naturally linked to both emotional fidelity and procreation so that, outside of this context, sex was essentially destructive of the potential for human flourishing: "the full sense of mutual self-giving and human procreation in the context of true love," as the encyclical *Gaudium et Spes* put it.

But suddenly, a new twist had been made to this argument. There was, it seems, *in nature,* a group of people who were "definitively" predisposed to violation of this natural law; their condition was "innate" and "incurable." Insofar as it was innate, this condition was morally neutral, since anything unchosen could not be moral or immoral; it simply *was.* But always and everywhere, the activity to which this condition led was "intrinsically disordered and [could] in no case be approved of." In other words, something in nature always and everywhere violated a vital part of the nature of human beings; something essentially blameless was always and everywhere blameworthy if acted upon.

The paradox of this doctrine was evident even within its first, brief articulation. Immediately before categorically asserting the intrinsic disorder of homosexuality, the text asserted that in "the pastoral field, these homosexuals must certainly be treated with understanding and sustained in the hope of overcoming their personal difficulties and their inability to fit into society. Their culpability will be judged with prudence." The difficult doctrine of a blameless condition's leading to activity that is always abominable was then further elaborated: "This judgment of scripture does not of course permit us to conclude that all those who suffer from this anomaly are personally responsible for it, but it does attest to the fact that homosexual acts are intrinsically disordered and can in no case be approved of." Throughout the passage, there are alternating moments of extreme alarm and almost passive acceptance; tolerance and panic; categorical statement and prudential doubt.

It was therefore perhaps unsurprising that, within a decade, the Church felt it necessary to take up the matter again. The problem could have been resolved by a simple reversion to the old position, the position maintained by fundamentalist Protestant churches: that homosexuality was a hideous affliction of heterosexuals, which should always be resisted and which could be cured. But the Catholic Church doggedly refused to budge from its assertion of the natural occurrence of constitutive homosexuals — or from its compassion for and sensitivity to their plight. In Cardinal Joseph Ratzinger's 1986 letter, "On the Pastoral Care of Homosexual Persons," this theme is actually deepened, beginning with the title.

To non-Catholics, the use of the term "homosexual person" might seem a banality. But the term "person" constitutes in Catholic moral teaching a profound statement about the individual's humanity, dignity, and worth; it invokes a whole range of rights and needs; it reflects the recognition by the Church that a homosexual person deserves exactly the same concern and compassion as a heterosexual person, having all the rights of a human being, and all the value, in the eyes of God. This idea was implicit in the 1975 declaration, but was never advocated. Then there it was, eleven years later, embedded in Ratzinger's very title. Throughout his text, homosexuality, far from being something unmentionable or inherently disgusting, is discussed with candor and subtlety. It is worthy of close attention: "[T]he phenomenon of homosexuality, complex as it is and with its many consequences for society and ecclesial life, is a proper focus for the Church's pastoral care. It thus requires of her ministers attentive study, active concern and honest, theologically well-balanced counsel." And here is Ratzinger on the moral dimensions of the unchosen nature of homosexuality: "[T]he particular inclination of the homosexual person is not a sin." Moreover, homosexual persons, he asserts, are "often generous and giving of themselves." Then, in a stunning passage of concession, he marshalls the Church's usual arguments in defense of human dignity in order to defend homosexual dignity:

> It is deplorable that homosexual persons have been and are the object of violent malice in speech or in action. Such treatment deserves condemnation from the Church's pastors wherever it occurs. It reveals a kind of disregard for others which endangers the most fundamental principles of a healthy society. The intrinsic dignity of each person must always be respected in word, in action and in law.

Elsewhere, Ratzinger's document refers to the homosexual person's "God-given dignity and worth"; condemns the view that homosexual persons are totally compulsive as an "unfounded and demeaning assumption"; and argues that "the human person, made in the image and likeness of God, can hardly be adequately described by a reductionist reference to his or her sexual orientation."

Why are these statements stunning? Because they reveal how far the Church had, by the mid-1980s, absorbed the common sense of the earlier document's teaching on the involuntariness of homosexuality—and had the courage to take this teaching to its logical conclusion. In Ratzinger's letter, the Church stood foursquare against bigotry, against demeaning homosexuals either by anti-gay slander or violence or by pro-gay attempts to reduce human beings to one aspect of their personhood. By denying that homosexual activity was totally compulsive, the Church could open the door to an entire world of moral discussion about ethical and unethical homosexual behavior, rather than simply dismissing it all as pathological. What, in 1975, had been "a pathological constitution judged to be incurable" was, eleven years later, a "homosexual person," "made in the image and likeness of God."

In one sense, then, the Church had profoundly deepened its understanding of the involuntariness of homosexuality, the need to understand it, the need to care for homosexual persons, and the dignity of people who were constitutively gay. But this was only half the story. The other half was that, simultaneously, the Church strengthened its condemnation of any and all homosexual activity. By 1986, the teachings opposed to the approval of homosexual acts were far more categorical than they had been before. Ratzinger had guided the Church into two simultaneous and opposite directions: a deeper respect for and understanding of homosexual persons, and a sterner rejection of almost anything those persons might do.

At the beginning of the 1986 document, Ratzinger bravely confronted the central paradox: "In the discussion which followed the publication of the [1975] declaration . . . an overly benign interpretation was given to the homosexual condition itself, some going so far as to call it neutral or even good. Although the particular inclination of the homosexual person is not a sin, it is a more or less strong tendency ordered toward an intrinsic moral evil and thus the inclination itself must be seen as an objective disorder." Elsewhere, he reiterated the biblical and natural law arguments against homosexual relations. Wisely avoiding the problematic nature of the Old Testament's disavowal of homosexual relations (since these are treated in the context of such "abominations" as eating pork and having intercourse during menstruation, which the Church regards with complete equanimity), Ratzinger focused on St. Paul's admonitions against homosexuality: "Instead of the original harmony between Creator and creatures, the acute distortion of idolatry has led to all kinds of moral excess. Paul is at a loss to find a clearer example of this disharmony than homosexual relations." There was also the simple natural-law argument: "It is only in the marital relationship that the use of the sexual faculty can be morally good. A person engaging in homosexual behavior therefore acts immorally." The point about procreation was strengthened by an argument about the natural, "complementary union able to transmit life," which is heterosexual marriage. The fact that homosexual sex cannot be a part of this union means that it "thwarts the call to a life of that form of self-giving which the Gospel says is the essence of Christian living." Thus "homosexual activity" is inherently "self-indulgent." "Homosexual activity," Ratzinger's document claimed in a veiled reference to AIDS as a kind of retribution, is a "form of life which constantly threatens to destroy" homosexual persons.

This is some armory of argument. The barrage of statements directed against "homosexual activity," which Ratzinger always associates with homosexual sex, is all the more remarkable because it occurs in a document that has otherwise gone further than might have been thought imaginable in accepting homosexuals into the heart of the Church and of humanity. Ratzinger's letter was asking us, it seems, to love the sinner more deeply than ever before, but to hate the sin even more passionately. This is a demand with which most Catholic homosexuals have at some time or other engaged in anguished combat.

It is also a demand that raises the central question of the two documents and, indeed, of any Catholic homosexual life: How intelligible is the Church's theological and moral position on the blamelessness of homosexuality and the grave moral depravity of homosexual acts? This question is the one with which I wrestled in my early twenties, as the increasing aridity of my emotional life began to conflict with the possibility of my living a moral life. The distinction made some kind of sense in theory; but in practice, the command to love oneself as a person of human dignity yet hate the core longings that could make one emotionally whole demanded a sense of detachment or a sense of cynicism that seemed inimical to the Christian life. To deny lust was one thing; to deny love was another. And this dilemma forced me to reassess whether the doctrine made sense even in the abstract.

A whole set of questions presented themselves. Let me, several long years later, elaborate them. One might begin by looking for useful analogies to the paradox of an inherent homosexual dignity that, as a behavior, becomes homosexual iniquity. Greed, for example, might be said to be an innate characteristic of human beings, which, if acted upon, is always bad. But the analogy falls apart immediately. Greed is itself evil; it is prideful, a part of Original Sin. It is not, like homosexuality, a blameless natural condition that inevitably leads to what are understood as immoral acts; greed is a blameworthy feature in anyone and is immoral at every instance of its manifestation. Moreover, there is no subgroup of innately greedy people, nor a majority of people in which greed never occurs. Nor are greedy persons to be treated with respect as a peculiarly troubled group. There is no paradox here, and no particular moral conundrum.

What, perhaps, of a mental or physical illness that is itself morally neutral, but that always predisposes people to culpable acts? Here, again, it is hard to think of a precise analogy. Down's syndrome occurs in a minority and is itself morally neutral; but when it leads to an immoral act, such as, say, a temper tantrum directed at a loving parent, the Church is loathe to judge that person as guilty of choosing to break a commandment. The condition excuses the action. Or, take epilepsy: if an epileptic person has a seizure that injures another human being, she is not regarded as morally responsible for her actions, insofar as they were caused by epilepsy. There is no paradox here either, but for a different reason: with greed, the condition itself is blameworthy; with epilepsy, the injurious act is blameless.

Another analogy can be drawn. What of something like alcoholism? This is a blameless condition, as science and psychology have demonstrated. Some people have a predisposition to it; others do not. Moreover, this predisposition is linked, as homosexuality is, to a particular act. For those with a predisposition to alcoholism, having a drink might be regarded as morally disordered, destructive of the human body and spirit. Accordingly, alcoholics, like homosexuals, should be welcomed into the Church, but only if they renounce the activity their condition necessarily implies.

Unfortunately, even this analogy will not hold. For one thing, drinking is immoral only for alcoholics. Moderate drinking is perfectly acceptable, according to the Church, for non-alcoholics. On the issue of homosexuality, to follow the analogy, the Church can hardly say that sex between people of the same gender would be — in moderation — fine for heterosexuals but not for homosexuals, at least not without cracking a smile. In some respects, in fact, the Church teaches the opposite, arguing that the culpability of homosexuals engaged in sexual acts should be judged with prudence — and less harshly — than the culpability of heterosexuals who engage in wanton "perversion." (At other times, the Church's pastors have suggested that homosexual acts can be more dangerous for those inherently predisposed to homosexuality, for such acts are more likely to lead to a settled pattern of behavior than the activities of the "opportunistic homosexual.") But for the most part the Church eschews any nuanced argument, stating baldly that the immorality of homosexual sex does not lie in its effect on the character of the particular homosexual, but in the fact that, like masturbation, extramarital sex, or premarital sex, homosexual sex is not open to the possibility of procreation in a divinely blessed marital union.

But the analogy to alcoholism points to a deeper problem. Alcoholism does not ultimately work as an analogy because it does not reach to the core of the human condition in the way that homosexuality, following the logic of the Church's arguments, does. If alcoholism is overcome, by a renunciation of alcoholic acts, then recovery allows the human being to realize his or her full potential, a part of which, according to the Church, is the supreme act of self-giving in a life of matrimonial love. But if homosexuality is overcome by a renunciation of homosexual acts, the opposite is achieved: the human being is liberated into sacrifice and pain, barred from acts of union with another that the Church holds to be intrinsic to the state of human flourishing. Homosexuality is a structural condition that restricts the human being, even if homosexual acts are renounced, to a less than fully realized life. The gay or lesbian person is considered disordered at a far deeper level than the alcoholic: at the level of the human capacity to love and be loved by another human being, in a union based on fidelity and self-giving. The homosexual person's dignity does not extend to being able to participate in the highest goods of human life—which is perhaps why the Church understands that such persons, even in the act of obedient self-renunciation, are called "to enact the will of God in their life by joining whatever sufferings and difficulties they experience in virtue of their condition to the sacrifice of the Lord's cross."

This suggests another analogy: the sterile person. Here, too, the person is structurally barred by an innate or incurable condition from the full realization of procreative union with another person. One might expect, following the precise logic of the Church's teachings on the essential nature of openness to procreation in a marital relationship, that such people would be regarded in exactly the same light as homosexuals. They would be asked to commit themselves to a life of complete celibacy and to offer up their pain toward a realization of Christ's sufferings on the cross. But that, of course, is not the Church's position. Marriage is available to sterile couples or to those past child-bearing age; these couples are not prohibited from having sexual relations.

There is, I think, no rational distinction to be made, on the basis of the Church's teaching, between the position of sterile people and that of homosexual people with regard to sexual relations and sacred union. If there is nothing morally wrong, per se, with the homosexual condition or with homosexual love and self-giving, then homosexual persons are indeed analogous to those who cannot reproduce. With regard to the sterile couple, it could perhaps be argued, miracles might happen. But miracles, by definition, can happen to anyone. What the analogy to the barren suggests, of course, is that the injunction against homosexual union and commitment does not rest, at heart, on the arguments about openness to procreation, but on the Church's failure to fully absorb its own teachings about the dignity and worth of homosexual persons. It cannot yet see them as it sees sterile heterosexuals: as people who, with respect to procreation, suffer from a clear, limiting condition, but who nevertheless have a potential for real emotional and spiritual self-realization, in the heart of the Church, through the transfiguring power of the sacraments. It cannot yet see them as truly made in the image of God.

For many homosexual Catholics, life within the Church is a difficult endeavor. In my twenties, as I attempted to unite the possibilities of sexual longing and emotional commitment, I discovered what many heterosexuals and homosexuals had discovered before me: that it is a troubling and troublesome mission. There is a lamentable tendency, when we discuss both homosexual and heterosexual emotional life, to glamorize and idealize the entire venture. To posit the possibility of a loving union is not to guarantee its achievement. And I was not the first human being to think I understood a human experience before being foiled by its fickleness, its comedy, and its risk.

But it must also be true that to dismiss the possibility of a loving union at all—to banish from the minds and hearts of countless gay men and women the idea that they, too, can find solace and love in one another—is to create the conditions for a human etiolation that no Christian community can contemplate without remorse. What finally convinced me of the wrongness of the Church's teachings was not that they were intellectually so confused, but that in the circumstances of my own life—and of the lives I discovered around me—they seemed so destructive of the possibilities of human love and self-realization. By crippling the potential for connection and growth, the Church's teachings created a dynamic that in practice led not to virtue but to pathology; by requiring the first lie in a human life, which would lead to an entire battery of others, they contorted human beings into caricatures of solitary eccentricity, frustrated bitterness, incapacitating anxiety—and helped to perpetuate all the human wickedness and cruelty and insensitivity that such lives inevitably carry in their wake. These doctrines could not in practice do what they wanted to do: they could not both affirm human dignity and deny human love.

This truth will one day, I pray, overcome the current doctrine of the Church on the matter of homosexuality. To say that is not to oppose the Church, but to hope in it, to believe in it as a flawed institution that is yet the eternal vessel of God's love. It is to say that such lives as mine and those of countless others must ultimately affect the Church not because our lives are perfect, or without contradiction, or without evil, but because our lives are in some sense also the life of the Church, and because, in time, the truth about such lives will overcome the distortion in ourselves and in others. Slowly and surely, as Catholic family after family comes to terms with its gay and lesbian members, as parish after parish begins to recognize the human beings within its midst, this lesson will have to sink in. If there is any meaning to the term *sensus fidelium*, this has to be a part of it.

I remember, in my own life, the sense of lung-filling exhilaration I felt as my sexuality began to be incorporated into my life, a sense that was not synonymous with recklessness or self-indulgence—although I was not immune from those things either—but a sense of being suffused at last with the possibility of being fully myself before those I loved and before God. I remember my family's coming to terms with the love that we had for one another, a love that I had progressively distanced from myself as adolescence set in. I remember the hopefulness of friendships restored and lies undone in a life that, for all its countless fallibilities and iniquities, was at least no longer premised on a lie covered over by a career. I remember the sense a few months ago in a pew in a cathedral, as I reiterated the same pre-Communion litany of prayers that I had spoken some twenty years earlier, that, for the first time, the love the Church had always taught that God held for me was tangible and redemptive. I had never felt it fully before; and, of course, like so many spiritual glimpses, I have not felt it since. But I do know that it was conditioned not on the possibility of purity, but on the possibility of honesty. That honesty is not something that can be bought or won in a moment. It is a process peculiarly prone to self-delusion and self-doubt. But it is one that, if it is to remain true to itself, the Church cannot resist forever.

MARY JO WEAVER

Feminists and Patriarchs in the Catholic
Church: Orthodoxy and Its Discontents

The title of my essay is autobiographical, historical, and interpretive: it comes from attempts to make sense of my own oxymoronic existence, describes a complicated situation with extensive ramifications, and leads to a set of religious issues that, in an extrapolated form, reach beyond the constraints of this particular paper. My basic question is a simple one: What does it mean to have been reared to *patriarchy*, to be deeply committed to *feminism*, and to be inexorably *Catholic*? Like the plot of many a good story, this one is triangular: two of the characters are fighting with each other for the love and attention of the third. Although the outcome is not clear, the death of the beloved is a real possibility. And although I would like the narrative action to resemble the graced movement of genuine self-understanding in Dante's *Purgatorio*, I am afraid that it is actually much closer to the shoot-out at the O.K. Corral.

Patriarchy and feminism exist in the Catholic Church as competing ideologies within a larger religious framework. Insofar as either of them claims to be the only authentic voice, or attempts to silence or exclude the other, they are heretical ideologies that violate the very essence of Catholicism by closing off discussion. Orthodox Catholicism, in other words, should be larger and more embracing—more catholic, if you will—than either patriarchy or feminism. Yet Catholic orthodoxy can stay alive only by welcoming the claims and counterclaims of these two arch-enemies. Astute readers will notice that I have now introduced a fourth player—orthodoxy—to an already complicated set of terms. Further-more, I have hinted that these four characters—patriarchy, feminism, Catholicism, and orthodoxy—achieve their most authentic identities only when they work together.

Patriarchy and feminism are often defined in the worst possible ways by their opponents. For angry feminists, patriarchy is a rapacious reli-gion bent on the destruction of the planet. Those enraged by the women's movement picture feminism as a malevolent plot devised by resentful, unfulfilled lesbians to destroy the family. In these pages I am attaching patriarchy to institutional intransigence: patriarchs are those men and women who support the status quo in the Catholic Church, sometimes by making an idol of the past. Feminists, on the other hand, work for new structures of gender relations that will lead to greater indi-vidual autonomy: they support change in all institutions, sometimes by discarding the past as useless or by making an enemy of it. In one way of looking at things, therefore, the arguments between patriarchs and feminists about the present and the future are really altercations about the nature of the past. Is there an orthodox way to approach the past? A Catholic one?

Orthodoxy and catholicity are not interchangeable terms. Indeed, catholicity is one of the traditional "marks of the Church" that testi-fies to universality, whereas orthodoxy, which means "right thinking," is usually perceived as a system of belief and behavior that conforms to established doctrine. In other words, catholicity is theoretically com-patible with pluralism, while orthodoxy is single-minded; catholicity can welcome debate, but orthodoxy stifles it; and catholicity is open to new registers, while orthodoxy restricts itself to a defined range. In the very exercise of making these distinctions, I must point to a fun-damental problem of slippage in the popular use of these terms. Most people—liberals and conservatives alike—link orthodoxy and catholicity, as in the phrase "orthodox Catholicism," and proceed to invest that phrase with the power to resist challenges of any kind. They then use this functional definition to explain their own relationship with the Church: as liberals resisting or as conservatives welcoming the rigidity that they take to be an essential feature of orthodox Catholicism.

What if it were possible, however, to interpret orthodoxy as a mode of spirituality and social formation rather than as a set of doctrines? According to Rowan Williams, in the best reading of the Christian tradition, orthodoxy is an encompassing term concerned with deepening religious understanding and enlarging religious discourse. "We habitually oppose orthodoxy to conflict, doubt, or provisionality," he says, but "there is an aspect of Christian orthodoxy which is precisely a negative moment." At its heart is the confrontation with an image of loss, or Logos rejected by the world. The central paradox is that the Word becomes a universal hope and attains meaning only as it is lost and abandoned and buried.[1] As the terms "Catholic orthodoxy" and "orthodox Catholicism" play through this paper, I want them to exhibit a more ancient and, ironically, less certain face than one typically associates with them. I wish to bring that aspect of openness to some current debates between patriarchal and feminist understandings of Catholicism because I believe that the struggle between patriarchy and feminism engages issues in the Church that go far beyond the gender divide. The historical accommodations of patriarchy and the contemporary challenges of feminism together raise questions that can put orthodoxy in touch with the ironies of its own position, knowing itself totally only to the extent that it knows itself as incomplete.[2]

The test of orthodoxy should have something to do with its potential for authentic comprehensiveness and with its confidence in the power of its own source narrative. It is crucial to remember that Christianity has its roots in a highly dramatic *question* and that it evolved into a community that drew its followers into a realm of some ambiguity and paradox. The earliest Christians—from Paul to Augustine—had to deal with the fact that God's purpose was somehow made manifest in the flesh of a condemned man, that "the new age" had dawned with "the slaughter of the Anointed at the hands of those who controlled the religious constructions of meaning."[3]

It is worthwhile to linger on this point. Catholic Christianity claims, rightly, to have a unique perspective on the great human questions. Because of its involvement in the life, death, and resurrection of Jesus, it proclaims with some authority that it has time-tested and often wise ways to deal with love and death, egocentricity and community, sin and suffering. At the same time, because of its faithfulness to its bewildering source narrative, the Church can never claim to have an absolute or total perspective. Its continuing existence depends upon its ability to remain open to new levels of meaning, and even to profound change. The Christian Church, in other words, has provisional (not ultimate) "answers" to universal questions. Put another way, since there are deep questions at the heart of faith, it is still possible for God to surprise us.[4]

Christian history has often glossed over the wrenching difficulties that Jesus presents to a believer not only about his death, but about the nature of God and the way God works in the world. The human need for coherence, the historical demands for clarification, and the administrative problems of institutional operation led the medieval Church to make the astonishing claim that it knew God's ultimate word and could reproduce it as clear and authoritative teaching. Although I find this assertion understandable and comforting to a certain degree, I believe that it undermines rather than supports orthodoxy because it admits that Catholicism came to prefer the conceptual economy of limited explanations over the transformative and frightening "otherness" presented by the spectacle of a crucified God.

Perhaps this understanding of orthodoxy can unsettle the hardened presuppositions that seem to govern disputes within the Church. Conventional wisdom says that orthodoxy must use its power to eliminate conflicting interpretations, but it is possible that orthodoxy must welcome conflict in order to survive. And while Catholicism has been shaped by its own theological history to view theism as totally capable of rational demonstration, or spirituality as a manageable system of divine/human interaction, it is more likely that God and human interactions with God are mysterious, elusive, and often terrifyingly unclear.

The institutional pronouncements of the Catholic Church make it appear as if its future depends upon the elimination of troublesome questions—like those raised by feminists—yet I would suggest that without feminism the Catholic Church is in danger of falling into idolatry, "a disease of the human spirit" rooted in terror and in a comical desire to defend the Omnipotent.[5]

Although my focus is on the relations between patriarchal Catholicism and feminism, I could be just as easily describing the battlegrounds defined by liberals and conservatives or reflecting on the contested accommodations of the Second Vatican Council. Contemporary Catholicism is marked by conflict, and like the American Protestant communities described by Robert Wuthnow, Catholics seem divided into factions that stare at one another as if across an abyss.[6] Still, the contestation over the place or the role of women in the Church raises almost everyone's hackles and is a flash point in modern American Catholicism, which is precisely why it is the best source of deeper theological reflection. The antagonistic and fearful exchanges between feminists and patriarchs push Catholics toward theological reflection because the guts of the Catholic tradition demand a radical openness to mystery, just as the divine self-communication to the world—recognized by Christians in the Christ event—demands the embrace of "the Other," or what in the feminist/patriarchal wars might be called "the enemy."

The feminist critique of Roman Catholicism got off to a running start in 1968 with Mary Daly's groundbreaking book *The Church and the Second Sex.* Over the twenty-five years since then, the women's movement in the Catholic Church has stimulated a provocative series of intellectual and activist engagements that have made common cause with liberationist, communitarian, ecological, and other grassroots movements. Women in the Church, like women in the society at large, have analyzed various patterns of women's subordination and have organized themselves for the purpose of changing them. Although I could name a number of highly sensitive issues attached to feminist activism—reproductive choice and sexuality, for example—the most visibly *religious* altercation has erupted over the issue of women's ordination.

The first modern invitation to conversation about women in the priesthood came from St. Joan's Alliance, an international group founded in 1911 to work for women's rights. In 1962, the Alliance sent a carefully worded petition to the preparatory committees for the Second Vatican Council asking them only to consider the question of women priests. Needless to say, nothing came of this initial overture. Perhaps the prelates thought they had gone about as far as they could by allowing four women auditors to attend Council sessions, at which they would not be permitted to speak.[7] If the Council fathers were not interested in the question of women's ordination, however, scholars were. In the years after Vatican II, theologians, canon lawyers, and biblical critics all interrogated the tradition and found no persuasive reason why women should not be ordained.[8] In addition, women enrolled in divinity schools and studied at seminaries in astonishingly large numbers—nearly half the seminary students of the 1970s were women—and so were prepared intellectually and psychologically for ordination. Finally, the experience of many Catholic women—that they actually had vocations to be priests—intersected with a crisis in the priesthood itself: with fewer men being ordained and many leaving the priesthood to marry, there seemed to be a real need to consider women's ordination. By the mid-1970s, the Church—freshly described as "the people of God," or a "pilgrim community"—was becoming rattled by a comprehensive challenge to the way things had always been done.

Let me interrupt the story here to say what I think was demanded from orthodoxy or catholicity at this point, namely, an exploration of faith in freedom: put in modern terms, an openness to dialogue. Church officials had three choices in this matter. First, they could have agreed with the case for women's ordination. Far-fetched as this may seem now, it was not an unreasonable hope in the early 1970s, when even the Vatican's own biblical commission found no Scriptural objection to women priests and historians were finding consistent evidence of women's leadership and power in early and medieval Christianity. Second, Church officials could have declared that they were unsure of how to proceed. Admitting that they were caught between powerful arguments in favor of women's ordination and their own experience as part of an all-male tradition would have gained them some sympathy for the difficulty of the question and would have engaged interested Catholics in a protracted and thorny but, one hopes, constructive debate. It would also have opened a dialogue about the nature of religious authority and the nature of tradition that might have forestalled some of the acrimony of the 1980s.[9] Third, Church officials could have used their power to try to suppress any further discussion, saying either that the question did not merit serious attention or that it was somehow scandalous.

None of these alternatives was without problems; but my argument rests upon acceptance of the fact that some problems are inherent to the very meaning of Christianity, which, in its early years, was not afraid to build its tradition on the paradox that fidelity demands not unconditional attachment to old forms, but perspective-shattering engagement with new options.[10] In my list of possible responses, the first and the third operating modes—where religious authorities rule absolutely either for or against women's ordination—would have settled the matter before it had a chance to become a question. From a sociological perspective, one might say that these two options represent diametrically opposed responses to the profound social crisis generated by the women's movement. The immediate concern might be the shortage of priests, but the galvanizing issue is feminism within the Catholic Church. Feminism and patriarchy, therefore, could represent radically different paths proceeding from a shared desire for an authentic and speedy resolution to a critical situation. The first one is utopian, innovative, and future-oriented; the second predicates its route upon timeless, eternal truth and follows in the footsteps of the past. As Martin Riesebrodt has argued, while feminism tends to be optimistic about human nature and is basically an "ethic of conviction," patriarchy emphasizes obedience and is more properly described as an "ethic of law."[11]

If these two alternatives generally describe the poles of feminism and patriarchy, perhaps the refusal to resolve the question without discussion defines the position of orthodoxy or catholicity. This last option would open up a highly complicated, emotionally painful issue for the express purpose of exploration and understanding. As I think about the future in practical terms, it is hard to believe that ordination will not eventually be granted to Catholic women. Since that issue is part of a larger conflict over the structure of social relations, and since diversity and conflict are not going to disappear, those who choose to live with them will eventually have to engage in cooperative interaction to solve their problems. Patriarchs and feminists will finally have to learn to work together toward a model that goes beyond rights talk (as in "women have a right to be ordained") and beyond claims about an absolute moral order (as in "priests have always been men; therefore, priests must always be men"). Since the moderate alternative requires genuine openness to positions that are often uncomfortably at odds with one's cherished views, the status quo (what I am calling patriarchy) may seem to have more to lose here than feminism; but I am not altogether sure that this is true. In my understanding of orthodoxy, both sides have something to learn from one another, both may be broken open to discover new self-understandings.

In religious terms, this alternative—admitting confusion and inviting dialogue—would be the orthodox choice. The messy, complicated testing of the power structures of its own tradition is what characterizes catholicity, and it is what teaches people what it means to be part of a living tradition. In the process of wrestling with the women's ordination question, Catholics might learn that their religion welcomes opportunities to pursue new avenues of meaning by engaging its members in the project of reconciling their beliefs and judgments with the authority of Scripture, the writings of the fathers and doctors of the Church, the official teachings of popes and councils, the liturgy, and the consensus of the faithful over the centuries. The Catholic tradition is orthodox because it is both faithful to its past and, under the guidance of the Spirit, always seeking final answers. If tradition is a means of accessing the creative events at the source of a community's life, then an orthodox tradition is one that keeps a community authentically attentive and answerable to something above and beyond its present life. In other words, its present self-understanding, including its understanding of the past, is "always liable to be brought into question by the abiding possibility of retrieving the original points of novelty, distinctiveness, and discrimination which brought it to birth."[12]

The feminist project, in its creative applications of new hermeneutical and archeological insights, claims precisely to be retrieving something of the original experience of the Christian Church.[13] If that is even a remote possibility, then orthodox Catholicism has a mandate to take it seriously, no matter how disruptive its consequences. Indeed, there is no warrant in either Jesus' life or his teachings to hold tightly to an idea so as to avoid risks. The timid servant in the Gospel of Matthew, who buried his "talent" in order not to lose it, was condemned as *unfaithful*.[14] If we can extrapolate that point to the ordination issue, it seems reasonable to conclude that faith requires risks on the part of all concerned, including the guardians of the tradition. When they hold to it so tightly as to repulse any challenges to it, they effectively bury it. By contrast, feminist interpreters and theologians whose work supports the moral power of women's ordination call upon the Church to venture itself. When its officials refuse to take the risk, they violate the very tradition they are trying to protect. The catholic, orthodox tradition is not one of self-protection and consolation; rather, it is one that proffers itself for questioning in and on the presence of God's self-communication. Deciding in advance which questions are legitimate or worthy is an act similar to that of the servant in Matthew's story: it is timid and, worse yet, unfaithful.

I am not arguing that the institution has to be taking risks all the time, or that Church officials can or ought never make judgments, or even that orthodox Catholicism has no right to condemn certain ideas or practices. Indeed, the fact that the tradition has a center, and a history of trying to keep itself authentically faithful to that center, protects it from collapsing into a relativistic mess. I am saying, however, that Church officials and feminists both made mistakes in the way they handled the question of women's ordination. What the eventual outcome of a genuine dialogue would have been, one cannot say. It is easy to see what has happened without that dialogue: feminists and patriarchs have become, if anything, more suspicious of one another and have grown further apart. Women's ordination is no longer a question that invites dialogue; it is a jagged edge that divides liberals from conservatives. As a continuing source of discontent, it has become a symbol for great underground oceans of ambivalence about the ways in which Vatican II has or has not lived up to its dizzying potential.

It is possible to trace a tragic pattern of reaction and counter-reaction between feminists and patriarchs on the ordination issue. In the early years—from the mid-1960s to the mid-1970s—feminist questions were addressed to Vatican officials in subdued, respectful language, and scholarly support of women's ordination was the product of dialogue with the tradition. Given the response of Church officials, however, courtesy did not long remain a defining characteristic of the feminist approach. When the first "Women's Ordination Conference" was announced, the hierarchy organized itself against it. Answering the question before it could be asked, as it were, Archbishop Joseph L. Bernardin, president of the National Conference of Catholic Bishops, issued a statement affirming the traditional ban against women's ordination one month before conference participants convened in Detroit in 1975. The first WOC meeting, therefore, occurred in a highly charged atmosphere that stimulated angry rhetoric and led some speakers to question the very desirability of being ordained into such a community. There is good reason to think, said Rosemary Ruether, that "the present clerical and institutional structure of a Church so constituted is demonic and itself so opposed to the Gospel that to try to join it is contrary to our very commitments." [15] At the same time, the dominant themes were equal rights, elaborated in criticisms of past practice, and motivation for change. In keeping with some of the new theology of church-as-sacrament, Anne Carr told conference participants that she hoped for "a church [that] would embody the Christian message of equality, freedom, and love as a causally effective sign to itself and to the world." [16] It was not to be. The "message" from Rome was condemnation.

The Vatican "Declaration on the Question of the Admission of Women to the Ministerial Priesthood" (15 October 1976) was a blow both to those who had hoped for ordination and to those who had hoped only for dialogue. The careful work of scholars was dismissed, testimony on women's spiritual and theological preparedness for the priesthood was scorned, and the risk-taking mandates of orthodoxy were ignored. Women's ordination was forbidden on the grounds that it had never been done and that priests had to represent Jesus anatomically—absurd and dangerous arguments that made Catholicism look ridiculous and treated its symbol system as if it were somehow in danger of depletion. In issuing the declaration, the Sacred Congregation for the Doctrine of the Faith was operating from a pre-conciliar model of a benevolent authority ruling over grateful and obedient subjects. They relied on the old motto—"Roma locuta, causa finita"—rather as the postcolonial upper classes continued to rely on the caste system, blissfully ignorant of how ineffective it had become. Indeed, in the case of women's ordination, as Leonard Swidler noted about the Vatican's forbidding it, the revised motto might read "Roma locuta, causa stimulata."[17]

Today, the situation appears to be thoroughly intractable. The two sides are clearly at war with one another, and neither the supporters of patriarchy nor the advocates of feminism are eager to engage in "conversation" on this issue. For sheer anger, it would be hard to surpass Donna Steichen's antifeminist unmasking of "the hidden face of Catholic feminism" in *Ungodly Rage*, which posits the ultimate feminist objective as the obliteration of Christianity.[18] At the same time, it must be admitted that those who castigate feminism as an anti-Catholic conspiracy insidiously infiltrating the Church do not do so without impressive supporting quotations from those Catholic feminists who have made incendiary statements about the Pope, the liturgy, and other aspects of the tradition that represent male domination. Mary Daly's later work has been deliberately blasphemous, and feminist conferences have typically been open to and celebratory of beliefs and practices condemned by the Catholic Church.[19]

Feminists and patriarchs engaged in warfare cannot *imagine* dialogue: they find one another so alien and abhorrent that they long only for victory. Some frustrated feminists have become active in the Womenchurch movement, which describes itself as a community in exodus from patriarchy, following what its members see as the authentic stream of the Jesus tradition. Those who support patriarchal Catholicism and wish it were a good deal *more* uncongenial to feminism sometimes think of themselves as remnants or holdovers, waiting for the restoration of order. Both groups are reacting to what I see as a flawed understanding of "orthodox Catholicism." Both perceive it as a rigid, uncompromising system sustained for the express purpose of maintaining total control of doctrine and practice in the Church. Neither faction perceives catholicity—a fundamental mark of the Church—as having a stake in keeping questions open. Neither understands orthodoxy as something that must "preserve a spaciousness of perspective" and that entails "a sensitivity to the varieties of Christian experience in history which regularly unsettle uncritically hierarchical models of leadership."[20] Apparently equally ignorant of the best parts of their own tradition, each group has moved to close off dialogue. In the end, everybody loses.

The practical losers are those Catholic women who believe they have priestly vocations. The conceptual losers are feminists and patriarchs, who tend to see the question of women's ordination as one of gender rights rather than as a challenge to create a more catholic community. The pastoral losers are the people in those parishes who can find neither priests nor any way out of this impasse. The ultimate loser is Catholic orthodoxy, consigned to a dusty and dysfunctional definition that obscures its possibilities and so puts its transformational power out of reach just when it is most needed.

Women who want to be ordained have three choices. They can remain within the institution, praying for change; leave to seek ordination in a Protestant denomination; or remain but become openly heretical by celebrating the Eucharist for communities of disenfranchised or disgruntled Catholics. Like the options for religious authorities outlined earlier, all three choices leave something to be desired. Waiting for patriarchy to change appeals most to the saintly and the naive, who tend to see the women's ordination issue as a matter of textual reinterpretation and practical readjustment, failing to appreciate the extensiveness of the cultural crisis that undergirds it. Renouncing one's Catholic heritage to seek ordination in a Protestant denomination has the advantage of allowing women to fulfill *part* of their vocation, but only at an enormous price. This avenue is, in effect, a withdrawal from the struggle and an admission that nothing can ameliorate the situation of Catholic women with vocations to the priesthood. The third alternative is an openly heretical but strangely compelling one since, as I have argued elsewhere, it has biblical resonances and evokes the courage rooted in religious experience.[21] If an orthodox tradition provides a way for a community to clarify its distinctive vision and also serves as a dialectical means by which to change it, then women who pursue their priestly vocations invite debate and, insofar as they are exemplary ministers, can also function as effective symbols of a new order. Of course, they may simply invite condemnation, which puts us back at square one — or back at the O.K. Corral, where it's smarter to shoot first and ask questions later.

Feminists and patriarchs are caught up in this horrendous struggle because it is larger than the question of women's ordination. The issue of women's role in the Church is about more than power, which is why feminism might do better to position itself in relation to orthodoxy rather than in relation to patriarchy. If feminists could see the genius of catholicity as the ability to stay with the question, they might find more fruitful avenues toward change than are currently available in the debate over women's gaining the same rights that the Church has traditionally reserved for men. If patriarchy cannot tolerate a plurality of moral orders — which is, I believe, what is ultimately at stake here — orthodoxy can. It legitimizes a process that welcomes honest dialogue about difficult questions and stresses the participatory character in which they are worked out.

The best solutions to difficult religious problems — women's ordination, language about God, liturgical practice — are orthodox Catholic ones, distinguished by a particular set of attributes. Orthodoxy is possessed of a measured confidence based on the accumulated wisdom of the ages and the consequent capacity to take the long, historical view. Orthodoxy does not have to resolve every question that comes its way, but it is not afraid to examine current arrangements in the light of a radical question at the core of its faith. As Rowan Williams concludes, orthodoxy is a *tool:* "In the Catholic tradition, orthodoxy has kept the saints, the contemplatives, and the radicals, the poets, scientists, and revolutionaries . . . plugged into the project of discovering the conditions for hope."[22] In encouraging the discombobulating encounter between contemporary believers and the mystery at the heart of their faith, orthodoxy can enforce certain rules of discourse, not the least of which is that it be fundamentally irenic, tentative, and constructive. Orthodox Catholicism is the language of a community with shared symbols and hopes, a community in which people can disagree about how those symbols currently embody its hopes. Catholic orthodoxy is conserving and creative, rooted in the past even as it remains open to the future.

I began by admitting my own complicity in patriarchy, as someone brought up to respect the buttressed certainties of that tradition. It took a long time and a great deal of thought to arrive at a more embracing view of orthodoxy and an acceptance of the Augustinian notion that Christianity is an endless journey of the imagination and intellect propelled by desire. Orthodoxy is not a world unto itself: like the Christianity it represents, it is answerable to something beyond itself of which it is but a pale image. When I first encountered feminism, I could not see how I might accept its arguments without relinquishing my religious beliefs, including my confidence in the concept of tradition and the value of the past. Indeed, much of my work over the last fifteen years has been an attempt to take my old Catholic sensibilities into the feminist critique of patriarchal religion and bring my feminist consciousness to bear on the patriarchal resistance to change. The only way I can see to hold both my old sensibilities and my new consciousness to the demands of dialogue is to invoke a reading of orthodoxy or catholicity that knows when to bow to paradox and believes that it can find, in the ironies of human fallibility, a more capacious language and a more graceful vision of the divine/human interaction than either patriarchy or feminism, alone, dares to imagine.

NOTES

I presented an earlier version of this paper as the annual Hugh McCloskey Evans Memorial Lecture at Tulane University. I wish to thank the chair of Judeo-Christian Studies at Tulane for permission to publish it here. I have benefitted greatly from the critical responses of Robyn Wiegman and Mary Favret (who try to teach me new languages of discourse), from Susan Gubar and Donald Gray (who keep prodding me to clean up my old ones), and from my new colleague in Religious Studies, David Brakke (who knows the languages of the ancient world).

1 Rowan Williams, former Lady Margaret Professor of Divinity at Oxford, is now the Anglican Bishop of Wales. While much of his work has been directed toward a new reading of the history of spirituality and new ways of understanding old terms, the best single article I have found on the genuinely expansive and open-ended nature of orthodoxy is his "What Is Catholic Orthodoxy?" in *Essays Catholic and Radical*, ed. Kenneth Leech and Rowan Williams (London, 1983), 11–25. I have written on catholicity as an expansive term in "Overcoming the Divisiveness of Babel: The Languages of Catholicity," *Horizons* 14 (Fall 1987): 328–42.

2 Rowan Williams, " 'Know Thyself': What Kind of Injunction?" in *Philosophy, Religion and the Spiritual Life* (Royal Institute of Philosophy Supplement 32), ed. Michael McGhee (Cambridge, 1992), 211–27. The great Augustinian paradox about the quest for self-knowledge is that one arrives there only by seeking to arrive there. Not unlike earlier patristic writers—Gregory of Nyssa, for example, who argued that one's knowledge of God, in whose image the soul is made, is always incomplete, eternally open, expanding—Augustine makes a clear argument for the *process* of self-knowledge. It is never finished; it can and must be always open to new questions.

3 Rowan Williams, *The Wound of Knowledge* (Boston, 1990), 3. The way in which religious authorities control meaning is not simply a religious issue. An angry riff on the conflict between the way that the "priests" see or teach things and the way they "really are" can be heard on Sinead O'Connor's 1992 compact disc, *am I not your girl?* At the end of the final song, she indicts priests as liars, connects their lies with the "Holy Roman Empire," and says, "They told us lies to take us away from God." Her point is more violent than mine—quoting the Scripture that Jesus came to bring not peace but a sword—but is not dissimilar: we both resist the notion that priests (or anyone else) occupy a privileged position that allows them to ignore or reject our experience as irrelevant or irreverent.

4 I would also argue that it is possible for God to be surprised by *us*. See the title essay in my *Springs of Water in a Dry Land: Spiritual Survival for Catholic Women Today* (Boston, 1993), 55–75. In Ron Hansen's powerful fictive account, *Mariette in Ecstasy* (New York, 1991), a young stigmatic who was dismissed from her community as a disruptive influence writes a

letter thirty years later to an old friend, saying how her life has conformed to the contours of the tradition in every way. At the end of the letter she describes her relation to Christ by saying, "We try to be formed and held and kept by him, but instead he offers us freedom. And now when I try to know his will, his kindness floods me, his great love overwhelms me, and I hear him whisper, Surprise me" (179). What would it mean to believe that one could "surprise" God?

5 For an explication of the oppositions of idolatry and grace, see Luke Johnson, *Faith's Freedom: A Classic Spirituality for Contemporary Christians* (Minneapolis, 1990), 60–77.

6 See Robert Wuthnow, *The Restructuring of American Religion* (Princeton, 1988).

7 Had the Council fathers known more about the history of the women's movement in the United States, they might well have reconsidered their decision to disallow women's voices. The first women's rights convention in the United States—held in Seneca Falls in 1846—was organized by Elizabeth Cady Stanton after she was not permitted to speak at international antislavery meetings in London. The fact that she had worked for the abolitionist cause for many years and then was barred from addressing the assembly *because* she was a *woman* enraged her and galvanized her into action on behalf of the rights of women. The rest is history, as they say. At Vatican II, one of the foremost authorities on economics and world hunger, Barbara Ward, was asked to prepare a paper for the Council, but she was not permitted to read it herself.

8 See chapter four of my *New Catholic Women: A Contemporary Challenge to Traditional Religious Authority* (San Francisco, 1985), where I outline the history of the women's ordination movement in terms of its shift from petitioning for "equal rights" to demanding structural change in the institution. See also, for example, Haye van der Meer, *Women Priests in the Catholic Church: A Theological-Historical Investigation* (Philadelphia, 1973); Ida Raming, *The Exclusion of Women from the Priesthood* (Metuchen, NJ, 1976); and Edward Kilmartin, "Apostolic Office: Sacrament of Christ," *Theological Studies* 36 (1975): 243–64. For a general set of reactions from scholars and activists in favor of women's ordination, see *Women and the Catholic Priesthood: An Expanded Vision*, ed. Anne Marie Gardiner (New York, 1976).

9 An excellent introduction to the concept of "tradition" as a changing and remarkably malleable concept can be found in Gershom Scholem, *The Messianic Idea in Judaism and Other Essays on Jewish Spirituality* (New York, 1971), 282–303. In Roman Catholic terms, tradition refers to the whole

process of handing on the faith to each generation: it is Catholicism's lived and living faith.

10 The most obvious supporting story from the New Testament—found in the Acts of the Apostles—recounts the early community's being divided over Gentile Christianity within a Jewish-Christian framework. The wrenching question had to do with Jewish dietary laws, as specified in the Torah: What could be done about laws that God had enacted for all time? Peter's dream—in which God told him that *no food* was impure—was breathtakingly disruptive because God had thereby countermanded the Torah specifically and the accumulated traditions of Judaism generally. Yet, in spite of the fact that such a change seemed to entail cultural suicide and would in any case arouse bitter opposition, Peter, James, Paul, and the other leaders of the early community somehow found the dream liberating, perhaps because it opened up new possibilities for building the Christian community and for understanding its relationship with the God of Israel.

11 Martin Riesebrodt, "Fundamentalism and the Political Mobilization of Women," in *The Political Dimensions of Religion*, ed. Said Amir Arjomand (New York, 1993), 243–71.

12 Williams, "Catholic Orthodoxy," 14.

13 The most important contributions to this project are clearly Elisabeth Schüssler Fiorenza's *In Memory of Her: A Feminist Theological Reconstruction of Christian Origins* (1983); *Bread Not Stone: The Challenge of Feminist Biblical Interpretation* (1984); and *But She Said: Feminist Practices of Biblical Interpretation* (1993). The work of feminist biblical scholars should not be viewed as isolated or exclusive to their field; on the contrary, it is continuous with the newest scholarly directions in social history and so engages the attention of a wide range of scholars. Feminist biblical scholarship is not, in other words, a "women's issue," but a rich vein of academic interest. On the other hand, we may wonder what will happen to this argument if feminist exegetes are simply wrong. If Christianity never welcomed women into positions of leadership and shared spiritual growth, then I would use that "fact" to press the central question of this paper—that is, why must orthodoxy always be seen as preservation of the past rather than as movement toward the future?

14 Indeed, one reading of this parable is to see the "talents" as forms of authority within the early community and to suggest that nothing is gained without their (risky) exercise. *The Jerome Biblical Commentary* says that "this paradoxical saying indicates that the powers conferred on the disciples grow with use and wither with disuse" (107).

15 Rosemary Ruether, "Ordination: What Is the Problem?" in Gardiner, ed., *Women and the Catholic Priesthood*, 33.

16 Anne Carr, "The Church in Process: Engendering the Future," in Gardiner, ed., *Women and the Catholic Priesthood*, 79.

17 See Leonard Swidler, "Commentary on the Declaration of the Sacred Congregation for the Doctrine of the Faith on the Question of Admission of Women to the Ministerial Priesthood," in *Women Priests: A Catholic Commentary on the Vatican Declaration*, ed. Leonard Swidler and Arlene Swidler (New York, 1977), 3-18. Swidler and Swidler's book overall is a gold mine of information on the declaration, including its history and status.

18 See Donna Steichen, *Ungodly Rage: The Hidden Face of Catholic Feminism* (San Francisco, 1991). The book is interesting because of its combination of research—Steichen attended many feminist meetings, talks, workshops, and liturgies—and undiluted rage. Her language is loaded: feminists are often "lesbian leftists" or "childless," and they do not so much speak as "thunder," "twitter," "screech," or "fume and rage." Steichen is worried, with good reason, about the slippage from Catholicism to feminist liturgies to goddess worship and witchcraft; but her chance to invite the kind of dialogue that might help both "sides" clarify their positions and attempt to understand why they tend to unnerve each other is lost in an angry case selectively made.

19 I once interpreted Mary Daly's work as the guerrilla theater of the women's movement. In a way, it is not fair to include her here since she has been calling herself a post-Christian feminist for more than twenty years. At the same time, many of her themes and targets are specifically Roman Catholic. See my *New Catholic Women*, 170-77. Catholic feminist conferences—"Womenspirit Bonding" at Grailville in 1982 and various Womenchurch meetings—have usually included affirmations of lesbian relationships, prochoice activism, goddess spirituality, and liturgical experimentation.

20 Williams, "Catholic Orthodoxy," 23.

21 See my *Springs of Water in a Dry Land*, 37-54.

22 Williams, "Catholic Orthodoxy," 25.

KATHY RUDY

The Double-Effect/Proportionalist Debate

As a Catholic, I speak for a large community that has a long
tradition of welcoming strangers and giving them a home, and
of holding itself up to judgment for the quality of that welcome;
a community which has learned painfully that the extent to
which we close our homes and hearts and lives to others, and
especially to children, is precisely the extent to which
we have placed ourselves beyond the reach of a loving God.
— Michael Garvey

When those jerks down at the rectory start delivering groceries
when I deliver the babies, then I might think about more. But I
got caught with the first one when I was seventeen. I had big
plans until then; I was going to nursing school. Then comes the
second. But the next time it happened I took care of it. What
does the pope know? Is he paying our doctor bills? Is he getting
me a raise?
— "Annamarie," from *No Turning Back*

In the 7 October 1984 issue of the *New York Times,* an advertisement sponsored by Catholics for a Free Choice called for open dialogue
among American Catholics on the issue of abortion. The ad claimed
that

> [s]tatements of recent Popes and of the Catholic hierarchy have
> condemned the direct termination of pre-natal life as morally
> wrong in all instances. There is a mistaken belief in American
> society that this is the only legitimate Catholic position. In fact,
> a diversity of opinions regarding abortion exists among committed
> Catholics.

This declaration incited unprecedented anger among many Roman Catholic Church officials who believed that it was entirely erroneous. Condemnation of abortion had always been indisputable. In fact, the Vatican disagreed so strongly with the claims of the advertisement that it commanded the twenty-four signers to publicly retract their statement or face dismissal from their congregations. What this ad calls "a diversity of opinions" some American Catholic theologians call "proportionalism."[1]

Until the Second Vatican Council (1962–65), Catholic theologians around the world understood that they were not to debate the validity of a ruling that the Vatican had pronounced, even when that pronouncement was not made ex cathedra. They might debate interpretations, but they could not challenge the teaching directly by favoring an alternate methodology. All of this changed with Vatican II. Although the documents produced then took virtually no notice of abortion, the "new" spirit mandated by the Council set the stage for much of the debate that followed. The post-conciliar Catholic, "while committed to the faith, [was] more 'independent-minded,'" as Richard Neuhaus put it, "and quite prepared to challenge both governmental policies and church doctrine on matters such as birth control and premarital sex."[2]

Thus, by the time of the 1968 encyclical *Humanae Vitae* (which upheld the Church's restrictive attitudes toward sexual matters), attitudes toward formal dissent had changed dramatically.[3] After Vatican II, many American Catholics felt that it was not only their responsibility to dissent, but also their Christian obligation to do so. As Maureen Fiedler, one of the "Vatican 24" (a signer of the *New York Times* advertisement), put it, "Adult, responsible Catholics have the right, even the duty, to speak out for what they believe is the good of the Church."[4] The *New York Times* ad, one of the first public declarations of dissent, grew out of this distinctly American sense of obligation.

Not only did the Vatican force the religious signers to recant, but in their "Resolution on Abortion" the National Conference of Catholic Bishops in the United States claimed that "no Catholic can responsibly take a 'pro-choice' stand when the 'choice' in question involves the taking of innocent human life."[5] American Catholics who refused to follow this teaching increasingly found themselves denied Communion, threatened with excommunication, or dismissed from their orders. Within this struggle over moral authority and ecclesiastical power lies a complicated tangle of philosophical and cultural conflicts whose contending factions are not simply fighting about whether abortion is right or wrong: they also deeply disagree over what it means today to be a Catholic in America.

In 1979, a Catholic woman from rural Pennsylvania—I'll call her Betty—got pregnant. She loved the baby's father and would have married him, but he was already married to someone else. Not knowing precisely what she should do with the rest of her life, she moved to the nearest city, had her baby in a Catholic home for unwed mothers, and left the baby with a nice couple from the parish each day while she searched for work. She waitressed for a while and had a few other odd jobs, but grew dissatisfied with her life, as well as with the life she was barely providing for her son. One day, soon after the baby's first birthday, Betty simply didn't pick the boy up.

Betty went home to finish college and then went on to graduate school. She is now a friend of mine, a quite successful feminist academic, and, like me, no longer a Catholic. Of all the personal stories I heard in the process of writing this essay—all the broken relationships and botched abortions, all the regrets—hers is the most painful. She knew, she says, that her life ought to go somewhere, ought to be worth something. She also knew, she says, that she wasn't a very good mother. The couple from the parish provided a family to that child, which she could not. After hearing Betty's story, I began to think about the women I knew while growing up who had made similar choices. Two girls dropped out of my class in parochial high school to have babies, and at least half a dozen left the College of St. Rose to do the same. Most of these girls went to some other city to have their babies and then put them up for adoption through Catholic agencies.

However, while these decisions were undoubtedly painful, the women and girls who made such choices often did so because, as Betty articulated it, it was "part of her way to God." Inside the world of traditional Catholicism, a socially and theologically intertwined system of support existed that made these decisions not only possible, but necessary. This system sustained these women and directed them against the "easier" solution of abortion.

The philosophical principle of "double effect" is used by the Roman Catholic magisterium to determine the only conditions under which abortion may be found acceptable. It is a carefully reasoned, precise argument designed to determine, in situations where an act will have both good and bad effects, whether committing that act should be considered a sin. According to Church teaching, abortions that are unintended, such as miscarriages, are not sinful. In order to guarantee that the evil consequence of this particular act is unintended, traditional Catholic moralists suggest that we must be able to describe it without using the term "abortion" or any synonym for that term. An abortion is unintended only when the act under consideration can be described as something other than an abortion.

Currently, the magisterium finds only two types of abortive situations morally acceptable under the dictates of double effect: the case of a pregnant woman with a cancerous uterus (the fetus is then removed along with the uterus), and the case of an ectopic pregnancy, in which the fetus is lodged in a fallopian tube (the fallopian tube is then removed). These two cases are acceptable because something other than an abortion can accurately describe the surgical procedure. The indisputably unintended nature of these two exceptions is verified by the four conditions of double effect. The Catholic Church believes that by observing the parameters of these four guidelines, no Catholic will ever sanction an intended abortion:

1. *The act under consideration, independent of its context (action qua action), must be good or indifferent.* It is unacceptable, under this rule, to commit or perform an evil in order to achieve an ultimate good. According to adherents of the double-effect principle, if the description of the act signifies an evil, nothing can make that act morally good or indifferent. One cannot, for example, kill John in order to prevent him from killing Mary because killing, in and of itself, is an evil. If, however,

John assaults Mary, it might be argued that the act under investigation could be described as defensive, that is, the act of killing John would be defined as defending Mary. In this view, the evil designated as "killing" is replaced by the good of "defending."

2. *The moral agent must directly intend only the good effect of the action; the evil effect is only indirectly intended.* The intended effect (the one that is *directly* intended) must be morally good; only the unintended effect (the one that is simply permitted) may be evil. As in the example above, the good of "defending" Mary must be the only effect intended; killing John must be understood as simply permitted. This condition contains the logic that the entire principle of double effect is formulated to achieve; the other three conditions are designed to guarantee its smooth operation.

3. *The good effect is not produced by the bad effect.* In this condition, one must be able to narrate the act under consideration such that the good effect happens before or simultaneous to the bad. If the good effect flows from the bad in a subsequent manner, the act could be understood as the commission of evil to achieve good. Thus, if there were any other way of defending Mary, or any contravening measures that would ensure her safety, the killing of John could not be understood, according to this criterion, as indirect.

4. *There must be a proportionately grave reason for permitting the evil.* Here, the good effect of the act must be evaluated against the bad effect and found comparatively greater. For example, it would be morally wrong to kill John because he was about to cheat on a test, for the moral evil of killing would be proportionately greater than the moral good of saving John from cheating. (Proportionalism argues that this consideration is the only valid one for moral decision-making.)

In the licit cases of an ectopic pregnancy and a cancerous uterus, then, the criteria of double effect are met because: (1) the removal of a pregnant cancerous uterus or pathologically blocked fallopian tube is a good or at least morally neutral act; (2) since the intention is to remove the disease, the abortion is permitted, but not intended as such; (3) the removal of the defective organs can be called something other than an abortion; and (4) the abortion is permitted, proportionately, because it saves the life of the mother, and both fetal and maternal lives would otherwise be lost.

Any abortion performed outside these two instances would be illicit. Consider, for example, a pregnant woman who suffers from chronic hypertensive heart disease associated with severe renal insufficiency. If this woman does not receive an abortion, she will probably die from cardiac or renal dysfunction brought on directly by the pregnancy. However, under the conditions of double effect, even though this woman may die, an abortion is out of the question. Although she could argue that the procedure would save her life, the good effect would be produced by the bad—the abortion—which could not be called something else.

It is not coincidental, of course, that the double-effect criteria with respect to abortion not only express traditional Catholic theology, but also "ordinary" understandings of the way that God works in the world. Stated differently, the philosophy that underpins traditional Catholicism in relation to abortion is enmeshed in a cultural system that both produces and is produced by the philosophical convictions. For example, traditional Catholics surround themselves not only with children, but with pictures of and prayers to saints; they create a "household of faith," which historian Ann Taves has described as a "network of affective, familial relationships between believers and supernatural 'relatives,'" a gathering that implies that life is designed to be lived in community, and that all should be welcomed.[6] In this social, domestic, neighborhood context, abortion is wrong because no child is or ever could be "one too many." The existence and bounty of large Catholic families vividly demonstrate that abortion is unnecessary.

Human bodies do not exist "out there," waiting to be organized into governing cultural systems; indeed, the logic of any such system tries to account for actual bodies, which reproduce themselves in their children. How many children we have is in some measure determined by the size and shape of the space allotted to them within the ideological system that grips us. While the number of children produced in many traditional Catholic families may be in some respects a result of official interdictions against abortion and contraception, the size of these families also serves to signify membership in Catholicism and to reflect Catholic beliefs about God's work in the world. Stated quite simply, the existence of seven or nine or perhaps even twelve siblings usually tells us something about where this family goes to church and, consequently, what it believes. The issue of abortion in Catholic America must be understood in relation to this cultural identity. Big families, and the philosophies and interdictions that inform their lives, are part of what it means to be Catholic. According to the way Catholic theology sees the world, there is always enough to go around, always room for one more. Or as Dorothy Day, cofounder of the Catholic Worker movement, once suggested, "[A] baby is always born with a loaf of bread under its arm."[7]

Although applying the principle of double effect is the only official method for determining licit abortions, many respected and thoughtful American Catholic scholars have spoken and written in favor of a different, unauthorized method.[8] Proportionalism, proposed as a less rigid alternative to double-effect theory, permits abortions in many more cases. The term "proportionalism" is derived from the presupposition that evils must be weighed against each other and proportionally evaluated. Although still understood as a sin, an abortion may also be understood, according to proportionalists, as the lesser of two evils and may therefore be found morally acceptable. Just as the principle of double effect is endorsed and supported by the cultural precepts of traditional Catholic theology, the philosophical presupposition of proportionalism is produced by and reproduces the convictions of assimilated American Catholicism.

In 1968, Father Charles Curran asked the following question about double effect: If, according to Catholic thinking, an ectopic pregnancy can licitly be removed along with the pathological fallopian tube that holds it, why can't the fetus simply be removed from the tube (assuming this to be surgically possible) without taking the tube?

> By removing just the fetus, the doctor does not impair the child-bearing ability of the mother. The doctor knows that the fetus has

no chance to live and sooner or later will have to be removed. The logical solution would be to remove the fetus and save the tube if possible.[9]

Double-effect thinking permits abortion in the case of ectopic pregnancy only if the tube is also removed, for it is the pathological nature of that tube and its necessary removal that allow the abortive procedure to be understood as unintended. What *is* intended is the removal of the pathological tube. Curran bypassed the discussion of intent and moved directly to an application of proportionalist reasoning. In this thinking, a result that left a woman with both of her fallopian tubes (and consequently her ability to bear children) intact was obviously preferred over one that did not. Curran's reasoning reflects the idea that evil must sometimes be committed in order to achieve good, an idea that is anathema to proponents of double effect.

A formal critique of the idea of intent associated with double effect was introduced in 1973 by the premier scholar of proportionalism, Richard McCormick, who articulated his "dissatisfaction with the narrowly behavioral or physical understanding of human activity that underlies the [traditional] interpretation of direct and indirect."[10] McCormick's alternative construct forcefully interrogated the philosophical naiveté of the double-effect view of intention and simultaneously reflected distinctly American ideologies. It is worth letting McCormick register his differences with double effect in his own voice:

> The rule of double effect is a vehicle for dealing with . . . conflict situations where only two courses are available: to act or not to act, to speak or remain silent, to resist or not to resist. The concomitant act of either course of action was harm of some sort. Now in situations of this kind, the rule of Christian reason is to choose the lesser of two evils. This general statement is, it would seem, beyond debate; for the only alternative is that in conflict situations we should choose the greater evil, which is patently absurd. This means that all concrete rules and distinctions are subsidiary to this and hence valid to the extent that they actually convey to us what

is factually the lesser evil. . . . Thus the basic category for conflict situations is the lesser evil, or proportionate reason.[11]

McCormick took Curran's practical application and expanded it into a moral methodology that, as he claimed, is self-evident, even for Christians. By rejecting intent as a measure of morality and by relying only upon the consequences of an act to determine the act's acceptability, McCormick launched the discussion of proportionalism.

The methodology of proportionalism is clearly contrary to the beliefs of traditional Catholics, who hold that doing good and avoiding evil are duties that cannot be compromised or negotiated. Their antipathy to proportionalism has been expressed in a series of accusations that include relativism, incommensurability, and utilitarianism.[12] These denunciations and the proportionalists' responses to them comprise a major segment of the published work in contemporary Roman Catholic moral theology. At stake in this conflict is not only method but authority, not only philosophical principles but cultural identity.

The most significant methodological difference between double effect and proportionalism can be viewed in cases where a therapeutic abortion is the only means of saving a woman's life (also known as the life-against-life dilemma). In the logic of double effect, abortion is to be avoided at all costs. A mother's faithfulness to God's commandments carries greater moral weight than saving her life. Even if a woman dies in childbirth, as long as she did not seek an abortion she can at least be assured that she did not sin. As double-effect proponent Josef Fuchs explains:

> The two obligations concerning a [life-against-life situation], to preserve the life of the mother and not to kill the child, only seem to contradict one another. There is in fact no commandment to save the mother at all costs. There is only an obligation to save her in a morally permissible way.[13]

Double-effect theory dictates that it is better to allow one woman to die—if you are the pregnant woman, to die yourself—than to kill a fetus.[14] Or, as many moral theologians and Church officials have articulated it, two deaths are better than one murder.

Proportionalists are unwilling to accept such exacting criteria. They promote awareness of and adaptability to multifaceted dilemmas and are willing to allow lesser evils for the attainment of greater goods. In most life-against-life situations, proportionalists believe that one death, even if it is accomplished by the sin of abortion, is less evil than two. Abortion performed under these or any conditions is clearly evil, yet proportionalists understand certain abortions to be less evil than the alternative. Although significant developments in medicine — most specifically, cesarean sections — have rendered most of these life-against-life situations obsolete, the methodological difference between the two ways of configuring moral behavior remains an issue, particularly because proportionalism's primary audience resides in and is produced by American culture.

According to recent statistics, American Catholics are practicing birth control and abortion at rates rivaling those of Protestant and secular Americans. Gallup polls indicate that a large percentage of American Catholics support legalized abortion.[15] Kristin Luker claims that "as a group, Catholics are increasingly using contraception in patterns very similar to those of their non-Catholic peers."[16] As more and more American Catholics choose abortion, the cultural space for a more liberal theory such as proportionalism widens. It is not that proportionalists write in direct response to the increase in Catholic abortions; rather, these events and principles emerge together as part of a pattern in what it means to be an American Catholic.

The ideology of a specifically American Catholicism comes into being as related bodies are reconfigured into "American-looking" families.[17] Catholics, if they want to become more American, have fewer children. My paternal grandmother, for example, who came from the old country when she was sixteen, raised her six children and cared for her elderly mother-in-law in a small, two-bedroom house in Syracuse, New York, "up near St. Vincent's Parish." After she died, my father gave the house to my soon-to-be-married brother and sister-in-law for their first home. Frank and Sue lived there happily until their first child came along, but, needing more room, they soon moved to the suburbs, after selling the house to Sue's single brother. His visitors now often remark on how perfect the house is for someone who lives alone. The changes that this little house has gone through indicate how my extended family keeps getting more and more American.[18]

In his influential history, *The American Catholic Experience,* Jay Dolan argued that Catholics have stood not in oppositional relationship to American ideology, but rather in a free and happy relationship, participating in all its aspects and eras.[19] If public values conflict with religious beliefs, Catholics are usually able, according to Dolan, to lay aside their "private" religious convictions. Their assimilation into American life has been made possible by the separation of church and state. On the side of "church," Catholic morality is perceived, in this interpretation, as a personal characteristic or conviction that is acceptable only if it does not conflict with the larger precepts of the American state. Allegiance and obedience to an ethic that pervades all aspects of life—such as the principle of double effect—are considered, in Dolan's narrative, "an old-world, European model of Catholicism."[20] In the "new and exciting, thoroughly American Church," Catholics respond to tensions and to anti-Catholic sentiments by publicly proclaiming their loyalty to everything the republic stands for: individual choice, freedom, pluralism, and democratization. This new Church blends beautifully into the existing American landscape.

Dolan's narrative is indicative of the influence that American liberalism has had on contemporary American Catholicism. Indeed, at the close of his history, Dolan suggests that pluralist attitudes give new life to Catholicism in America: "There is no longer one way to do theology, to worship at Mass, to confess sin, or to pray. There are various ways of being Catholic, and people are choosing the style that best suits them."[21] Catholics today are able to choose "the style that best suits them" because the choice of a *style* does not conflict with the overarching loyalty that Catholics must, in this narrative, grant to America. The portrayal of these theological "options" as one set among many to be consumed in accordance with personal taste poses no threat to the primary allegiance America requires—that is, to the conviction that the ability to make free choices is more important than any particular choice.[22] In choosing the style that best suits them, Catholics mirror the liberalism upon which proportionalism is founded.

This "new" Catholicism, then, differs from the traditional faith not only in that it offers the space for personal choice, but also because such personal choice (as long as it is in keeping with overarching American values) can be considered moral. Allegiance to the republic is formulated as the most fundamental moral value; hence pluralist Catholics are allowed to choose the values of America over traditional Catholic values and still remain moral. This wedding of American liberalism and Catholicism dictates that particular religious characteristics are acceptable only in private, and only as long as they do not conflict with the overriding commitments made in the public arena to the presuppositions of American ideology.

The benefits of the proportionalist methodology for American Catholic women, who need no longer be subject to unlimited duties of childbearing and child care, are patent. Proportionalism, along with the shift toward Catholic assimilation into American culture, offers women who find themselves with an unwanted pregnancy the freedom to pursue careers and other interests without being hampered by familial commitments. Catholic women are also able to liberate themselves from the burden of evil-doing with abortions sanctioned by the principles of proportionalism, which is itself sanctioned by American liberalism. However, while such liberation is clearly an advance for many women, other options have been closed off.

For example, fewer Catholic families envision their lives as being intertwined with those of unwed pregnant mothers in their parishes largely because there are fewer women with full-term, unwanted pregnancies. As more women choose abortion, the systems that previously existed to support those with unwanted pregnancies are being virtually disassembled.[23] Before abortion was legalized in America, most Catholic parishes sponsored or supported homes where such women could go to have their babies. Catholic adoption agencies and social services existed in most geographic areas as backups for those women who couldn't find housing for themselves or families for their babies. Every priest in every parish knew how to access these systems. When an unmarried, pregnant woman came to him for Confession or simply for guidance, the priest was immediately able to introduce her into these systems. Such networks of Catholic caretaking have been either greatly diminished or entirely dismantled. A priest once knew precisely where to send a woman with an unwanted pregnancy; now he is increasingly less certain about what her options are and perhaps, in some cases, less certain about her moral obligations as a Catholic.

This situation is not unrelated to the liberalism that underpins cultural accommodations. The logic that mandates cordoning off religious particulars in the private sphere also dictates the sequestering of particulars associated with femaleness or womanhood. Liberal ideology makes it acceptable for us to be women, perhaps even feminists, as long as we do so in private and only as long as our behavior as such doesn't interfere with our prior (more important) commitment: to keep such particulars out of public, political space. The traditional Catholic systems that supported women with unwanted pregnancies are disappearing because women, according to liberal ideology, are perceived as self-sufficient, isolated individuals. Private needs and affiliations, such as pregnancy and religion, are cordoned off in the private sphere.

In terms of abortion, the liberal paradigm attempts to maintain the pretext of equality by offering pregnant women the choice to be either like men (and not pregnant) or different from men (and pregnant). Abortion serves as a kind of equalizer; any woman who does not want a child can simply not have one and thus immediately restore herself to the *ur*-position of the liberal self—to the "same" condition as men. While abortion is an option that many of us choose, the choice between "being pregnant" (and coping on your own) and "not being pregnant" is not enough. What we often need is a community that financially, emotionally, and spiritually supports those of us who have unwanted pregnancies, but who do not want abortions. We need an option that allows us to carry these pregnancies to term and then assures us that our children will be cared for within a larger community or family.

What has been lost in the shift to proportionalism is the ability to respond to an unwanted pregnancy the way that Betty did. In some ways,

Betty had more options than "being pregnant" or "not being pregnant"; she had a way to deal with her situation that allowed her to be responsible both to her baby and to the family she called her church. Betty had the option of plugging into a network of support, and in doing so she felt that she wasn't abandoning her baby to strangers, but rather turning him over to a circle of care that was more often than not centered on her parish. Betty gave up her son not precisely because she couldn't care for him, but because she knew, from first-hand knowledge, that someone else could better care for him. With all of its faults and oppressive tendencies, she found the community that enabled this decision within the fabric of traditional Catholicism.

My own biological mother did as well. She carried me—unwanted— and turned me over to Frank and Rosamond Rudy, other Catholics like herself, to raise. She did this because, as a traditional Catholic, she saw the world as a place where there would always and undoubtedly be room for one more child, where "family" is more about sharing faith than sharing a household, and where sharing a household expresses such faith. My biological mother believed in a God who was accommodating and loving enough to provide for everybody, and she lived within a family founded not on blood relations but on these theological convictions. In taking me in, my adoptive parents taught me the virtue of welcoming a stranger and showed me how to see my Church, both my local parish and worldwide Catholicism, as one family. Even though my political quarrels with the Catholic Church have been severe enough to cause me to leave it, I also mourn the loss of the community and ideology that upheld and assisted both Betty and my mother.

NOTES

1 For an excellent review of this incident from the perspective of two signers, see Barbara Ferraro and Patricia Hussey, *No Turning Back: Two Nuns' Battle with the Vatican over Women's Right to Choose* (New York, 1990). For a more explicitly feminist analysis of the incident, see also Mary Hunt and Frances Kissling, "The *New York Times* Ad: A Case Study in Religious Feminism," *Journal of Feminist Studies in Religion* 3 (Spring 1987): 115–27.

2 Richard Neuhaus, *The Catholic Moment: The Paradox of the Church in the Postmodern World* (New York, 1987), 237.

3 The encyclical responded directly to the issue of abortion by claiming: "It is not licit, even for the gravest reasons, to do evil so that good may follow therefrom; that is, to make into the object of a positive act of will something which is intrinsically disordered, and hence unworthy of the human person, even when the intention is to safeguard or promote individual, family or social well-being." See "Humanae Vitae: On the Regulation of Birth" (25 July 1968), in *The Gospel of Peace and Social Justice: Catholic Social Teaching Since Pope John,* ed. Joseph Gremillion (Maryknoll, NY, 1976), 434.

4 Maureen Fiedler, S.L., "Dissent within the U.S. Church: The Case of the Vatican '24,'" in *Church Polity and American Politics: Issues in Contemporary American Catholicism,* ed. Mary C. Segers (New York, 1990), 306.

5 U.S. Bishops Meeting, "Resolution on Abortion," *Origins* (16 November 1989): 395.

6 Ann Taves, *The Household of Faith* (Notre Dame, 1986), vii.

7 Critics of Catholicism sometimes suggest that Catholic positions against birth control and abortion serve primarily to populate or overpopulate society with Catholics. These critics do not take into account, as Susan Nicholson points out, "the superior position accorded virginity in Catholic doctrine." See her *Abortion and the Roman Catholic Church* (Knoxville, 1978), 3. That is, large Catholic families are not the only way for Catholics to live faithfully; indeed, in a history filled with asceticism and monastic celibacy, those who reproduce abundantly do not even attain the highest spiritual status. It is my belief that the large Catholic family reflects not moral or spiritual loftiness, but rather a uniquely Catholic understanding of God and God's creation. Catholics do not have large families because they conspire to take over the world; they do so because they believe that God will provide and care for each and every precious child.

8 It should be noted that the debate between double effect and proportionalism is reserved primarily for moral theologians. While the mandates and writings of moral theology both here and abroad either directly or indirectly control the behavior of many American Catholics, few nonacademic Catholics understand the philosophical parameters of this debate. This is related, of course, to the fact that graduate education in the moral theology tradition has been largely restricted to (male) clergy.

9 Charles E. Curran, "Absolute Norms in Medical Ethics," in *Absolutes in Moral Theology?* ed. Charles E. Curran (Washington, DC, 1968), 113.

10 Richard McCormick, "Ambiguity in Moral Choice," in *Doing Evil to Achieve Good,* ed. Richard McCormick and Paul Ramsey (Chicago, 1978), 33.

11 Ibid., 38.

12 On the charge of relativism, see William May, "Contraception, Abstinence and Responsible Parenthood," *Reason* 3 (1977): 34–52. For a proportionalist defense against relativism, see Lisa Cahill, "Teleology, Utilitarianism, and Christian Ethics," *Theological Studies* 42 (December 1981): 611. On the major critique of proportionalism as incommensurable, see *Doing Evil to Achieve Good,* ed. Richard McCormick and Paul Ramsey (Chicago, 1978).

13 Josef Fuchs, *Natural Law* (New York, 1965), 131.

14 The moral distinction between killing and allowing someone to die has been debated in both the long history of Roman Catholic moral reasoning and the emergent field of medical ethics. For positions that support the moral relevance of the distinction, see Phillip Devine, *The Ethics of Homicide* (Notre Dame, 1979), 129. For positions that contest this distinction, see Nicholson, *Abortion and the Roman Catholic Church,* 72.

15 As cited by Mary C. Segers, who suggests that less than 15 percent of Catholics oppose abortion under any circumstances. See her "The Loyal Opposition: Catholics for a Free Choice," in *The Catholic Church and the Politics of Abortion,* ed. Timothy Byrnes and Mary Segers (Boulder, 1992), 182.

16 Kristin Luker, *Abortion and the Politics of Motherhood* (Berkeley, 1984), 210. Indeed, Luker's estimate of the percentage of Catholics who receive an abortion is conservative. According to the Alan Guttmacher Institute, for example, Catholics are 30 percent more likely than Protestants to have abortions (cited in Ferraro and Hussey, eds., *No Turning Back,* 252).

17 I use "American Catholicism" here and throughout to refer to Catholics who have been "assimilated" into American life, in contradistinction to "traditional Catholics." Although the difference between these two groups can be at times unclear, my argument is that abortion and reproductive patterns help to delineate the boundary between them.

18 It is not the case, of course, that American Catholics began using birth control only in the last two decades. Indeed, a significant number of Catholics, in their desire to become assimilated into the American middle class of the 1950s, began using various forms of birth control and even abortion in order to maintain their class position or to "get ahead." What made these contraceptive acts different from those of assimilated American Catholics of the 1990s is that the earlier generations expressed a sense of guilt about their practices; indeed, in some instances that guilt led them to break off

their relationship with the Church. Their use of birth control and abortion caused varying degrees of erosion in their identification with traditional Catholic formulations of morality. In the cultural milieu of American Catholicism today, however, proportionalism at once rationalizes and reflects the changes made in the lives of many American Catholics, changes that have made it possible for Catholics to use birth control or abortion and still consider themselves to be in good standing with "the Church." Whether such Catholics *are* in good standing with the Church depends, of course, on how one defines "the Church." According to the magisterium and other officials in Rome, people practicing abortion or birth control are in a state of sin. According to American moral theologians like McCormick and Curran, precedent exists within the Church's history for the methodology of proportionalism, and therefore people who use birth control and abortion are, in certain circumstances, still under the auspices of traditional Catholicism. This conflict is related to a struggle over who gets to define what constitutes Church membership.

19 This strand of analysis originated with John Courtney Murray; see especially *We Hold These Truths* (New York, 1960). Most commentaries on the history of Catholicism in America reiterate Murray's premises. See, for example, John Tracy Ellis, *American Catholicism* (Chicago, 1970); William Halsey, *The Survival of American Innocence* (Notre Dame, 1980); and David O'Brien, *Public Catholicism* (New York, 1989).

20 Jay P. Dolan, *The American Catholic Experience: A History from Colonial Times to the Present* (New York, 1985), 294.

21 Ibid., 453.

22 This free-market model could also be extended to an investigation of American attitudes toward worship. Many Americans today "shop" for a church until they find one that is in keeping with their personal tastes. Denominational affiliation is thus becoming, in many segments of the American population, a superfluous consideration. Consequently, many contemporary Catholic churches feel that they must "compete," alongside and as equivalents to Protestant denominations, for members. Worship, like moral methodology, has become subject to a market economy.

23 For an account of how *Roe v. Wade* affected the adoption industry, see Ricky Solinger, *Wake Up, Little Susie* (New York, 1993).

DAVID PLANTE

My Parents, My Religion, and My Writing

I was born and brought up in a small Franco-American parish in Providence, Rhode Island, the center of which was the brick church, where Monsieur le Curé could not speak English, only French. At the brick parochial school, the nuns, les Mères de Jésus-Marie, taught in French in the morning and in English in the afternoon. After school, at the table in the kitchen of our clapboard house, I wrote poems and stories in a notebook. I wrote in English.

I wrote about the parish, surrounded by circles within circles. Each increasingly inward circle concentrated the parish more and more on its past, on the North American forests in which it had evolved since the arrival of my ancestors from France in the seventeenth century. And each increasingly outward circle expanded the parish more and more into the future of twentieth-century America, in which it would disappear.

At supper time, my mother would tell me I had to clear away my writing and set the table with plates and knives and forks. She never worried about disturbing me when I was writing.

My father would never disturb me when I was writing, even if he needed me to help, say, with getting the storm windows up for the winter. I knew this, and took advantage of it. I wouldn't offer to help, but would sit and write while he struggled, with my younger brother, to carry the storm windows out of the cellar into the yard. My mother would tell me, "You've got to close your notebook and help your father." He was always surprised when I, knowing he was about to do a job around the house, put down my writing and spontaneously said, "I'll help you, Dad."

When I turned sixteen, my mother said I should get a job for the summer. "You've got to work," she said, "you can't do nothing all summer." My father said, "He'll read and write. He'll do a lot of work." Yet I hated my father and loved my mother, and, translating my feelings into stories, wrote in my notebook about my hatred and my love. That my father seemed to support me in my vocation and my mother seemed to think of my vocation as secondary to living didn't occur to me.

When my poems and stories appeared in the literary magazine of the college I attended, the Jesuit Boston College, I always brought a copy to my parents to show them. My mother took some interest in my stories and was privately amused by them. ("Oh, how could you write that?" she'd laugh. "You weren't brought up to know such things.") My father, after he put his glasses on, the lenses pitted by the iron filings that flew up from the machine he worked at in the file shop, read them carefully, then set them aside without saying anything. It was only when my aunt—or, in the one-word honorific, Matante—Cora was visiting that he would take the most recent piece from the desk in the parlor where my mother had put them and hand it to my aunt, his jaw stuck out and a thin smile on his lips, saying, "Read this." His appreciation of my writing was public. My mother, embarrassed, would say, "Oh, it's only a college magazine."

My Aunt Cora always looked at the poem or story, but said that because of her cataracts she couldn't read it. Then she would say about my writing, "C'est un don" ("It's a gift"). Being my Aunt Cora, she meant a gift from God. To be a writer was to have a vocation in the same way a priest had a vocation, though not quite so elevated. My father agreed with her. "Oui, c'est un don."

And I agreed with both of them.

God Himself chose a person to give a vocation to, so it wasn't something you could ask for. But you could pray to God to let you know, to illuminate you, if you did have a vocation and were uncertain about it. I would pray to God for illumination of the *don* I had, illumination of exactly how I should act on it, because I didn't really know. I liked to think that to be a writer was to enter an order, a strict one, and that the vows required would be: never, ever write for money; always write purely, innocently; and, most difficult, always write about what was greater than yourself.

How else could I explain to myself my wanting to be a writer except that it was my vocation to be one? How else, coming from the barely literate background I came from? My father could hardly write, my grandmother not at all. What prompted me, at the age when I first could, to write stories and poems in a large script on ruled paper, and always, because of the underlay or overlay of French, spelling strangely, with an "e" at the end of many verbs: "controle," "demande," "refere"? Had any of my ancestors, from no matter how far back, written a poem? Perhaps no one ever had? And what inspired me to go to the public library and take out books and read them? What made me want to buy books and have a small bookcase to put them in? Did I know of anyone else in the parish who did this? There must have been some, but I didn't know them.

After I started college, my mother's only criticism of my writing or reading so much was to say to me, "Don't you want to go out? It's such a beautiful day, you can't want to stay cooped up." As I'd only shrug and continue, she'd modify her objection, if that was what it was, to, "At least, from time to time, look up and stare out as though at the horizon; that'll save your eyes." Could my mother have been made to believe by my father that I had a vocation?

The only conceivable reason my parents might have had for reading books—I think of the three shelves of books in the glassed-in breakfront top of the desk in the parlor, French novels such as Prosper Merimée's *Carmen* and Ludevic Halévy's *L'Abbé Constantin,* which my father said were good literature, as if he were the custodian of good literature and wouldn't allow anything less in the house—was to be morally and spiritually uplifted. There was no other reason. Good literature was not far removed from religious literature, and its effect was not far behind that of religious literature, such as the *Lives of the Saints*. Bad literature, best-sellers read only for entertainment, had nothing, but nothing to do with good literature. Books were a religious experience, and so was writing. My writing *had* to be a vocation that came from God.

If you didn't read a book for moral and spiritual uplift, what else would you read it for? My parents wouldn't have understood: for truth. Sometimes I did have abstract conversations with my mother, though never with my father, about reading and writing for truth. I might have said, Well, a person reads or writes to see through life's illusions, to see the truth of life, no matter how hard. Even my mother, less intelligent than my father but more educated because of her family, would have responded: the truth of life? Their idea of truth was based on an ancestral truth: the tree stump would not be uprooted, the snow storm would not stop, the doctor would not arrive in time to save the sick mother. Their truth was simple: what was impossible was true. That the deepest meaning of a book should be the great awakening that truth and beauty and love were illusions, and life a brutal fact, my parents would have found incomprehensible. They had no illusions, not because they saw that goodness and beauty and love were lies, but because the truth of the impossibility of life, the basic truth of their inherited, primitive culture, was as self-evident to them as a stone, as death. They didn't have to read to find this out.

So was it *for* illusion that they imagined a person read (or wrote) a book? The illusion of possibility? That was too sophisticated for them. They would repeat: a good book lifts the reader (and the writer) morally, spiritually. And how does it do that? By praising God. And so I, in trying to write, tried to praise God.

If I believed my writing had to do with God, it was my religion that gave me this belief. If I believed the images that occurred to me while writing had meaning, not in me as a writer, and not even in the reader's subjective appreciation of them, but in something impersonal and objective, something not inward but outward, as distinct from the writer's and reader's world as another world entirely, this was because of my religion. If I believed that that other world was a world of awareness, depthlessly dark because depthlessly clear awareness, which itself existed apart from me, like eternity, I was merely extrapolating from my religion, and I believed every image that came to me had its meaning in it. Without it, writing was nothing, as my religion taught me that life was nothing without God.

And now, years later, confirmed in my atheism, I know that whatever depth there is to my writing has to do with my religion. I imagine that whenever I write I do so over a plane that lies beneath all my writing like a pane of glass, and what shows up on that plane is not light but darkness, and I see every letter I write against it. When I am writing on that darkness, I am writing in a state of ecstasy, because I am not writing in terms of what I want my writing to be, or of any belief I would like my writing to convey, but entirely for that darkness, which gives my writing a depth that I myself would not be able to give it. For my writing to be true, I must be able to see through it to the darkness that inspires it, through the letters, between the lines, between the paragraphs, all about the page. If I work on the writing, it is to let that darkness shine up through it as clearly as possible, which means trying to make my writing as clear as possible. The truth of my writing—the spiritual truth for which I write—is all in that darkness, so clear in its depth that there is, like God in eternity, no seeing to the end of it.

STANLEY HAUERWAS

A Homage to Mary and to the University
Called Notre Dame

Just seven. With that answer I knew this was going to be different. I had just been hired to teach in the theology department at the University of Notre Dame. It was one of the obligatory occasions to meet "the faculty." I assumed they were, like me, academics before they were anything else. I confess I thought it curious that the economist who sought me out actually thought *Rerum Novarum* might have something to do with economics, but what caught me completely off guard was his answer to the ritualistic question asked on such occasions when you are desperate to find something in common: "How many kids do you have?" "Just seven."

With that "just" I knew I had entered a strange new world. Nothing in my old world had prepared me for that "just." Even being from the South was insufficient to prepare me for all that "just" involved. My father was one of six bricklaying brothers, but that was "back then." One of the brothers, Rufus, had five children, but Aunt Christeen was from an East Texas farm and was used to it. Even then all their cousins thought five was a lot. No one in the family would have thought "just five." Not even Uncle Rufus. Catholics were going to be different.

Of course, from my growing up I was not entirely without knowledge of Catholics. After all, I had played "war" and tried to figure out what "sex" was with Charlie Jurek. Charlie said he was Catholic, but that did not seem to make much difference in Pleasant Grove, Texas. There did not seem to be enough of them to make any difference. I knew there were more Catholics than Charlie since he told us that he went to a church weirdly called Saint August-stein, or so we pronounced it. I assumed what it meant to be Catholic was going to a church that did not have a real name—like Pleasant Mound Methodist. Of course, as I got older I learned that Charlie was Czech, or something foreign, and he could do anything he wanted during the week and get forgiven for it on Saturday with no sweat.

By the time I got to Notre Dame I thought I was more knowledgeable, if not sophisticated. I had been to Yale Divinity School and had gotten a Ph.D. in theological ethics. I knew a lot about Catholics, or at least something called church history. I was even an "expert" on Aquinas's *Summa*. I had actually read the whole damn thing, which is more than many Roman Catholic theologians can claim. I had studied *Rerum Novarum* as well as the other social encyclicals. Hell, I was ready to go.

But that "just" threw me. What kind of people would produce that "just"? Of course, as I would learn over the next fourteen years, many Catholics would have nothing but disdain for that "just." The kids I had in class, who were the "just," now explained the "just" as an "ethnic thing" that they had no intention of repeating. After all, that was why they were at Notre Dame—to become good Americans, who had small families who could get ahead. Yet for good or ill, whether they had learned to hate it or love it, that "just" was part of their history.

By God's grace it is now part of mine. Although I did not realize it at the time, coming to Notre Dame was going to change my life. I thought I was simply making a "vertical move," up from Augustana College (Rock Island, Illinois) to a "real" university. I did not anticipate that I was going to have to think about, let alone even to begin (to be sure, in a hesitant and awkward way), becoming "religious." My theological training had not prepared me for this development.

At Yale you are trained to be a theologian by writing books about other people's books. There is nothing wrong with such training, but it always has the danger of becoming an end in itself. For example, you can easily forget that the subject of theology is God. There are good reasons to forget that, moreover, given the character of the modern university. God, to put it mildly, does not sound like a university subject. How do you study that?

Of course, this is a good theological question. Most of Christian theology has insisted that we know God more by what God is not than by what God is. All positive predication of God's attributes is qualified by the negative apophatic reminder. What I learned, however, was that this means something quite different when said by a priest who begins each day in prayer than it does when I say it. There is no substitute for being around significant practitioners. Notre Dame was filled with such practitioners.

No doubt such practitioners were at Yale, and even in Texas, but I did not notice them and, if I had, would probably have ignored or dismissed them as "pious." What made Notre Dame different is that you could not miss them. They were simply there in the way the "just" was simply there. Mary requires that they exist. Without them you would not know what it means to pray to Mary and how such prayer produced such people as those called Catholics. For what I was learning is that "Catholic" names not a set of "beliefs about God," but a world of practices called the Church. It simply had not occurred to me that "church," that is, practices as basic as prayer or having children, is intrinsic to what we mean by God. Suddenly, Wittgenstein had implications that I had not anticipated.

For good or ill, what it means to be a "Catholic" is to be a member of the Church. I can illustrate the difference by calling attention to what it means to be an atheist in Judaism, Protestantism, and Catholicism. When Jews say they do not believe in God, they mean that God is an unjust son of a bitch and they will be goddamned if they will worship him. When Protestants say they do not believe in God, they mean that this is all there is. You might as well eat, drink, screw, and die. When Catholics say they do not believe in God, they mean that they are angry at the Church.

Thus I soon learned that ex-Catholics disbelieved with an intensity I could only admire. Boy, could they ever get angry at the Pope about the teaching on contraception, or at the priests for being such pricks, or at the nuns for the way they had taken out their frustrations on the kids in the second grade, and so on. What was remarkable, however, was that they had been part of a people who had actually marked them for life. The deepest marking for most was, of course, having been among the "just." What a wonderful gift—even if it took the rest of your life to get over it.

Such was the world I entered as one of the first Protestants to teach theology at Notre Dame. Of course, there were many non-Catholics at Notre Dame, but not many in theology. I was so new to the Catholic world that I did not even realize I was an "experiment." I just thought any "good department" would want someone as smart as me. What a shit I was. Of course, in some ways my blissful arrogance worked out well for everyone since it never occurred to me that I ought to hedge my bets. Even if it had, I probably would not have known how to do so.

It is important to note, for those unfamiliar with the Catholic world, that the very presence of a theology department at Catholic colleges and universities, and in particular at Notre Dame, is a relatively new development. Theology was what you taught priests in the seminary. Why would good Catholic kids, most of whom knew better than to think about becoming priests, need to know anything about theology? That was what priests, or at least some theologians, and the Church were for. All that everyone else needed to know was when to show up for Mass. The Jesuits, of course, never thought that was enough. They thought smart Catholics ought to know something about philosophy. So the Catholic laity got taught Plato to make them Catholics. What a world.

Theology as an undergraduate subject became necessary for Catholics to answer Protestants' questions. After all, Catholic Americans live in one of the first countries whose intellectual and cultural habits, for good or ill, were established by Protestants. So when graduates of Notre Dame went to live in the South, they encountered Southern Baptists who asked them if it was really true that they obeyed a guy in Rome or worshiped Mary. No graduate of Notre Dame knew how to answer questions like that. Praying to Mary was as natural as being a Notre Dame football fan. It simply came with the territory.

So the very existence of theology at Notre Dame was a response to the Catholic break-out from the "ethnic" ghetto. The department had originally been founded to provide more or less advanced catechism. After Vatican II they thought it ought to be more scholarly, which meant hiring some smart guys from Europe. That was not a bad idea, but most Notre Dame undergraduates were not overly impressed by theology done with a foreign accent. So I got hired.

What a strange department it was. I discovered that we were granting a Ph.D. in liturgy. Moreover, those involved in teaching such courses were damn smart. It just did not sound like an academic subject to me, but then I thought, "What do I know?" After all, in the general run of things my field of Christian ethics is probably no less weird. Just ask the faculty at Duke.

I even discovered that one department member's specialty was ecclesiology—not only ecclesiology, but a subspecialty called Mariology. He was personally stiff, theologically conservative, but also one of the leaders of the Catholic charismatic movement. The Spirit sure could play tricks on folks. Over the years I learned to love him, and I hope he even learned to care for me a bit. Our relationship had not started well, I later discovered. During my initial interview at Notre Dame I had introduced myself to him by saying, "Hi there. My name is Stanley Hauerwas. I am from Texas. You know, that is where it takes four syllables to say 'gawddamn.'" I was not aware then that this could be offensive. Indeed, it meant so little to me that it was only later, when others told me the story, that I knew I had offended him. Of course, it was not long afterward when the same man refused to serve me the Eucharist at a university-wide Mass. I just got into a different line.

Yet this same man was otherwise unfailingly courteous to me. He could be vicious toward his more liberal Catholic colleagues, but he was pastorally sensitive in his dealings with me. I always thought he had no use for the Catholic liberals because they should have known better, but since I had had the disadvantage of being brought up in a false religion, he could be more patient in the hope of winning me to the true Church. As I reflect on my time at Notre Dame, I take great comfort in the thought that he believed I might make a Catholic.

My hiring had been one of the last official acts of my chairman, a priest in the Congregatio à Sancta Cruce (C.S.C.) order, prior to his becoming provost of the university. James Burtchaell was and is an extraordinarily impressive person, having done his Ph.D. in New Testament at Cambridge. I learned by watching him that those who have been humbled by Mary do not have to be afraid of exercising authority. I thought that, being urbane and cultured, he would be for "openness," but instead he used his bully pulpit to insist that Notre Dame remain Catholic. At the time, I could not conceive of Notre Dame as any more Catholic than it already was. The student body was 98 percent Catholic, there were priests all over the place saying Mass, and Catholics made up the majority of the faculty. Nevertheless, as things worked out, he was right.

I began to know what Catholicism was, however, only by learning to know the acting chairman of the department—Charles Sheedy, C.S.C. Charlie was a professor of moral theology, but had spent years as the dean of the college. Charlie had become a moral theologian because he was the last to speak up when his friend, and the new chairman of the new theology department, Theodore Hesburgh, C.S.C., had been passing out the jobs. He probably thought Charlie was a good candidate for moral theology because he also had a law degree from Catholic University. Of course, Charlie was too fascinated by all things human to be tied down to one field—there were all those French novels to read, and baseball season was always just around the corner. I always thought the order was wise to keep Charlie active in the novitiate and seminary after his retirement. The young priests were too tempted to be mirror images of the old priests—rather than giving conservative answers, they thought they had to give liberal answers. Charlie, who had always fought against his own alcoholism, knew that he had few answers, but he knew he was a priest.

Some said Charlie was that piece of humanity thrown into the gears of Catholic and university bureaucracy to bring them to a halt. He was surely that, but for me he was a friend and my priest. Long retired, suffering from emphysema, bored with the crassness of Notre Dame, he comes vividly to mind during our last conversation. I was teaching at Duke by then and had not seen Charlie for over a year. We agreed to meet on a bench in front of the Dome. Charlie was never one for small talk: "What do you think Heaven is going to be like, Stanley?" was the first thing he said. He is now in the process of learning.

David Burrell, C.S.C., a philosopher, became the department chair, serving for the next nine years. They were exciting and intellectually stimulating years. David was already a friend, as our offices in the basement of the library were close to one another. Through David I had become an active member of the philosophers' seminar at Notre Dame. I had never been around people who took argument so seriously. We spent a whole year reading the *Investigations* line by line. I thought Notre Dame was intellectual heaven.

It took me several years to discover that Notre Dame had its fair share of faculty who were intellectually dull. On the whole, however, I kept meeting interesting people who believed that being Catholic ought to make a difference to how they thought and taught. Even people in the law school and the business school thought that being a Catholic mattered to what they did as scholars and teachers. Burrell was also the kind of chairman who believed that ideas mattered for what we did. Convinced that Judaism could not be either just the "background" to Christianity or just another "religion," we became committed to hiring in Judaica. I found myself so engaged in the building of a department that was neither denominationally confessional nor "religious studies," I forgot I was not Catholic.

I became a theological anthropologist. My Catholic colleagues complained about the lack of diversity, by which they meant non-Catholics, in the student body. In contrast I felt as if I were part of a people zoo with no cages. I never knew this many different people existed. I discovered Eastern Europe, the Philippines, Mexico, Central America, South America, and, in an odd way, a Texas I had never really known, through colleagues and students at Notre Dame. Notre Dame, it turns out, does not serve a state, nation, or ethnic group; it serves Mary wherever she appears.

At the time I did not realize that I was becoming Catholic. It was certainly not anything I was trying to do. It just seemed after a while more important to read *Cross Currents* than *Theology Today*. Even though I was developing a C.S.C. prejudice against the Jesuits, I even read *America*. Catholicism constituted a world into which I was inextricably drawn. The intelligence and charm of Irish priests like Ernan MacMullin and Enda McDonagh were hard to resist. In fact, I was beginning to wonder if my liver would survive the goodbye parties for those who, from time to time, returned to Ireland.

What makes this world possible, of course, is the Mass. I had actually begun to go to church again when I taught at Augustana. The Lutherans, at least Swedish Lutherans, had a wonderful liturgy. When I moved to Notre Dame the only people I could find who worshiped like the Lutherans were the Catholics. I had gotten used to having the Eucharist every Sunday, and I was damned if I was going to give it up. I am not sure why I thought the Eucharist so important, but I was sure that if Christianity made any sense, it must be because of something to do with eating that meal. Or, paraphrasing Flannery O'Connor, "If it is just a symbol, screw it." I also had a son, Adam, to raise. He was at that rambunctious age when it is difficult, if not impossible, to stay still. Much to his and my delight, I discovered that I could take him to Mass each Sunday in the pit of Grace Hall. Burrell said Mass there for undergraduates sleepily hung over, so the noise my kid made along with the many other families who had discovered this system made a positive contribution. Adam simply assumed that you were supposed to stand alongside the priest during the great thanksgiving.

As an anthropologist utilizing the participant-observer method, I noticed that Catholics worship quite differently from Protestants—

Catholics are noisy and not particularly "worshipful." Although I was at first bothered by this, I began to realize that Catholics do not have to be "holy" at worship because they think God is going to show up anyway. If the priest gets it right, there is not a thing they can do to prevent God from being present in the Eucharist. In contrast most Protestants believe in the "real absence" rather than in any presence. Accordingly, we have to be especially "holy" because otherwise we are afraid "God" will go away. I suspect that one of the reasons why Protestants are so serious in worship is our unacknowledged presumption that there is no difference between what is happening in our subjectivities and God. Although I would have difficulty spelling it out, I think this has to do with the Protestant inability to really party the way that Catholics can.

As Adam got older, we discovered we liked going to Mass at Sacred Heart. I remember as a kid growing up that I seldom liked going to church. It was just so boringly wordy. In contrast I do not remember Adam ever suggesting, even on the coldest and snowiest mornings, that he did not want to go. It was, after all, a feast for the senses. Processions with flags and horns, smells and bells, thrilling music, and a meal to eat. What a way to find out what Christianity is about. I was learning right along with my kid.

Of course, there were things that bothered me. The maleness of it all was often a bit overwhelming, yet I kept meeting all of these strong women who, I thought, should not be there given the maleness of Catholicism. For example, my summer school classes were filled with sisters from all over the country—Sisters of St. Joseph, Franciscan Sisters of the Perpetual Adoration, Sisters of the Sacred Heart, and so on. I have often wondered if anyone in Catholicism has any idea how many orders there are. What I discovered in these women was the strength that comes from doing hard but good work well. There is no question that the future of the orders is grim. The reasons are no doubt complex, but I suspect that it has most to do with the loss of the work to do. However, I was at Notre Dame when civil rights and the Vietnam War, not feminism, dominated the social agenda. I do not know how it would feel to be there now. At least at that time, a time when undergraduate women were first admitted, I did not notice that docility was rampant in them; what I noticed instead was how the intellectual quality of my classes rose.

More troubling for me during this time than questions to do with the role of women were the dramatic gestures we were expected to make in worship. I was beginning to get used to prayers addressed to Mary, but on Good Friday I found that I was supposed to not only adore the Cross, but kiss it. Moreover, it was a crucifix. I did it, but I did not like it. I kept thinking that the Italians must have started this to make the Germans feel uncomfortable.

It took ten years, but I did finally discover that I was a Protestant. I do not know what it means for me to be a Protestant, but some folks at Notre Dame eventually got nervous about the theology department's having so many strange people in it. They appointed a Catholic liberal, a non-C.S.C. priest, to be our chairman. It was his job to make the department more Catholic—which is how I found out that I was a Protestant. He told me so, and I guess he was right. He said that under Burrell we had been trying to be a nondenominational department of theology, but from now on we would be denominationally Catholic. Of course, given my experience in universities formed by Protestants, I think our attempt to form a theology department that took God seriously was possible only because we were sustained by the Catholic Church—not just another Protestant denomination. Now I was being told that Catholics were going to try to be like Protestants. I suppose that is the way you have to go if you are going to make it in America, but I found it very sad. After all, what can you expect when your new chairman proclaims, in print no less, that if he had not become a theologian, what he would have most liked to be was a United States senator?

Of course, that message had been there all along. The subtext of Notre Dame has always been that Catholics can now make it in America. After all, the Protestant establishment is running out of energy, or at least kids. They sure as hell do not know what makes them Protestant anymore, unless it is class, so the Catholics might as well seize the opportunity. Notre Dame says that Catholics can become as rich and powerful as Protestants—only Catholicism means using that wealth and power to do "some good."

So I left Notre Dame. It was a sad leaving, but I am glad that the years there left their mark on me. For even though I am not a Catholic, I feel what it means to be one in the contemporary university. I suspect that the last legitimate prejudice on the American campus is against the Catholics. After all, they continue to remain members of a hierarchical institution that maintains some extraordinarily conservative moral practices. As hard as they try to be good Americans, Mary just keeps following them around.

THOMAS J. FERRARO

A Pornographic Nun: An Interview
with Camille Paglia

CAMILLE PAGLIA   I was born into an extremely religious Italian Catholic family, and for Italians, Catholicism is as much cultural as
it is religious. Italian Catholicism is very analogous to Judaism in this
respect. I have many intellectual friends who are Jews and who don't
believe in God, but who nevertheless adhere to Jewish practices and
transmit them to their children because Jewish history is the history of
the religion. The religion is the history of their people. The same thing
with Italian Catholicism: I have enormous respect for it; I feel Italian
Catholic and will be Catholic until the day I die because it is inextricable from my cultural identity as an Italian American. I think the
strong ritualism of all Mediterranean Catholicisms, of Spanish Catholicism as well, goes back to the early Mediterranean cultures. I feel there
is a direct line between the heavy ritualism of Roman religion—and
Etruscan before it—and modern Italian Catholicism. In this respect,
Roman religion was quite different from ancient Greek religion, which
wasn't so ritualistic. Roman religion was more like Egyptian religion,
which was ritual-heavy. My Italian Catholicism has given me a sense of

rapport with Egyptian culture since I was a tiny child. I feel I am Italian Catholic in my bones.

My earliest memories are of being in church—public occasions at St. Anthony of Padua Church in Endicott, New York, where I was born. It's in a mainly Italian, working-class neighborhood. The church is just this beautiful thing, under the grey skies of upstate New York. It's the snow belt up there, steel-grey skies—and this gorgeous church, in warm, orangey stucco, which is the color of architecture in the Mediterranean—all these stained-glass windows, and incredible numbers of polychrome statues, all holding mystical signs and with cryptic symbols all over them. I've written in *Sexual Personae* and elsewhere about the impact those statues had on me. Number one, St. Sebastian, who was up near the altar: You were supposed to be thinking about Jesus in a Catholic church, but St. Sebastian's figure was just overwhelming. It was a semi-nude young man with a loincloth slipping off his hips, and the look on his face was one of mild pleasure, as opposed to the pain you'd expect if your body were penetrated by all those arrows. And so there was, I now feel, a kind of sadomasochistic or homoerotic sensuality about the image that completely derailed any feeling I had for the Jesus, Joseph, and Mary triad. I mean, I have absolutely no identification with that because the images of the saints were so powerful to me. The other statues in the church were of St. Michael the Archangel—who remains my favorite saint to this day—in armor, trampling down the Devil. And next to St. Michael was St. Lucy, holding out her eyeballs on a platter. This is extraordinary—this sort of horror-movie image that every child would see. And in a sacred context. The garishness, the grotesquerie is so different from the experience of someone who is Protestant. No Protestant person of my memory has ever had *that* in a sacred space. Seeing someone holding her eyeballs out to you on a platter—it's amazing! We've never fully analyzed what impact that has on someone's imagination.

So as the years passed, I began to realize that the elements in the Italian Catholic church that I loved so much were the very things Martin Luther threw out of the Renaissance Catholic church because he regarded them as intrusions—foreign intrusions, pagan intrusions—into the purity of what we now call primitive Christianity. And I think Martin Luther was *right*. So this has led to my mega-theory, which is that Italian Catholicism is this fantastically complex thing that is not merely Christian, but is a unique fusion of Christianity with paganism. And that the things in Italian Catholicism that really formed my imagination were the pagan elements, in particular the saints. I was so excited when I eventually learned that Luther was especially opposed to the cult of the saints, who were late accretions and played very little part in the New Testament. And I realized that they are versions of the pagan gods; it's polytheism. In some cases this turned out to be literally true.

THOMAS FERRARO   Right.

CAMILLE PAGLIA   For example, there was a whole book I discovered in college about the Greek saints, saints of the countryside, who in many cases are exact transformations of ancient local gods. We know this about San Gennaro of Naples—Januarius—going all the way back to Janus, the Roman god, and so on. I eventually developed my huge narrative theory about Western culture, which is that paganism was never, as history books claim, defeated by Judeo-Christianity. In fact, paganism was simply driven underground and has erupted at three key moments in our history. The first key moment was the Renaissance—most people would agree with me; everyone acknowledges that Botticelli's *Birth of Venus*, let's say, is a revision of the Gothic Madonnas. But I go on to claim that the second great eruption was Romanticism, and this would be of the buried chthonic, or daemonic, element. The third eruption I see is in modern popular culture; I call the twentieth century the age of Hollywood. Everything in current popular culture that feminism finds most unpalatable—the sex and violence—I have reinterpreted as religious motifs coming up from the buried pagan past. Religion is at the heart of my interpretation of culture. For me, art began as religion, in cave paintings and magic, and the history of religion and the history of art are completely intertwined. I think that is the contribution I am currently making. So it's very peculiar, because I rebelled against the Catholic Church. I left the Catholic Church, like many people of my generation of the 1960s, impatient with the sexual censorship and the prudery of 1950s American Catholicism. Many other people have reported this, other Italian Americans, particularly the film directors — Coppola, Scorsese, and DePalma. There are so many people who see the repressions of the Church as a source of their rebellion. The irony is I thought I was leaving the Church and now I'm like a pornographic nun, or a nun with a lascivious mind. I've often used that phrase. I'm being true to Italian Catholicism in my own way. With all my interest in pornography, I've never left the Church; I've simply penetrated to its heart.

THOMAS FERRARO   Should the institutional Church be made nervous by a pornographic nun?

CAMILLE PAGLIA   Let me say this about Catholicism in America. One of the things I haven't liked about the history of Catholicism in the last thirty years is its drift toward Protestantism. I began feeling this in the 1950s already. The beautiful church that I remember so well, St. Anthony of Padua, was quite unlike the churches I attended with my parents when we moved to Syracuse, New York, which was a very Protestant city. The churches were getting blander and blander. In building a new church or renovating and restoring an old one, there has been a tendency in this country to systematically remove all the polychrome statues. It's a kind of airline-terminal effect, a warehouse look. You go into these Catholic churches now and there's hardly an image — except for a modernistic metal image of Christ, maybe. It's just appalling, the banality. The altar looks like a barbecue pit. How can these buildings ever develop the imagination and cultivate the aesthetic instincts of any child? The whole artistic heritage of the Catholic Church in this country has been thrown completely out the window. There is a real banalization, a homogenization, a kind of bourgeois mediocrity that's descended on the Catholic churches that I think is more the cause now of driving people away from the Church than was the original sexual repressiveness. And the Church has become very conscious in the last twenty years of the old charge of elitism against it in this new period of social activism. So the priests have put away the magnificent, ornamented, jeweled garments that they customarily wore during my youth. I've always been very interested in fashion. I'm not a fashion plate —

I'm rather dowdy—but I've always been very interested in clothing. I've always understood the ceremonial aspects of clothing, probably because, again, of my Catholic background. In my youth, every season of the religious year had its color-coding, so there were certain weeks when the priest was wearing green garments, beautiful emerald-green garments; at other times violet, black, or white, magnificent, with jewels, glittering. All those things are gone in America; it's considered bad taste, provocative. And the priests come out in these plain-looking things; they're trying to look like the original priests of primitive Christianity. Of course, the altar has been lowered. The priest no longer turns his back to the congregation; he's down there looking at you. And there are all these horrendous things now, like people having to shake hands.

THOMAS FERRARO   Like therapy culture, they talk about kisses of peace.

CAMILLE PAGLIA   The kiss of peace. My mother *loves* the kiss of peace. She loves the handshake, and the "Peace be with you," and all that. I find it so banal. The Catholic Mass in America is indistinguishable from an EST session, or one of those companies that helps you overcome bad eating habits. A kind of mundane social-welfare ideology has overtaken the Catholic Church in this country. The priests are no longer being trained in terms of learning or theology; they're no longer expected to have a mastery of history, as they once were. Instead they're supposed to be social service workers, doing *counseling*. It's an enormous loss. My father taught at a Jesuit school, Le Moyne College—the job he spent over twenty-five years in. He was in the Romance Languages department. The school was staffed by Jesuits and run by Jesuits. I took a course in logic one summer from the Jesuits at Le Moyne during my college years—I was attending the State University of New York at Binghamton. That rigorous intellectuality of the Jesuit tradition is now lost. Whether you're talking about academe or the Catholic Church, all intellectuality is quite gone. People mistake Lacan, Derrida, and Foucault for intellectuality, which is ridiculous, *absurd*. That's just verbal game-playing without knowledge, without historical learning. I feel very critical of the Church. Some people say, well, the Church had to change because it had to make itself accessible, and it had to modernize itself in order to bring in people again. And people like me who've left the Church have no business saying it shouldn't change; it has to adapt to changing circumstances. Actually, the Church is very powerful right now.

I *despise* the way gay activism has set itself against the Church. Despite my own problems with the Church, I feel that's one way gay activism has mortally injured itself. It's going to pay a price for its disrespect—breaking into St. Patrick's, throwing the Host on the ground—for thirty years. There's a kind of *jeering* going on against the Church, which seems very cheap indeed. I still feel the Catholic Church is an enormously grand institution. At a conference on homosexuality and biology two months ago [March 1993] at the Harvard Medical School, the whole day long all this jeering was going on from everyone who took the stage—catty remarks inducing jeering from the audience. Finally, I just lost my temper. When I got to the stage, I yelled at them. I thought, this is very peculiar, that I should be in this position of defending the Church. I said to them that I was not going to sit and allow these cheap, juvenile remarks to go on against the Church. I said, it's *suicidal* for gay activism to get itself into this mode. I said, if culture has a choice between the Catholic Church and gay activism, the Catholic Church will win, and should win, because it has two thousand years of spiritual experience and wisdom inside it, and gay activism is very shallow at the present moment. There's no one in gay activism, I pointed out, who has the dimensions or stature of a Martin Luther King, Jr., or a Gandhi. Both these great men drew on the spiritual past. Both were playing on their spiritual heritage. King was a minister; Gandhi returned to the tradition of the Hindu monk. So I'm in this peculiar position. Despite my criticism of the Church, I have ended up publicly defending it.

The power of the Church is amazing. Just go into a Catholic church in the suburbs, or anywhere. You can see the power of it, and the way it is growing in power. For young families raising children, it is a very powerful, organizing spiritual force. You can't help but feel this is not an institution that is staggering under the attack of gay activism. On the contrary. There's also a problem faced by people of my generation who left the Church. I'm not married; I don't have children, so I don't have to make these choices. But people who left the Church now have to decide how to raise their children. Are they going to raise them without religion, or what? Very wisely, a number of people I know have decided, oddly enough, to raise their children in the Catholic way, to send them to parochial school. Let them get all of the rules—to give them something to rebel against. I think that's important. Children raised without religion, the ones I'm getting in the classroom now, are lost. They're lost souls. At least Catholicism gives you a structure; it organizes your mind metaphysically and philosophically. That's really true about me, Madonna, Robert Mapplethorpe, Andy Warhol—it gave us a structure.

THOMAS FERRARO   Right. I wanted to ask you, anticipating the second part of the book, on pop culture and the question of a gay sensibility, to talk about Warhol and Mapplethorpe for a moment.

CAMILLE PAGLIA   I have constantly said that Catholics, or ex-Catholics, make the best pornographers. Catholicism gives you the sense of taboo—and the best pornography is based on taboo. That's part of the power of my imagination. Many people in the 1960s had this idea that sexuality would flourish when there were no restrictions whatever on it—that somehow the problem of sexuality in history is that it's simply a force that is trying to escape limitation. That is naive, and I'm afraid it's one of Foucault's major errors, among the many other errors he made. As I said in *Sexual Personae,* there's nothing less erotic than a nudist colony. Very censored imaginations can burst out into lurid pornographic forms. That's why I'm so attracted to the French decadents. The decadents usually ended up religious, like Huysmans, who became a monk. And Aubrey Beardsley, converting to Catholicism on his deathbed. There's a real intertwining here. The blasphemies of the Marquis de Sade depend on the existence of a structure of virtue to pollute and defile. That's why, as I pointed out, he has that parallel between Justine and Juliette—Justine the pure, and Juliette the profaner of Justine's purity. There's no doubt that *Sexual Personae* is ultimately a Catholic book. The structure of it, the enormous vision of it, the cosmology, the philosophy, the mega-philosophy of it, and the all-inclusiveness of it descend from the medieval worldview. It descends from the Scholastic, all-encompassing worldview of the Catholic Church. People who are so attracted to Lacan, Derrida, and Foucault are actually searching for something to give them this huge, all-encompassing meaning; but, my God, they're looking in the wrong place! The history of religion contains all these things.

THOMAS FERRARO   You've almost got a book of wonders there, in which not only do you have an argument—more than an argument—not only do you demonstrate the way in which Catholic paganism does burst out in these times, but you perform it. That is, you're doing art criticism catholically or paganistically, in some way, no?

CAMILLE PAGLIA   I think that art criticism—the great theory of iconography that was developed by Panofsky—fits perfectly into this view of art as religious. That's essentially what I'm doing. I'm treating every painting, or everything that I look at, as an icon, to be interpreted.

THOMAS FERRARO   You're moving by metaphor, analytically; that is, the intransitive sentence that juxtaposes two things that belong to different times and spaces; nonetheless, that's where the power of your writing comes from. Your writing is an eye itself, no?

CAMILLE PAGLIA   I think there's definitely a religious impulse in everything I do—even though I don't believe in God. It has transferred over from Catholicism. Art and religion began together. I've simply taken my religious feelings and put them into the religion of art. That's why I'm so influenced by the art-for-art's-sake tradition. What I'm doing, usually, is a homage. It's a homage to the artwork or to the sexual persona of Elizabeth Taylor or Rita Hayworth. They're like odes. Or what I do with the Nefertiti bust: it's essentially a meditation on an image. I feel very close to what Teresa of Avila was doing, or St. Ignatius. There's definitely a contemplative religious thing going on. My style is to make notations, to try to recreate in the reader these same feelings of awe or mystery, and admiration, veneration. That is intrinsic to my view of art. Veneration and respect. That's why my work is such a departure from French theory, which has been going on now for over fifteen years, and whose method is, basically, to *trash*.

THOMAS FERRARO   To trash, so that there are no heroes, there are no heroines; the artwork itself isn't resplendent. You take it apart, and there's only the critic.

CAMILLE PAGLIA   Exactly. And you used the word "resplendent." There's no doubt that I have this feeling for the numinous. I remember reading about the religious idea of the numinous when I was in college and thinking, "That is charisma; that is the charisma I'm seeing in the Hollywood stars." That is also what I'm doing. I'm looking at an artwork or an advertisement on TV, or a movie, or whatever it might be, and I'm reinterpreting it; or rather, I'm re-seeing it to discover its numinousness. Everything is glowing when I'm done with it. It could be glowing with hellfire; it could be daemonic, when I'm done with it. But I think that's the function of the critic. The critic is there to make you *see* better. The point of criticism seems to me to be expanded vision, or enlarged vision. And French theory got way off track.

Of course, one must break through the conventions of one's own time. That's why people go to college; they go in order to have their parochial assumptions deconstructed. But then one must build. One cannot just destroy the worldview of the person who comes into the classroom; you have to offer something bigger in its place, something cosmopolitan, something international, something cosmic, and its failure to offer that is the major bankruptcy of criticism in the last twenty years. That's why I consider French theory sacrilegious; I consider most of the literature faculty at Harvard, Yale, Princeton, and everywhere else—including Duke, okay?—lost souls. And I think that what they have done is evil. I really do. I don't believe in absolutes of good and evil; obviously, I don't believe there is a God in Heaven, or any transcendent system of power, but I do feel that what has been done by the most prestigious universities and the most prestigious professors of humanities in the last twenty years is indeed evil. They have destroyed the minds of a whole generation of young people. I know this to be true because I've received letters from the ones who have been driven out of graduate school. And I have to talk to them when they end up in the media, people with Ivy League educations who know nothing. And they are just wandering; their minds have been mutilated. How different that is from the kind of education I got at Harpur College at Binghamton. In the 1960s, we were all interested in Hinduism and Buddhism. We had left our own organized religions, impatient with their limitations. But we were still on a religious quest, a spiritual quest. Unfortunately, that 1960s spirituality survives today largely in the New Age movement, where it's become very sanitized and Americanized —

THOMAS FERRARO   And Protestantized, too —

CAMILLE PAGLIA   And Protestantized.

THOMAS FERRARO   It's that sort of secularized Protestantism that produces the therapy culture, and the kind of psychobabble — the language. Nobody has any ear at all in the New Age thing. I guess it's because they're not pressing against a vocabulary that's really rich, but rather playing with what is most easily available.

CAMILLE PAGLIA   I agree with that completely. I do feel that modern therapy, the obsession with it in America, is a substitute for religion. We've known for a long time that Freud made his greatest impact here in America, that Freud became an enormous pop hero of the 1920s, in ways he was not able to achieve in Europe. We've always been vulnerable to cultism. America has been a religious country, a country in search of religion, right from the start. I don't like the psychobabble aspect of current therapy. I am a Freudian — not a strict Freudian, but I believe that Freud's insights about character are still applicable. There's a storminess and pessimism, and a darkness, in Freud's view, that seems to me very true about the spiritual life. All these elements have now been purged away in therapy. That's the whole problem with current therapy, as with the current Catholic Church. All the darkness that was suggested by the statues of tortured saints and the polychrome statues of Christ on the Cross, dripping blood, and St. Lucy with her eyeballs; the violence and the barbarism of those images were true to life because violence and barbarism are part of everyday experience. So what's happened? Modern popular culture has risen up to fill this gap. All the violence and atrocity missing now from therapy and from the Catholic Church—you just turn on the TV and see the latest air crash, the latest car crash. Every kind of horror is now represented on the news, and that's the place where people go for a dose of reality. So for me, the sensationalism of TV, which serious people tend to dismiss, is part of the religious perspective of TV. Popular culture now offers the cosmic view, the complete view: "love and romance" *and* barbarity, rape, mutilation. It's like a catalogue of horrors, every time you turn on the TV. There is a horrific aspect to existence—what Hinduism calls the cycle of birth and death—that current therapy—feel-good, coddling, hand-holding—is not dealing with. But classic Freudianism did. The conflict, the combat—Freud's idea of ambivalence, the way you have love-hate, these complicated relationships to your parents and your lovers—it's not just one-dimensional. But current therapy, the psychobabble aspect of it, is addicted to the idea that we can all get along. If we all just understand each other and tolerate each other, everything will be fine. I call this the Mary Poppins or Betty Crocker view of life, which current feminism is a victim of.

THOMAS FERRARO   Let me ask you about the 1950s and the impact of a no-offense culture. It seems to me that one of the things that's happened in art and literary criticism is the refusal to name the spiritual energies, the religious energies that come from one tradition rather than another, and that in an effort to democratize the institutions of the academy, we have agreed not to talk about this stuff, not to name what might separate. In other words, there's a soft pluralism that the 1950s generated, a niceness academically registered, where you don't call what you're doing Catholic or pagan-Catholic, to make links, because that then separates you from Jews or Protestants and those descended from Eastern religions.

CAMILLE PAGLIA   Well, there's a couple of things in what you say. First of all, this idea of democratization: there is a terrible problem with the idea of hierarchy in many areas of inquiry of the last twenty-five years. "Hierarchy" has become a dirty word.

THOMAS FERRARO   The dirtiest word of them all.

CAMILLE PAGLIA   Which is why "hierarchy" is one of the most common words in *Sexual Personae*. It's there a million times because it's one of the failings that I saw in my own 1960s generation, which was pushing a kind of incipient egalitarianism. You can see that in the films of Woodstock—everyone is equal, a million people sliding in the mud, that sort of thing. And the egalitarian theory is now flourishing in feminism. That is where it has taken very deep root. Many feminists seem to believe that a totally egalitarian world is possible. You have these hilarious experiments in egalitarianism that are starting to be reported on in comic tones by the press. Two years ago, a huge lesbian feminist convention in Atlanta tried to run itself by egalitarian principles. As a consequence, when no one is taking charge, a discussion that should take ten minutes takes two hours; one that should take two hours takes seven hours, and you have a total breakdown. It's like early communism. It's a wonderful idea, but a communal or tribal organization can work only in very small groups. This is the origin of my most notorious sentence—"If civilization had been left in female hands, we would still be living in grass huts." Now, "grass huts" is a metaphor. It's a metaphor for the little tiny circle around the home-fire; it's a metaphor for this theory of egalitarianism, which I think does not work. And the fake leftist people in the academy who constantly talk in these terms, I want to say to them, "Oh, you believe in egalitarianism? Then renounce your rank. Renounce your rank of professor, and return to the rank of lecturer, or of assistant professor, with all the benefits thereof." And you know they won't; they're hypocrites. If you have something to teach—and I believe that as a teacher one should have something to teach, or what is one doing there?—then one has to accept that one is in a hierarchical relationship to everyone else. And I have no problem with that whatever. Of course, I was raised Catholic! And the strict hierarchy of the Catholic Church is a direct descendant of the hierarchical organization of the Roman Empire. We know that it was St. Paul who transformed the Palestinian sect into a Mediterranean and a world religion by modeling the early structure of the Christian Church on the administrative structure of the Roman Empire. And he was correct. And then we had the transfer of power from Jerusalem to Rome. And so the Catholic Church is a shadow image of the Roman Empire. I have meditated on this question for decades now. I'm constantly in combat with administrative incompetence in the universities and colleges I've been associated with. It's quite obvious that people either have a gift for administration or they don't, whether you're talking about the chairman of the department, or a dean, or a provost, or whatever. The kind of disorder that a pseudo-egalitarianism can cause in any institution is amazing to me. So academics who are very naive, coming out of literary studies, who have not studied political science, not studied the history of institutions, not studied how culture arose and became more complex in Mesopotamia, have this idea that somehow we could all get along fine, without any ordering from above. But there is no living species that is not hierarchically organized; it's something instinctual. People who can't control a class, who can't control a meeting, are incompetent. And they're often passive-aggressive. There is something deeply disordered about their views of the world. The egalitarians are the most hostile and vicious bitches of my entire experience. A person who is very organized is usually the most just because he or she is able to run a department or a meeting, or to run a college, so that there are minimal frictions within the body politic. Hierarchy is the great guilty secret, the great unexamined issue. You have to go all the way back to the earliest development of complex economic structures to see how we escaped from our original parochialism, living in isolated little villages. There had to be a complex hierarchical structure that allowed for the beginning of economic prosperity, that led to military protections for the weak, which included children and women. All these things depended upon hierarchical organization. We know that the irrigation projects of the Tigris-Euphrates valley were made possible by hierarchical organization. People went from poor, drought-stricken villages to a flourishing valley culture that led to art. How? Through hierarchy. Now, of course, hierarchy carried to extremes becomes fascism. But that's my view of history: that there's an oscillation between order and disorder, between Apollonian and Dionysian forces. Every time we veer too much toward one side, we have to correct, going back toward the other side. My generation, trifling and toying with the idea of egalitarianism, managed to produce a descent into barbarism, a descent into lawlessness, which in turn provoked the conservative reaction. So the whole Nixon-Reagan-Bush era was the result of my generation's not correcting soon enough its tilt toward lawlessness. Civilization cannot function in the Dionysian mode. Civilization cannot function *without* Dionysus, but there has to be a kind of modulation, a kind of reconciliation, between these two principles: the Apollonian, which goes toward order, and which is very structured and hierarchical, and the Dionysian, which is all the wild energies of emotion, sex, and nature.

THOMAS FERRARO   You have a real notion of cyclicity in the way in which history works, as opposed to the kind of progressivist storytelling that has a Protestant dimension to it and that has been the long-term stock-in-trade of historians, particularly academic historians in this country, where history itself is told as a kind of decline and fall—there's a Garden of Eden, and then we go forward, and everything changes, with no sense of return.

CAMILLE PAGLIA   I do see things in terms of cycles, and I feel that's what you see if you get outside of the literature department and study art history. It's very easy to make all kinds of stupid statements about art if all you know is words. My view of culture comes from art history, where you can clearly see the invention of motifs, their development, their reaching a high point, and then their decay or decadence. I do believe in organic cycles, and I think the Roman Empire is a great example. We're now back to that point in history—we're in a kind of Hellenistic period. It's like the Roman Empire, where we have a sharp contrast between very religious and traditional elements of culture—the Moral Majority and so on, which is like the republican morality that was still very strong in Rome—and then the fast-track, decadent circles, sophisticated, promiscuous, existing simultaneously. There is such a stark polarity in America right now between, let's say, the gay male world and what is going on just a few miles away in the suburbs, where you have very pious people, with their family lives and their Roman republican virtues. I love that famous phrase—those who don't learn from history are condemned to repeat it. You repeat the errors of history if you haven't studied them. That's what I think is happening now.

THOMAS FERRARO   *Sexual Personae* is a combination of what I called before this "book of wonders" and the autobiographical in your voice— that is, the up-front, in-your-face passion that *makes* that book. That's already part of the kind of writing that you were doing.

CAMILLE PAGLIA   In-your-face? [Laughs]

THOMAS FERRARO   Yeah, well, it's a combination of a confession of a passion—that is, a spiritual autobiography—and a review of the pageant of Western culture, which is the way that I understand the book to be written. So, in that sense, autobiography was already in play.

CAMILLE PAGLIA   My idea of autobiography is coming from Pater and Wilde: the critic is at the center, but not in the sense that French theory has it, where the critic is imposing his or her will on the text and reshaping it. Rather, the work works on you in a sensory, almost seductive or sexual way, and you transmit that sensory reverberation to the reader. That's what you do. So I feel very happy that my instincts were right. I think it's partly due to the Italian veneration for art. I always had this love of art, early on. I was doing this when it was unfashionable, and I just feel so lucky. By the time I was done with my work, which was going totally against the grain of what was expected in the late 1960s and 1970s and so on, by the time the book finally appeared in 1990, after endless problems, it was at exactly the right moment. People were tired of what they had been doing for the last twenty years.

THOMAS FERRARO   Yes, that's the great irony.

CAMILLE PAGLIA   They were looking for something else. I was so into all this gay stuff, when no one was even mentioning it twenty-five years ago. I was pursuing all these themes I had an instinct about. And boom, by the time the book came out, it was smack in the middle of the moment when people were thinking about sadomasochism, acting it out, interested in gay stuff, interested in Oscar Wilde, and there it was, all ready. I had really despaired in the 1980s—the book was done in early 1981, you realize—and the book was rejected by seven major New York houses. It was just endless. By the time the thing came out, I had given up thinking it would be published in my lifetime. I always had the sense that I was writing something for an audience that didn't exist yet, but I had great confidence that the audience would exist for it later.

THOMAS FERRARO   This is the vocational thing, the monkish vocational thing.

CAMILLE PAGLIA   Exactly. What sustained me through all that was absolutely my sense of the monastic vocation.

THOMAS FERRARO   You do this because it's going to really matter; it's going to matter after you don't; things don't end when you die; you give legacies.

CAMILLE PAGLIA   That's right. It's the idea of labor, the monastic tradition of isolated labor that you do for a greater cause, something that's greater than merely the contemporary, merely the present, and you are the custodian of the inherited past. It was the monks who preserved so many of the Greek texts, just copying them over again. The idea of a scriptorium, the laborious copying over—I think of that all the time. I copy out things, and the muscular copying out is in some way an act of respect. So there's no doubt my sense of vocation as a scholar was very much animated by the Italian Catholic past. My mother was born in the town of Ceccano, about twenty miles north of Monte Cassino— the great abbey where St. Thomas Aquinas was educated. This is our tradition. That's why I've been so contemptuous of the Ivy League. My attitude toward the Ivy League is totally disrespectful. Not because I'm a populist, because I'm not, as a scholar. I'm an elitist, as a scholar—I believe in the best and the greatest. Talent is something that is inborn, and I believe in the elitism of talent. But my sense of the tradition of scholarship long predates Harvard or Yale. So that's why I just spit defiance at these full professors at Harvard or Yale. I delivered a lecture at Harvard—to eight hundred people crammed into their biggest theater—called "What's Wrong with Harvard?" And here's this person from this unknown school in Philadelphia, going up there and slamming them and slamming them and slamming them—by name. I was naming names of people on their faculty, and slamming them. And the crowd was laughing and applauding and cheering. I thought, this is really something, because even Harvard itself knows that it's become corrupt or bankrupt or whatever. I'm a reformer, like Savonarola or my great role model, Teresa of Avila, who wasn't famous until she was in her forties. She went against the whole establishment. She fought the bishops and the Pope. She singlehandedly started the reform of the Spanish convents. People said to me early on, "Oh, what can you do? One person can't do anything." And I said, "Excuse me, one person can move mountains." That's the example of the saints.

THOMAS FERRARO   It's a great-woman theory.

CAMILLE PAGLIA   Yes. The earliest great women were the saints. And the saints were not pleasant people. They were not saintly.

THOMAS FERRARO   They were not *nice,* that terrible American word.

CAMILLE PAGLIA   They were not nice. They were troublemakers, they were loudmouths; they went against convention, they defied convention, and they had faith.

THOMAS FERRARO   One of the dimensions of Catholicism that interests me is the ceremonialness of the Mass itself; that is, the Mass as a ritual made up of pieces where you sit down, and stand up—you know the way it works—particularly the way it worked when it was still a Latin Mass. I'm just old enough to have a visceral memory of the Latin Mass. One of the places where I find those pleasures still in play is in rock & roll performance.

CAMILLE PAGLIA   I don't think it has much relationship to the Mass. I interpret the rock concert as a pagan form. The Christian Mass is itself part of pagan mystery religion, like the cult of Dionysus or Osiris, as we see in *The Bacchae*. There are lots of influences coming from pagan mystery religions into Catholic ritual, as in the Communion service, where we're dividing Christ's body into many pieces —

THOMAS FERRARO   Where we do cannibalism.

CAMILLE PAGLIA   —Right, that is obviously Dionysian omophagy, where you eat the god and he becomes part of you. There's a principle of identification operating in mystery religion that wasn't in the cults of the Olympian gods. So I would say that rock concerts are simply part of the pattern that my generation followed of leaving the organized religions behind and making a new kind of religion. A rock concert is very close, sometimes, to the Eleusinian cults, where you would be in total darkness, with the flames lit. People light lighters now and hold them up. The Eleusinian secrets were kept by most people, so we're not sure, but we do know that torches were involved and that the symbolism of light and darkness was being used. It's the whole idea of going down into the bowels of the earth, and that's what you feel in these giant rock concerts. The great masses of people, and the way ten thousand people become one and are being played upon by these great rhythms. That's not like the Catholic Mass at all. The big earth rhythms striking you and pounding you, the whole excitation of the sexual impulse—it's all purged out of Catholicism, it's nowhere in the Catholic Mass. That's one of the aims of a rock concert—to arouse, sexually arouse, and to flaunt the body in lewd, exhibitionistic pagan ways. I would say the rock concert has risen up as a new religion. And unfortunately it's a dangerous one too, since it's so easily manipulated.

THOMAS FERRARO   Let me ask you about the occasional pieces in *Sex, Art, and American Culture*. What's the relationship between being Italian Catholic and your position on date rape?

CAMILLE PAGLIA   The connection would be the idea of personal responsibility. There's a principle of self-criticism that you get as a Catholic, because of the self-examination leading to Confession. Madonna has commented on this too, that a Catholic has this power of self-analysis, of looking at yourself from the outside. You're trained to do that as a tiny child, to look at your life, to review your life, to assess it at certain intervals—originally, every week—and then to transfer that into verbal form. There is a kind of self-consciousness that Catholicism gives you, and also a sense of personal responsibility from childhood. You're expected to be responsible as a moral being from the age of six or seven, from your first Holy Communion on, right? And unfortunately in our culture there's a sliding of adulthood into your twenties now. A girl in college, eighteen or nineteen years old, gets drunk, dressed in a Madonna-style outfit, and ends up having an unpalatable sexual encounter at a fraternity house, and we're supposed to, like, excuse her! "Oh, poor dear, oh my gosh, those bad boys, gee, we're going to punish them," and so on. This is not Catholic.

THOMAS FERRARO   It's blame culture; it's litigation culture; it's always somebody else's fault.

CAMILLE PAGLIA   Yes, yes. But also this endless prolonging of childhood into late teens and into your twenties. Anita Hill was twenty-six; she was a graduate of Yale Law School. And even if what she alleged Clarence Thomas to have said to her were true—now there's some doubt even about that—even if it *were* true, the man never laid a hand on her. He was simply joking about pornographic materials. Big deal. Ten years later, she's still talking about her passivity. Passivity seems to be predicated in our culture now, where something's being done *to* you.

THOMAS FERRARO   Right. Whine culture.

CAMILLE PAGLIA   Whining culture. I'm constantly talking about the problems with whining. You're expected as a Catholic not only to examine yourself, but to take action on the basis of your faults. And moral adulthood is expected of you very early. And I think that is certainly behind my date rape thing, and my impatience with the childishness that is foisted on you in this culture, where everyone is all-forgiving. Well, everyone is not all-forgiving in Catholicism. Everything was very coded. You know, if you said this many Hail Marys, you could get a soul in Purgatory three years off, or something. It was all worked out like that, and it's rather hilarious now. The catechism itself, which I loathed when I had to memorize it for Confirmation—I just hated it, having to memorize the questions and the answers to the *Baltimore Catechism*—but I've realized that it's behind a lot of my writing. I'm constantly posing rhetorical questions, and then answering the questions. The rigor, the intellectual rigor of it.

THOMAS FERRARO   The aggressive formulations, which are both illuminating and infuriating to your readers, are a corollary of the way Italian kids are raised, no?

CAMILLE PAGLIA   Oh yes.

THOMAS FERRARO   —Which is that it produces both provocation and discipline at the same time.

CAMILLE PAGLIA   Yes, and I think the way Italian kids are raised is exactly right. That is, "no" *does* mean "no" in an Italian home. The liberal way kids are raised in America produces whiners in adulthood. It's a problem with authority—this goes back to the hierarchical thing again, where the parents want to be the equal of the kids. Well, that's never the attitude in Italian families. It's just like in Chinese culture: the elders are to be respected—it goes back to their ancestor cults. Similarly, in Roman ancestor cults, you kept the ancestral masks in the atrium of the house and marched with them on one holiday every year. It goes back in turn to Etruscan culture.

One of my favorite moments is the scene in *La Dolce Vita,* where there is this decadent Roman party at the end of the film. The aristocrats have been partying all night long at their villa, and suddenly it's dawn. The matriarch, the mother, appears with their family priest on the way to chapel for Mass. She abruptly summons these middle-aged aristocrats: "Come on, time to go to Mass"—and, boom, they suddenly leave the party and fall in line behind the mother on their way to the chapel. And all the other party-goers are gaping, with their mouths hanging open. The aristocrats are going from the orgy to the chapel not because they believe in God. The religion and the family culture are completely intertwined. You can see it there. There's a respect for the mother; respect for the family, that's your identity. And it doesn't matter whether in your heart you believe in God or not.

NOTE

The interview was conducted by telephone on 27 May 1993. A special thank you is extended to Carolyn Gerber, who transcribed it.

PAUL CROWLEY, S.J.

An Ancient Catholic: An Interview
with Richard Rodriguez

The following interview is the distillation of several conversations
with Richard Rodriguez in San Francisco.

PAUL CROWLEY   In the opening chapter of *Days of Obligation*
you write about Indians. Do you think of yourself as an Indian?

RICHARD RODRIGUEZ   Yes, I do—though only lately. For most of
my life I accepted the European (albeit the liberal) version of the
New World. I thought the Indian was dead or was off playing bingo
in Oklahoma. Oh, I knew I carried Indian blood (knew Mexico was
mestizo), but what did that mean? If I was an Indian, then weren't
you a Druid? I began rethinking the Indian role in history as the five
hundredth anniversary of the Columbus landing approached. I kept
hearing all this white guilt about what the European did to the poor
Indian. I was in Mexico City one day when I had my "vision": In the
capital of Spanish colonialism there were Indian faces like mine everywhere. Where, then, was the conquistador?

PAUL CROWLEY   The thesis of that first chapter seems to be that the
Indian is swallowing the European.

RICHARD RODRIGUEZ That's right. I think the European has ro-manticized the dead Indian, has felt guilty about what he did to the poor Indian. In five hundred years it has not occurred to many Euro-peans that maybe the Indian is alive—maybe the Indian was inter-ested in the European, maybe the Indian beckoned, maybe the Indian approached. My mother is, after all, Pocahontas; my grandmother is Marina la Malinche. And then there is Guadalupe—the Virgin Mary, dressed as an Aztec princess, sending the Indian to convert the Span-ish bishop, thereby reversing the logic of colonialism in 1531. Today, the dead Indian has become the mascot of the international ecology move-ment. But, I assure you, the Indian is alive, having babies, frightening Planned Parenthood. And Indians keep running across the border—Californians call them "illegal immigrants."

There may be a feminine impulse within colonial history that we do not understand. It's not as simple as two males butting heads—one wins, the other loses. Perhaps there is such a thing as seduction. Conversion. Perhaps cultures absorb one another. If it is true that the Franciscan padre forced the Eucharist down the Indian's throat, maybe she forgot to close her mouth. Maybe she swallowed the Francis-can priest. After all, the churches of Latin America are crowded with Indians today. It is Europe that has lost its faith. The great churches of Europe are empty tombs, art treasures for humanists—tourist attrac-tions. Anglicans charge tourists £4.00 to enter St. Paul's Cathedral.

PAUL CROWLEY In your first book, *Hunger of Memory*, you wrote against bilingual education and affirmative action. What happened to your Indian part? Many educators today consider you a neoconservative.

RICHARD RODRIGUEZ I'm not much interested in political labels. Bi-lingual education is a bad idea for Hispanic children—that's why it hasn't worked after thirty years. And affirmative action made us lose sight of the true minority—the poor.

Left or right—who cares about these designations? What interests me, these days, is the interplay of theologies in my life. I am a Catholic in a Protestant country. Two pronouns war within me—the American *I* and the Catholic *we*. Sometimes the tension is creative. There are other times when I feel Catholicism urging me toward a grammar and understandings that are un-American.

PAUL CROWLEY   As in *Days of Obligation,* where you distinguish between the "comic" spirit in Protestantism—the belief in self-invention —and the tragic spirit within Catholicism—the sense that we are bound by history, by inevitability, by sin.

RICHARD RODRIGUEZ   Catholicism, especially the Irish and Mexican versions that shaped me, always took the implications of Good Friday (life is suffering). Whereas Protestantism seems to me centered on the Easter promise (you can be born again). What is happening right now in Latin America is that an entire generation is turning to Low Church Protestantism.

PAUL CROWLEY   Why?

RICHARD RODRIGUEZ   In something like the way Protestantism took fire in Europe in the sixteenth century with the rise of the city, today Protestantism is spreading throughout the Latin South. Especially in monster cities like Mexico City or Lima, people find themselves alone, cut off from centuries of ancestors. Protestantism makes sense of urban loneliness, interprets it as individualism, the precondition of redemption. And Protestantism seizes on the experience of discontinuity—the peasant's feeling of being cut off from tradition. Discontinuity becomes a holy event.

PAUL CROWLEY   What about the United States?

RICHARD RODRIGUEZ   Oddly enough, I think a Catholic moment approaches. Even while the Latin South turns Protestant, the United States seems to be coming to the end of its Protestant era. There is a deepening loneliness, a hungering for community, particularly as our nation grows middle-aged and the westward migration makes a U-turn at the Pacific Coast Highway. I've written about two manifestations of this new communalism. I sense it in the environmental movement's notion of a shared ecology—what you do to your garbage is going to change my nephew's life. Americans search among recycled cans and bottles for a vision of the whole.

I have also written about the change in the gay movement here in San Francisco. In the 1970s, the gay revolution was largely a circus of egoism. With the AIDS epidemic, with suffering, however, came a remarkable circle of compassion around the deathbed. An astonishing accommodation with death. Very Catholic.

PAUL CROWLEY   You write about the fact that you regularly attend your neighborhood parish church, but you are also discontent with post–Vatican Council symbols of "communalism" in the liturgy, the Kiss of Peace, the translation of the credo to "we believe." Do you think of yourself as some sort of ancient Catholic?

RICHARD RODRIGUEZ   Yes, I like that term, ancient Catholic, certainly more than the term *traditional Catholic*—more, alas, than *Christian,* which has no pomp about it. I grew up in Sacramento, California, in the 1950s, linked by my Mexican-Catholic parents and my Irish nuns to the Church universal. So deeply did we believe in our communal faith that we didn't need theatrical handshaking and the fake translations that characterize the vernacular Mass—*credo* does not translate to the first-person plural. I suspect that reminders of our communal faith are suddenly necessary because we no longer believe in anything like a Catholic world.

PAUL CROWLEY   In recent years, there has been a wild, sometimes heretical cultural Catholicism abroad in "post-Protestant" America. I'm thinking of Camille Paglia, Andy Warhol, Madonna, Martin Scorsese. Do you consider yourself part of this renegade Catholic movement?

RICHARD RODRIGUEZ   Yes. In blond, crewcut America, my soul is hairy and dark. And has a mouth! So I need to be a communicant; I am more than a "cultural Catholic." But yes.

PAUL CROWLEY   Say something about the priests and bishops running the church.

RICHARD RODRIGUEZ   Just because the chancery holds legal title to a church does not mean that a bishop or archbishop owns a church. A parish belongs to the old men and women and to the children who have warmed a church in winter with their breath.

I think priests and bishops—many of them—have no idea how patient the laity is with them. Week after week we sit in the pews and listen to inane homilies. We listen as adults might listen to children. It's really quite astonishing, the inability of many priests in the pulpit to say anything, offering rambling pieties of remembered family life— "I remember Mama"—to a laity desperately needing moral instruction for their real lives. In real life, Mama is in a rest home wetting her bed. And our darling son is on crack. We are not a happy family. Fact is, Oprah Winfrey has become America's moral teacher at a time when bishops consult with their lawyers.

PAUL CROWLEY   Is there anyone in the Church you regard as a moral example?

RICHARD RODRIGUEZ   A neighbor of mine—retired Navy officer. He smokes too much, drinks. Homosexual. He hangs out at gay bars, where he drinks with his buddies. But I met him once at a hospital. It turns out he visits the sick, takes Communion to them. He works in the rectory of his parish, helps the nun in charge of "community services." And every Sunday morning he drives several old women to Mass. There he sits, toward the back of the church—the head usher. His job is to assign a heterosexual couple to take up the bread and the wine at the offertory. He is what the Church will not accept officially. And yet, literally, he is the Church. His is the only smile of welcome parishioners meet. His are the hands dispensing the Body of Christ. His spirituality is active and companionate and interested. And—this is most important to me—he is cheerful at a time of despair in the rectory, among priests who claim to have heard the good news.

PAUL CROWLEY   You sound anticlerical. And yet, I remember a compassionate essay you did on the *MacNeil-Lehrer News/Hour* regarding sexual scandals in the rectory.

RICHARD RODRIGUEZ   I can't see the moral failures of any priest apart from the moral failure of the society around him. I also do not forget that some of the most heroic lives I have witnessed have been those of priests and nuns.

Maybe there is a vein of anticlericalism in me, as in many Catholics. I try to be as patient with the clergy as a nun is with the male hierarchy. I do think the Church's understanding of human sexuality, for example, is primitive. How many centuries did the Vatican require to learn from Galileo? Will it take that long for Rome to learn from Freud?

I am always struck by the fact that the homilies in my parish church on the subject of homosexuality insist on describing it as a behavior, an act, or, worse, a "lifestyle." Clearly, the priest is afraid, as Rome is afraid, of acknowledging that homosexuality is an emotive response — an emotion — transparently human. And transparently divine? Dare we call homosexuality *love?*

Here in San Francisco, one of the most animate parishes, one of the few Catholic churches where one senses the Spirit hovering, is Most Holy Redeemer — the "gay" parish — in the Castro district. I dare the bishop of Rome to visit Most Holy Redeemer, witness the spiritual seriousness of gay men and lesbians. I predict the Vatican will one day apologize to homosexuals, just as Rome has needed to apologize to Jews, for centuries of moral cowardice.

PAUL CROWLEY   If the clergy and the laity are at such variance, how do you understand the future of orthodoxy?

RICHARD RODRIGUEZ   I accept the fact that the Church, as an institution, is conservative — by definition resistant to change. But what that means is that the agents for change and growth in the Church are always the people in the pews, not the cardinals in their silk shrouds. The shepherd is moved by the sheep, even the sinner within the flock. Isn't that the point of the Guadalupe story? — the Spanish bishop is the last one to see.

PAUL CROWLEY   Speaking of Guadalupe. Do you foresee the possibility of some hemispheric reconciliation of Protestantism and Catholicism?

RICHARD RODRIGUEZ   If it happens, it will happen in a place like Tijuana, the border town that for decades was the nighttime meeting place of cynical Catholicism and hypocritical Protestantism. And if the reconciliation happens, it will be in ways that will mystify us.

Today's Indian convert to Evangelical Protestantism could turn out to be an ecumenical pioneer. By casting so wide a net over the Catholic South, after all, Protestant missionaries may be harvesting more than they want. The accretions of the souls they reap may be a cultural Catholicism. Some ancient Catholic sensibility is finding its way into Low Church Protestantism.

Every time a priest friend of mine passes the Evangelical church down the street, where they even have a side-chapel, my priest friend sneers with all the wonderful cynicism of the Catholic church: "I'll bet any money they have a statue of Guadalupe in there."

CONTRIBUTORS

PATRICK ALLITT teaches American history at Emory University. He is the author of *Catholic Intellectuals and Conservative Politics, 1950–1985* (1993) and *Catholic Converts: British and American Intellectuals Turn to Rome* (1997). He is now writing a book on the history of wintertime in America.

PAUL CROWLEY, S.J., is Associate Professor of Religious Studies at Santa Clara University in California. Currently a visiting fellow at Boston College's Jesuit Institute, he has published articles in *Theological Studies* and *Heythrop Journal*, and he is working on a project on Christian pessimism.

THOMAS J. FERRARO, Associate Professor of English at Duke University, is the author of *Ethnic Passages: Literary Immigrants in Twentieth-Century America* (1993).

JAMES T. FISHER, Danforth Chair of Theological Studies at St. Louis University, is the author of *The Catholic Counterculture in America, 1933–1962* (1989) and *Doctor America: The Lives of Thomas A. Dooley* (1997).

PAUL GILES, Reader in British-American Literature and Culture at the University of Nottingham, is the author of *Hart Crane: The Contexts of "The*

Bridge" (1986) and *American Catholic Arts and Fictions: Culture, Ideology, Aesthetics* (1992).

MARY GORDON is Professor of English at Barnard College. Her writings include best-selling novels — *Final Payments, The Company of Women, Men and Angels,* and *The Other Side* — as well as a book of novellas, *The Rest of Life,* a collection of stories, *Temporary Shelter,* and a book of essays, *Good Boys and Dead Girls.* She has received the Lila Acheson Wallace–Reader's Digest Writer's Award and a Guggenheim Fellowship. Her most recent book, *The Shadow Man,* a memoir, was published in May 1996.

STANLEY HAUERWAS is Professor of Divinity and Law at Duke University. His most recent books are *Christians among the Virtues: Theological Conversations with Ancient and Modern Ethics* (1997) and *Wilderness Wanderings: Theological Interventions and Interrogations,* forthcoming as part of a new series from Westview Press, Radical Traditions: Theology in a Post-Critical Key, coedited with Peter Ochs.

FRANK LENTRICCHIA is the Katherine Everett Gilbert Professor of Literature at Duke University and the author, most recently, of *Johnny Critelli; and, The Knifemen,* two novels published by Scribner.

ROBERT A. ORSI, Professor of Religious Studies at Indiana University, is the author of *The Madonna of 115th Street: Faith and Community in Italian Harlem, 1880–1950* (1985) and *Thank you, St. Jude: Women's Devotions to the Patron Saint of Hopeless Causes* (1996).

CAMILLE PAGLIA, Professor of Humanities at the University of the Arts, Philadelphia, is the author of *Sexual Personae: Art and Decadence from Nefertiti to Emily Dickinson* (1990), *Sex, Art, and American Culture* (1992), and *Vamps & Tramps* (1994).

DAVID PLANTE, an American novelist and essayist now living in London, is the author of *The Catholic* (1986), *The Accident* (1991), and *Annunciation* (1994), among other works.

RICHARD RODRIGUEZ, an essayist and memoirist who also works in print and television journalism, is the author of *Hunger of Memory: The Education of Richard Rodriguez* (1982) and *Days of Obligation: An Argument with My Mexican Father* (1992).

KATHY RUDY, Assistant Professor of Ethics and Women's Studies at Duke University, is the author of *Beyond Pro-Life and Pro-Choice: Moral Diversity in the Abortion Debate* (1996) and *Sex and the Church: Gender, Homosexuality, and the Transformation of Christian Ethics* (1997).

ANDREW SULLIVAN was editor of the *New Republic* from 1991 to 1996. He is currently at work on a book on friendship.

MARY JO WEAVER, Professor of Religious Studies at Indiana University, is the author of several books, including two on women's issues in the American Catholic church, *New Catholic Women* (tenth anniversary edition, 1995) and *Springs of Water in a Dry Land* (1993). Along with R. Scott Appleby, she is currently engaged in a three-volume project mapping American Catholicism at the end of the century: *Being Right: Conservative American Catholics* (1996), *What's Left: Progressive American Catholics* (in progress), and an untitled final volume.

INDEX

Library of Congress Cataloging-in-Publication Data
Catholic lives, contemporary America /
Thomas J. Ferraro, editor.
Includes index.
ISBN 0-8223-2031-2 (alk. paper). —
ISBN 0-8223-2043-6 (pbk. : alk. paper)
1. Catholics—United States—History—20th century.
2. Catholic Church—United States—History—20th century.
I. Ferraro, Thomas J.
BX1406.2.C363   1997
282'.73'0904—dc21   97-13810   CIP